Your Career
HOW TO MAKE IT HAPPEN
5TH EDITION

Your Career

HOW TO MAKE IT HAPPEN

5TH EDITION

JULIE GRIFFIN LEVITT

BUSINESS CONSULTANT, TRAINER, AND
NATIONAL PRESENTER
FORMER SUPERVISOR WITH BOISE STATE UNIVERSITY
BOISE, IDAHO

THOMSON
SOUTH-WESTERN

Australia · Canada · Mexico · Singapore · Spain · United Kingdom · United States

THOMSON

SOUTH-WESTERN

Your Career: How to Make It Happen, 5th Edition
By Julie Griffin Levitt

Editor-in-Chief
Jack Calhoun

Vice President/Executive Publisher
Dave Shaut

Team Leader
Karen Schmohe

Acquisitions Editor
Joseph Vocca

Project Manager
Penny Shank

Consulting Editor
Susan Carson, Last Word

Production Manager
Tricia Matthews Boies

Production Editor
Tim Bailey

Director of Marketing
Carol Volz

Senior Marketing Manager
Chris McNamee

Marketing Coordinator
Lori Pegg

Design Project Manager
Tippy McIntosh

Manufacturing Coordinator
Kevin Kluck

Editorial Assistant
Stephanie L. White

Production Assistant
Nancy Stamper

Internal Design
Kim Torbeck

Cover Design
Tippy McIntosh, Kim Torbeck

Contributing Authors
Richard Rapp
Karen Schneiter Williams
Shelley Metzger

Compositor
Techbooks (York, PA)

Printer
Courier Kendallville

TABLE OF CONTENTS

PART 4   YOUR INTERVIEW

Chapter 11   Interview Like a Pro

Chapter 12   Master the Art of Getting Interviews

Chapter 13   Be Prepared for Any Interview Style

Chapter 14   Navigate Interview Questions and Answers

Chapter 20 Make Successful Job and Career Changes

APPENDICES

CAREER ACTION ASSIGNMENTS

PART 1 PLANNING YOUR CAREER

PART 2   YOUR JOB SEARCH

PART 3   CAREER SEARCH DOCUMENTS

PART 4   YOUR INTERVIEW

PART 5   AFTER YOUR INTERVIEW

PERSONAL BEST FEATURES

Dear Reader:

Welcome to *Your Career: How to Make It Happen*—The Career Power Kit!

Typically, 97 percent of the students in my classes secure jobs using the techniques in this text—before they finish the course! This text is your career power kit. It contains all the tools you need to assess, plan, and succeed in achieving your job search and career goals.

Get the Competitive Advantage
Did you know that people who develop sound job search and career planning skills are **80 percent more successful** in landing jobs than those who don't develop these skills? *Your Career: How to Make It Happen* provides the career management/job search tools that give you this huge competitive edge!

Learn How to Make Your Career Happen
This text provides the most thorough, practical career management and job search advice and guidelines available on the topic today. These guidelines offer big career dividends for you—jobs, promotions, and career success! *Your Career: How to Make It Happen* shows you how to:

- Develop proactive success attitudes.
- Increase your self-motivation and confidence-building skills.
- Identify and focus on your job strengths and match them to the best possible job and career targets.
- Organize your job search and identify the best potential employers.
- Develop a strong career network.
- Prepare resumes and cover letters that get positive results.
- Prepare professional electronic resumes and cover letters.
- Develop a career portfolio that demonstrates your job readiness.
- Get interviews and interview skillfully.
- Negotiate for a fair salary and benefits package.
- Use the Internet to increase your career knowledge and employment potential.
- Succeed in the changing workplace.
- Know how to change jobs or careers successfully and how to seek a promotion professionally.

The success of these tools and guidelines keeps *Your Career: How to Make It Happen* in high demand. This fifth edition is completely updated and clearly reflects the needs of the twenty-first-century workplace.

Take charge of your career with these practical tools. Use them to gain a competitive advantage and to achieve your full career potential.

Sincerely,

Julie Levitt

Julie Levitt

PREFACE

"Attitude is everything! The first chapter, 'Reach Your Full Career Potential,' focuses on personal motivation and proactive skills. It's like a pep talk that prepares readers mentally for successful career development.
The remaining chapters guide readers clearly and accurately through all phases of career planning, job search, and job success. I recommend this book highly. It's a great tool!"

Jenny Nordin
Employment Consultant
Idaho Job Service

"A technological revolution is changing the way we engineer careers and look for employment. Your Career: How to Make It Happen *doesn't just look ahead to the twenty-first century—it is the twenty-first century! Cyberspace job search techniques, preparation of winning career search documents, Internet exercises, and career success strategies create new windows of opportunity for students to reach full career potential."*

Linda Welther
Education Supervisor
ITT Technical Institute

THE PURPOSE OF THIS BOOK

This text provides the necessary job and career management tools to reach your full career potential. You will develop essential career success skills and gain competitive advantage in the workplace through class activities, direct practice in the business community, and Internet activities.

KEY FEATURES OF THIS TEXT

The key features of *Your Career: How to Make It Happen* are listed below. The graphic icons you see here are also used throughout the text to signal types of reader activities.

Career Actions—Your Competitive Edge: Career Action assignments represent a major objective of the textbook title—the *How to Make It Happen* part. You are the one who ultimately makes your career happen, and the hands-on assignments in each chapter guide you clearly and explicitly in the right direction. These assignments take you into the business community to learn about employers and jobs in your field, provide important practice in meeting and interacting with businesspeople, and focus on the activities necessary to achieve your immediate and future career goals. Some of these assignments include the following:

- Effective job search organization

- Development of essential career Internet skills, such as networking electronically and finding information on careers, jobs, and employers

- Preparation of winning resumes, cover letters, and career portfolios

- Actual career networking to develop contacts and access information

- Interview practice

- **NEW Learner's CD:** The new Learner's CD contains the following: Career Action Assignment forms, Chapter PowerPoint Slides for interactive study and review, sample documents, and chapter case studies to reinforce essential chapter concepts. The icon indicates that you should access a form or document on your Learner's CD.

- **NEW Instructor's Resource CD:** This new CD offers a complete and customizable set of instructor resources, including teaching suggestions, chapter tests, chapter PowerPoint slides, case studies with solutions, teaching masters, and more.

- **NEW Personal Best Features:** Each chapter contains an important new "Personal Best" feature that highlights a strategic application or a key contemporary issue. These features focus on career management and communication skills that will help you achieve your personal best.

- **Internet Assignments:** *Your Career: How to Make It Happen* emphasizes the important role the Internet plays in successful job search/career planning by integrating guided Internet assignments throughout. This icon signals that an assignment involves use of the Internet.

- **Success Tips:** Over 100 easy Success Tips highlight the key steps you can take to achieve full job satisfaction and career potential.

- **Employer Quotes:** Quotes from leading employers and career experts introduce each chapter and highlight important concepts from the employer's perspective.

- **Career Management Files Binder:** A pivotal career management component of the textbook is the ongoing development of your own set of career management and reference documents. As you complete key Career Action assignments, you will be directed to save those considered to be most essential as references throughout your lifetime career. The binder icon indicates that you should file the completed assignment in your Career Management Files Binder.

- **Your Career Advantage Companion Web Site:** The *Your Career: How to Make It Happen* web site provides convenient access to over 100 of the most timely, value-added career and job information links. You can also find useful career-boosting articles on the "Bulletins" page of the site. For easy access to this career resource:

a. Go to www.levitt.swlearning.com.

b. On the *Your Career: How to Make It Happen* home page, click on the "Links" button. On this page, you can access links in the following categories:

- Self-assessment
- Career planning and job search information
- Jobs listing sites
- Efficient web-searching information
- Search engines
- Researching companies (and employers)
- Financial information

c. On the home page, click on the "Bulletins" button to access valuable career articles and tips.

- *Your Career: How to Make It Happen* **WebTutor:** The WebTutor is an optional online component for *Your Career: How to Make It Happen*. Visit Thomson Learning's WebTutor web site at e.thomsonlearning.com.

WHO CAN USE THIS BOOK?

This text is written for anyone seeking employment, a promotion, or a career change. This includes students (career and technical, college, and university level) as well those currently working in or reentering the workforce. This book is appropriate for traditional students as well as for adults reentering postsecondary systems to gain additional training or for those planning a new job, promotion, or career.

WHAT BENEFITS WILL YOU GAIN FROM THIS BOOK?

The authoring team conducts active, ongoing job seeking and career development research. They refine and enhance the instructional materials as re-

quired to meet the changing needs of the job market. This text reflects over 20 years of professional expertise in career management.

You will develop all the tools you need to manage your career successfully and gain the following benefits:

- **The right job and the right career moves:** This text will prepare you to land the right job or promotion and succeed in your career through practice and development of proven career management techniques.

- **Competitive advantage:** You will learn and apply strategies that give you the winning advantage when competing in today's job market.

- **Convenient career management skills/tools:** You will develop efficient job search and career management skills and tools that help you achieve current and future career goals.

You will also gain an important competitive and timesaving edge with these career management tools:

- **Career Management Files Binder.** As you complete the activities in this text, you will compile a set of documents and information you can use for future career activities. Your **Career Management Files Binder** will consist of personal data; content for resumes, cover letters, and applications; reference lists; and summaries of your qualifications, education, training, and more. You can use this base of information any time you seek a promotion, consider a new job, or pursue a new career.

- **Career Portfolio.** You will prepare a master set of documents and other items that provide evidence of your skills, abilities, achievements, experience, and other job qualifications. This Career Portfolio is designed to demonstrate and document your employability.

- **Interview Marketing Kit.** This professional looking binder or case contains selected items from your Career Portfolio for each job interview. You will tailor the contents of your Interview Marketing Kit for each interview by choosing items that match the specific needs of individual employers. This targeted evidence of your qualifications will greatly enhance your interview effectiveness.

WHAT SKILLS WILL YOU DEVELOP?

This text offers a unique combination of knowledge and practical applications designed to build skills for your job search and career development. You will learn:

- How to assess your occupational qualifications.

- How to identify and confirm the best job and career choices.

- How to use the Internet to increase your job search and career management success.

- How to prepare an electronic resume, cover letter, and online employment application.

- How to organize your job search to find the best possible job in the shortest possible time.

- How to research prospective employers and your career field.

- How to succeed in the application process (application, resume, and cover letter).

- How and where to look for a job.

- How to get interviews and succeed in them.

- How to follow up an interview successfully.

- How to adjust quickly and achieve peak success in a new position.

- How to apply techniques on the job that result in maximum career advancement.

- How to evaluate the pros and cons of changing jobs or careers or relocating and how to plan for such changes.

- How to deal effectively with being laid off, downsized, or terminated.

YOU WILL LEARN BY DOING

You can gain an 80 to 100 percent advantage over your competition by using this text. Through the practice assignments, you develop the essential job search and career planning skills that give you this competitive advantage. The goal of this text is to help you get the most suitable job possible and to

develop your career successfully. You won't just read about succeeding in a job search; you will practice the skills in your business community through class and outside Career Action assignments.

Some of these assignments include researching your career field and target job; submitting resumes and cover letters for evaluation; taking practice interviews in actual offices, and more.

THE INTERNET WILL BE YOUR CAREER PARTNER

Using the Internet is a must for a successful job search and for career management in the twenty-first century. This is why *Your Career: How to Make It Happen* incorporates important exercises to build your Internet skills. Job applicants who use the Internet for employer and industry research and for professional electronic communications with employers outdistance those applicants who don't use this important tool. You will be counted among the Internet-savvy applicants when you complete this text.

The *Your Career: How to Make It Happen* web site serves as your central Internet career resource. The site provides convenient, direct links to invaluable career information. You will also find useful articles on the "Bulletins" page of the site. For easy access to this career resource, go to: www.levitt.swlearning.com.

YOU ARE PART OF THE SCRIPT

Consider this book to be a partial script. You, the principal player in the development of your own career, will fill in the blanks. You will be carefully coached and directed through exercises that will help you identify, confirm, and realize your job and career goals. Good communication skills are vital to achieving career success. For this reason, you will be given ample guidance, practice, and real applications in developing winning resumes and cover letters and in developing verbal and nonverbal skills required to get and succeed in job interviews.

How to Get the Most From This Book

Before reading a chapter, review the learning objectives listed on the first page of the chapter to see exactly what you will learn. An overall summary is presented in the first paragraphs of each chapter to clarify the content.

The assignments are designed to focus on your personal job and career goals, not on generalized theories. Reading alone will not give you the practice you need to develop these skills adequately. You will be an active doer, taking charge of your own career success by following the guided steps necessary to ensure it. To get the best results, read each chapter and study and complete all the assignments. The path is clearly laid out for you to reach your job and career goals.

Evaluation

To assess your understanding of the principles of each chapter and to identify any areas you need to review, three levels of evaluation are provided with the curriculum for *Your Career: How to Make It Happen:*

Critical Thinking Questions are included at the end of each chapter. The purpose of these questions is to prompt your consideration of how the key concepts of the chapter apply directly to you and your career goals.

Chapter Tests are provided on the Instructor's Resource CD. Your instructor may use these tests to evaluate your mastery of the key concepts of each chapter.

Case Studies are provided on the Learner's CD. They are designed to give you practice in applying the essential career concepts for each chapter.

Develop Lifetime Career Skills and Information

Each chapter of this book contains Career Actions, special assignments to help you develop skills and compile information necessary for getting the job you want, succeeding in it, and advancing your career. Many of these assignments make use of corresponding perforated worksheets found at the end of the chapters. You can write your answers on these forms, or you can access the forms on the Learner's CD and complete them using your computer. Some assignments are to be prepared using separate paper. If possible, use the forms on your Learner's CD for easier completion of assignments. See additional detail regarding the Learner's CD under the headings "Content of the Learner's CD" and "Back Up Your Career Action Assignment Content."

The information you assemble by completing the Career Action assignments is essential for developing your resumes, cover letters, employment applications, networking lists, and so on, throughout your life. You will file your completed Career Actions in your Career Management Files Binder, creating a convenient collection of information you can quickly access and update any time you pursue a job or career goal. You will be making a smart investment in your lifetime career success as you create your personal base of career information.

Content of the Learner's CD

The all-new Learner's CD provides greater convenience and added value. The components are summarized below:

- **Career Action assignments** that contain forms are now available on the new Learner's CD, and content can be keyed into the forms instead of handwritten on the forms in the textbook. These Career Action forms are provided in both formats, however, for students who do not have ready access to computers.

- **Complete set of PowerPoint Slides** review key points of all chapters. These slides increase knowledge retention and serve as a convenient study guide.

- **Case Studies** and Case Study Questions are included for each chapter. These Case Studies are designed to reinforce key chapter topics through an application-focused exercise.

- **Model Documents** are provided, including selected model resumes, cover letters, and other career development resource materials.

Back Up Your Career Action Assignment Content

Because so much of the information you gain and so many of the documents you create while using the text will be useful throughout your career, you should back up your work. In this way, you will have convenient access to your basic resume, cover letter, networking information, and more. By backing up all files throughout the course on your personal storage media, you will create a kind of electronic "Career-to-Go." This media will contain all of your essential career data, which you can easily update or revise any time you seek a promotion or a job or career change.

Use the following procedures to back up your work:

- **Career Action Forms.** Selected Career Action forms are provided on the Learner's CD as read-only files, which you can retrieve and complete electronically. Permanently save your completed Career Action forms onto your hard drive or network drive, and then back them up on a personal diskette or CD.

- **Job Search Documents.** Also back up all other job search document files (cover and other job search letters, resumes, reference sheets, and so on) you create throughout the course onto a personal diskette or CD.

Storage of Backup Media. Store all of your backup media in your Career Management Files Binder. Also save your completed resumes and cover letters and the other career management documents you create in your Career Actions onto a personal CD.

A FINAL WORD OF ADVICE AND ENCOURAGEMENT

National studies verify that job seekers who are persistent, informed of current job market trends, and organized in their approach are at least 80 percent more successful in attaining their career goals than those without this training. The tools necessary to succeed in your job search and career development are conveniently organized in this book. Apply these tools to maximize your career potential and the quality of your working life.

It's YOUR CAREER—make it happen with the winning success tools presented in this text!

ACKNOWLEDGMENTS

This book reflects the influence of many people skilled in career management education. Foremost in this category is the thorough and professional writing and subject-matter guidance provided by:

Karen Schneiter Williams, Professor, Computer Business Technology Department, San Diego Mesa College. Karen strengthened the curriculum content and professional perspective by revising and updating seven of the chapters and by advising and assisting with editing on many topics in this fifth edition of the textbook. Karen is highly regarded in the business education community. She worked on the National Standards for Business Education in 1995 and 2001 and is currently one of the writers on a new publication providing instructional strategies for integrating the 11 areas in business, including career development. She also is serving as a contributing author and coauthor of an English grammar text and has served as a contributing author of technology chapters for three business communication texts.

Mr. Richard Rapp, Associate Vice President for Student Affairs and Director of the Career Center, Boise State University. Mr. Rapp contributed significantly by writing Chapter 20, updating Chapter 8, and editing and advising on the text.

Mr. Rapp has personally assisted over 20,000 people in finding appropriate career employment. He also serves in leadership roles in local and national career planning and placement organizations.

Shelley Metzger, Ph.D., Associate Director, Boise State University Career Center. With her expertise in career counseling and education, Shelley greatly enhanced the curriculum by revising and updating the chapter tests and WebTutor quizzes, developing the new Case Studies, assisting with revision of the model resumes and teaching activities, and assisting with research for the textbook.

In addition, the following people deserve recognition for their contributions to this curriculum. **Lynne Whaley,** textbook author and resume/career expert, researched and wrote many of the resumes and job search letters, developing excellent market-driven content. **Mary Seroski,** computer technology expert, network specialist, and programmer with The Network Group, provided important research assistance with computer technology and electronic resume topics and developed the set of motivational slides. **Ben Botti,** University of California at Davis, assisted with research and development of content regarding web resume technology. He also serves as the web master for the *Your Career: How to Make It Happen* site.

Grateful acknowledgment is made to **Dr. and Mrs. Richard Griffin,** the sources of inspiration and experience upon which Chapter 1 of this text is based.

Importantly, I wish to recognize **Dr. Monte Levitt,** who provided artwork and the personal support so essential to developing this comprehensive curriculum. Thank you, Monte, I am profoundly grateful.

I am also grateful to the following reviewers and instructors who offered valuable suggestions and support:

Gerry Ellis
DeVry University-Kansas City
Kansas City, MO

Terry Engleman
Spokane Falls Community College
Spokane, WA

Darien V. Hartman
Boise State University
Boise, ID

Lori L. Jacobson
North Idaho College
Coeur D'Alene, ID

Kevin LaMountain
DeVry University-Phoenix
Phoenix, AZ

Dr. Carolyn Paul
DeVry University-Pomona
Pomona, CA

Patricia A. Pou
Sanford-Brown College
Hazelwood, MO

"As a former Personnel Recruiter for a Fortune 500 company, I strongly recommend this book to anyone who is looking for a challenging, well-compensated career. I only wish this book was on the market when I was looking for a career!"

Darryl Wright
Leadership & Employee Development
Corporate Training & Education
Micron Technology, Inc.

ABOUT THE AUTHOR

Photographed by Sims Studios, Inc.

Julie Griffin Levitt is a corporate trainer and consultant, lecturer, and author of numerous educational and training publications. She teaches and consults throughout the United States and in Canada in the areas of career planning and job search skills, office occupations, written and oral communications, supervision, and personal motivation. Her home base is Boise, Idaho.

She has taught job-seeking and career planning skills at the secondary and postsecondary levels. The job placement ratio of her students is 97 percent or better.

chapter 1

REACH YOUR FULL CAREER POTENTIAL

In this chapter, you will:

 Set up a Career Management Files System.

- Use affirmation statements and positive self-talk to help achieve your goals.

- Identify techniques for successfully setting and achieving your goals.

- Improve assertive behavior and apply it in your job search.

 Access the Internet and complete a proactive success action plan.

"A sense of purpose generates action and movement in the direction of dreams and goals, while wishes generate only half-hearted intentions. Think about it. Purpose says, 'I will do this.' Wish says, 'If only I could.'

Life is not a spectator sport. Set your sights on what you want in your career and then make it happen. Now, what are you waiting for?"

Joan C. Borgatti, R.N, M.Ed.
Editorial Director
www.nursingspectrum.com

Chapter 1 provides guidelines to help you strengthen career-boosting skills, attitudes, and strategies that persuade employers to hire and promote. You will learn and apply nine strategies to give you the competitive edge in achieving career success and reaching your full potential.

GET THE COMPETITIVE EDGE WITH NINE SUCCESS STRATEGIES

Successful leaders in all fields, from business to entertainment, consistently use the nine success strategies discussed in this chapter to help them achieve their career goals. These strategies focus on positive attitudes and actions. Throughout the world, Olympic sports psychologists coach competitors to achieve maximum performance by learning and applying these strategies. Renowned motivational experts such as Anthony Robbins, Brian Tracy, Denis Waitley, and Stephen Covey teach these strategies to help business leaders, politicians, and performers reach their peak potential.

Use Nine Success Strategies

Review and use the nine strategies that follow to help achieve your full career potential. They profoundly affect career success at every step.

1. Positive Thinking and Behavior

2. Visualization

3. Positive Self-Talk

4. Affirmation Statements

5. Dynamic Goal Setting

6. Positive Action

7. Assertive Behavior

8. Self-Esteem Builders

9. Proactive Habits

These nine success strategies and behaviors are major career enhancers that help transform goals into realities. Pay close attention to any that are new ideas for you. They provide wide-ranging benefits; you can use them to:

- Create and sustain your inner drive.

- Increase your confidence.

- Provide mental and physical energy.

- Guide you toward goals.

- Help you project competence, enthusiasm, and presence.

- Improve performance.

It's shocking but true. The most qualified person is not always the one who gets the job or promotion. The person hired is the one the employer perceives to be the most qualified. Your experience, skills, resumes, and more—your entire job search package—are greatly enhanced by practicing these key success strategies.

SUCCESS TIP

The person hired is not always the most qualified, but the one perceived as most qualified. Nine success strategies enhance your ability to project winning competence.

Set Up Your Career Management Files Binder

To help you prepare for job search and career success, *Your Career: How to Make It Happen* guides you through development of your own Career Management Files. Your Career Management Files will include career development and job search documents (self-assessments, records of experience and skills developed, resumes, cover letters, job search organizational aids, and more) you can use throughout your career each time you seek a new promotion, a new job, or a career change. Career Action 1-1 is the first step in organizing this essential career information.

Complete Career Action 1-1

Improve Performance Through Positive Thinking and Behavior

Positive thinking is making a conscious effort to think with an optimistic attitude and to anticipate positive outcomes. *Positive behavior* means purposely

CAREER ACTION 1-1

Set Up Your Career Management Files System

Directions: In Appendix B, Career Management Tool 1: Career Management Files, follow the instructions to set up your own Career Management Files Binder. In this binder, store completed Career Actions specified throughout the book. When you have completed all of these, you will have a valuable collection of career-related information you can use throughout your life. Your completed binder will include records of your education and work experience, summaries of job- and career-related values and skills, resumes, cover letters, and more.

acting with energy and enthusiasm. When you think and behave positively, you guide your mind toward your goals and generate matching mental and physical energy.

Positive thinking and behavior are often deciding factors in landing top jobs: your first job, a promotion, a change of jobs—whatever career step you are targeting. That's because the subconscious is literal; it accepts what you regard as fact.

The function of your subconscious is to support your thoughts and behaviors by triggering matching physiological responses. Research has proved that positive thinking and behavior have a powerful impact on personal performance, confidence, and even health. This chapter explains how you can learn to use the power of autosuggestion to enhance your performance and career development.

Positive thinking causes the brain to generate matching positive chemical and physical responses, such as increased mental alertness and physical energy, improved respiration and circulation, and increased beneficial endorphins. Thinking positively actually boosts your ability to perform and to project enthusiasm, energy, competence, and confidence—the qualities interviewers look for when they hire and promote candidates.

SUCCESS TIP

Think and act positively. Doing so profoundly improves performance and outcome.

Figure 1-1: You project your positive self-image.

Negative thinking causes the brain to stimulate matching negative chemicals and physical responses, such as increased blood pressure, reduced mental alertness, increased anxiety, decreased physical energy, and fight or flight reactions. These responses decrease energy, creativity, and performance and simultaneously erode self-confidence.

Follow these steps to form the habit of positive thinking and to boost your success:

1. **Deliberately motivate yourself every day.** Think of yourself as successful, and expect positive outcomes for everything you attempt.

2. **Project energy and enthusiasm.** Employers hire people who project positive energy and enthusiasm. Develop the habit of speaking, moving, and acting with these qualities.

3. **Practice this positive expectation mind-set** until it becomes a habit. Applicants who project enthusiasm and positive behavior generate a positive chemistry that rubs off. Hiring decisions are influenced largely by this positive energy. The habit will help you reach your peak potential.

4. **Dwell on past successes.** Focusing on past successes to remind yourself of your abilities helps in attaining goals. For example, no one is ever born knowing how to ride a bicycle or how to use a computer software program. Through training, practice, and trial and error, you master new abilities. During the trial-and-error phases of development, remind yourself of past successes; look at mistakes as part of the natural learning curve. Continue until you achieve the result you want, and remind yourself that you have succeeded in the past and can do so again. You fail only when you quit trying!

> *"No pessimist ever discovered the secrets of the stars, or sailed to an uncharted land, or opened a new heaven to the human spirit."*
>
> Helen Keller

SUCCESS TIP

Interviewers say projecting enthusiasm and positive behaviors generate a positive chemistry that is a big hiring advantage.

Use Visualization to Your Advantage

Positive visualization is purposely forming a mental picture of your successful performance and recalling the image frequently. Visualization improves performance because the positive picture triggers your subconscious to generate matching positive physiological responses that increase performance.

Athletic champions and successful people throughout the world use positive visualization to boost their performance and achieve goals. The act of visualizing successful performance of any skill or activity in detail actually increases learning and skill development. This is because visualization serves as a form of mental practice or rehearsal that strengthens performance. Have you used it personally or in a group to help improve performance? This is definitely a technique you want to apply in all your career activities.

Apply the following visualization techniques to boost your success in job searches and interviews and in attaining goals:

1. **Relax.** Sit in a chair, close your eyes, breathe deeply, and clear your mind.

2. **Mentally draw a picture or create a mental video** that shows you succeeding in your goal. To project a positive and competent image, visualize yourself doing just that—walking and speaking with confidence, maintaining good posture, and performing optimally.

3. **Make the picture detailed and visualize success.** Do not permit any negative visions or thoughts (fear, failure, anxiety, or errors). See yourself as already having achieved your goal.

4. **Incorporate pictures, words, actions, and senses.** Mentally practice exactly what you plan to say or do. This mental rehearsal literally strengthens your actual performance.

5. **Dwell on the image; be able to recall it instantly.** Repeat the visual picture as often as possible before the actual event.

SUCCESS TIP

Visualize your positive performance. Your brain then triggers positive responses that enhance performance.

Practice Positive Self-Talk

Positive self-talk means purposely giving yourself positive reinforcement, motivation, and recognition—just as you would do for a friend. Congratulate yourself when you do well, and remind yourself of your abilities, accomplishments, strengths, and skills. Keep a to-do list, check off accomplishments, and review your progress periodically.

Make Self-Talk Work for You. What you habitually say to yourself has a profound impact on your self-image, your self-esteem, and your performance and success. Remember, your subconscious triggers physiological responses that match the pictures and thoughts you have of yourself to make them happen. Make this work *for* you by keeping your self-talk positive. For example:

- I did a good job on that report.
- I can do this.

Stop Negative Self-Talk. You may be quick to nag yourself because you want to be perfect. However, negative self-talk is damaging because the subconscious literally believes what you say about yourself. If you catch yourself using negative self-talk, stop and rephrase. Eliminate the negative words. Focus instead on the best course of action you can take and *do it.*

Make positive communication a habit. Focus on the positive in goal statements, self-talk, and all communications. Compare the following phrases and notice how the positive words convey confidence, commitment, and enthusiasm.

Negative	Positive
I'll try	I will
I should do	I will do
I must	I want to/I choose to

Winning athletes use visualization, affirmation, and positive self-talk to improve performance and reach their goals. You can too!

Focus With Affirmation Statements

Affirmation statements are positive self-statements or reminders to help achieve goals. They are positive messages with a punch, "mental bumper stickers" to motivate your subconscious to work for you. The following guidelines explain how to use this powerful mental reminder technique:

1. **Make the statements personal.** Use *I*, your name, or *you.*

2. **Keep affirmations short!** If you can't remember them, how can you use them?

3. **Phrase them positively.** The mind accepts as truth the words you give it. Use positive words only. Leave out negative words. For example:

   - **Negative:** I will not be nervous during my interview.
   - **Positive:** I will be calm and self-assured during my interview.

4. **Include a positive emotion.** A phrase that triggers a positive emotion strengthens the affirmation. Example: "My goal is *valuable* and it *excites* me."

5. **Phrase affirmations as fact.** Phrase a goal as if it is happening or has happened (even if you haven't achieved it yet). Your subconscious believes mental messages and works to make them reality.

   - I am making good progress on my goal.

   - I am strengthening my speaking abilities.

6. **Say your affirmations at least once a day.** Repetition enhances self-confidence, acts as a reminder, and stimulates your subconscious to help you achieve your goal.

> Complete Career Action 1-2

SUCCESS TIP

Use positive self-talk and affirmation statements to trigger matching positive physical responses that enhance performance.

Get Ahead With Dynamic Goal Setting

Career goal setting involves recording clear objectives and required actions to achieve them. The main rea-son people don't achieve goals is because they don't set any to begin with. Use the following steps to focus your efforts and to maximize your goal achievement. You can also use this process to set team or group goals.

1. **Define your goals clearly in writing.** Writing down your goals increases the likelihood of achieving them by 80 percent! Writing goals increases your sense of commitment, clarifies required steps in the achievement process, and helps you remember important details.

2. **Identify and focus on the benefits** (to you and others) of achieving goals. This is a strong motivator.

3. **Define the purpose of your goals.** Link your goals to a practical, specific purpose. To boost your own motivation, base your goals on inspiration, not just logic.

4. **Identify supportive forces for you.** Examples of supportive forces include instructors, books, training, people who encourage you to persevere, skilled coaches or mentors, and printed and online research materials.

5. **Develop an action plan, set deadlines, and act.** Establish subgoals. Divide each main goal into logical, progressive steps. Set deadlines for completing each step, and complete steps on time.

6. **Establish priorities.** Take action in order of priority.

CAREER ACTION 1-2

Practice Positive Self-Talk and Affirmation Statements

Directions: Access your Learner's CD or use a separate sheet of paper to write your responses.

1. Recall a goal you have been striving to achieve and on which you are making progress. Then write a positive statement about your progress.

2. Describe one or more of your work skills or abilities that fit the requirements of the job you are or will be seeking. Write complete sentences.

3. Write an affirmation statement to use as a reminder to help you achieve an important career goal.

7. **Make a public commitment.** If appropriate, share your goals with someone who encourages you to go the extra mile—to increase your sense of responsibility and provide motivation.

8. **Be realistic about limitations.** Don't set a short-term goal to get a job requiring more education. Set separate goals to get the education, take an interim job, and then reach the ultimate goal.

9. **Use positive self-talk and affirmation statements.** Do this every day! Write down your statements, post them prominently, and review them regularly.

SUCCESS TIP

Write down your goals and you'll increase their achievement by 80 percent! Focus on how achieving your goals will benefit you and others.

10. **Use positive visualization.** This boosts goal achievement.

11. **Practice.** Practice new skills regularly. Get additional information, training, coaching, and feedback on your progress.

12. **Evaluate and revise goals as necessary.** Evaluate your progress. Experiment with new methods if you're not getting the results you want, and, if necessary, revise your goals.

13. **Persevere.** Stay the course until you succeed!

14. **Reward yourself.** Rewards are motivators. As you make progress toward your goals, do something nice for yourself.

15. **Record progress on your goals.** As simplistic as it seems, a long series of check marks on a calendar can motivate you by providing a sense of accomplishment. However, don't let missing an occasional daily goal deter you. Keep focusing on the ultimate goal.

"When we set goals, the magic begins: The switch turns on, the current starts to flow, and the power to accomplish becomes a reality."

Wynn Davis
The Best of Success

Take Positive Action

When you take regular positive action (no matter how small) and make progress toward goals, you create real evidence of achievement. This increases confidence and creativity and boosts your momentum. Action fuels more action! Deliberately plan and regularly work toward your goals to maximize your success.

Say you have a long-term goal of specializing in a career field. You can take momentum-building intermediate actions, as follows:

- Research to learn exactly what skills you need to qualify in the specialty. Contact specialists in your area to learn what skills they require.

- Take courses to help you develop these skills. As you complete each one, you will be a step closer to your final goal.

- Work in an entry-level position for a firm noted in your targeted specialty area. Then get additional training or education to qualify for the specialty.

- Get help in arranging an internship or a work-study program with a firm noted in your target specialty area.

Complete Career Action 1-3

Develop Assertive Abilities

Assertive behavior is:
- Standing up for your own rights.

- Expressing yourself honestly, courteously, and comfortably.

- Observing and respecting the rights of others.

Assertive behavior promotes equality and a healthy balance in human relationships. Assertion is based on human rights—especially the right to be treated with respect in all situations. Every person has the right to be listened to and taken seriously, to say yes or no with conviction, to express his or her opinion, and to ask for what he or she wants.

Assertive Behavior Is Critical in Your Job Search.

Why is assertiveness critical to a successful job search and career potential? Assertiveness conveys self-esteem and capability.

Employers hire people who behave confidently and are able to convey their job qualifications comfortably and clearly. They want employees who strengthen human relations and project competence in the workplace through assertive behavior. They hire applicants who demonstrate assertiveness in interviews, resumes, and all communications. To reach your full career potential, be assertive and tactful in expressing yourself, and respect the rights of others.

Assertive Behavior Is Critical to Workplace

Success. Personality types fall into three general categories: nonassertive, aggressive, and assertive. Employers avoid hiring nonassertive and aggressive employees because they are often detrimental in the workplace.

- **Nonassertive People.** These people have difficulty expressing thoughts or feelings because they lack confidence. Nonassertive people may become unhappy because they permit others to abuse their rights. They project their feelings of unhappiness to others.

SUCCESS TIP

Behave assertively to enhance interview and career success.

- **Aggressive People.** These people violate the rights of others with domineering, pushy behavior. Their goal is to dominate because they fear loss of control. Overly aggressive employees drive business away; therefore, employers avoid hiring them.

- **Assertive People.** Assertive behavior is essential to achieving career success. Assertive people are confident, express their needs and opinions comfortably, and are sensitive to the feelings and needs of others. Employers want assertive employees because assertive behavior projects capability and promotes a healthy, productive working environment.

Building Assertiveness Skills. Being assertive requires having healthy self-esteem. Therefore, a key to improving assertiveness is to strengthen self-esteem. Because all the success strategies and behaviors discussed in this chapter build self-esteem, they also enhance assertiveness.

CAREER ACTION 1-3

Practice Dynamic Goal Setting and Positive Actions

 Directions: Access your Learner's CD or use a separate sheet of paper to write your responses.

1. Review and follow the guidelines for dynamic goal setting on pages 6–7. Identify a goal that is important to you.

2. Write down your goal and describe it by addressing goal-setting guidelines 1-5.

3. Identify three to five positive actions you can take in the next ten days to achieve this goal.

4. Follow up by actually completing all 15 guidelines.

Employers look for people who behave confidently and respect the rights of others.

practice showing respect for others more openly. The winning combination is *assertiveness + respect.*

Techniques for Developing Assertiveness. Review the following techniques for improving assertiveness. Practice expressing your feelings and needs calmly and clearly. Also demonstrate acceptance and respect for others by praising them when they perform or behave well.

1. **Initiate a friendship.** Invite a person you don't know well to have coffee or lunch. Take time to get to know him or her.

2. **Express your opinion** in a meeting or conversation, particularly when you believe strongly about the topic—even if everyone else doesn't appear to agree with you.

3. **Join a professional or service organization or club,** and volunteer to serve on a committee. What a way to network and build your assertive skills!

4. **Compliment someone** on a skill, a talent, an achievement, or a positive quality.

5. **Tell someone when he or she has offended you unfairly.** Evaluate first to be certain the person was actually unfair. Being overly sensitive can impair your assertiveness.

6. **Return faulty merchandise** to get an immediate replacement or a free repair.

7. **Initiate a conversation** with a stranger before or after a class, meeting, or social event. (Just try it; you'll like it!)

Complete Career Action 1-4

Practicing Assertiveness. Strive to deal with others in a confident, positive way without appearing boastful or overbearing. Force yourself to be more open, to express your ideas and needs, and to perform with greater confidence. At the same time,

CAREER ACTION 1-4

Improve Assertiveness

Directions: Review the techniques for developing assertiveness just discussed. Select at least two activities for practicing assertiveness—exercises provided in the chapter or others more pertinent to your needs. Access your Learner's CD to write out a plan for improving your assertiveness skills through the exercises you have chosen and follow through with your plan.

Enhance Your Self-Esteem

Projecting confidence requires a healthy self-esteem (belief in your abilities and your worth). Think how easy it is to project a confident, competent image when you feel good about yourself. By developing the success habits outlined in this chapter, you will strengthen your self-esteem.

Enhancing Your Self-Esteem. Begin by describing yourself in writing. You might want to ask a friend or family member to help. Make two lists: one of your positive traits and one of your negative traits. Which list is longer? If it's your positive list, you have a good base for self-esteem. If it's your negative list, you must work harder to develop a strong sense of self-confidence. By doing so, you strengthen your assertive abilities because good self-esteem makes behaving assertively easy.

Next, identify negative images you want to change. Begin with the trait you think you should improve first. For example, a negative trait may be a lack of initiative, expressiveness, or organization. Improving self-image often requires developing a positive habit, such as reading more to improve vocabulary or exercising to improve fitness.

After you identify the traits you want to improve, develop your action plan. Write your goal in positive terms, as shown in Figure 1-2. Write your Action Plan so you can evaluate it daily. This makes progress easy to evaluate and provides reinforcement. Put a check mark on your calendar each day you make progress toward your goal. This seems simplistic but it is surprisingly motivational.

Action Plan

Goal: To improve my public-speaking skills by enrolling in a workshop.

Personal Action Plan for Achieving Goal: On Tuesday afternoon, I will research dates and times for public-speaking workshops offered on campus. After I have the scheduling information, I will sign up for the workshop sessions that fit my schedule. Once I have completed and participated in the sessions, I will write a summary of the skills I learned. In the summary, I will identify the three most important points to use in my public speaking. My next goal will be to practice my public speaking!

Time Frame for Action Plan: I will write the public-speaking workshop session dates and times in my planner. I will attend all sessions offered this semester.

Figure 1-2: Action Plan

PERSONAL BEST

Maintaining Work and Life Balance

Balancing the demands of your work and personal life can sometimes feel like a juggling act. As you identify career goals that are important to you, consider how these goals impact:

- **Your values.** What do you consider important in your life—family, personal interests, work, education, community service, spiritual development, and so on?

- **Your priorities.** Based on your values, which daily tasks are most important to you? Which are least important?

- **Your physical health.** With a fit body, you are better able to deal with emotional stress and physical strain.

- **Your stress level.** Are your goals achievable? Be realistic about what you can accomplish in one day.

Today many employers are sensitive to the importance of personal and professional balance. They know that employees who achieve a healthy balance in life are happier and more productive. Explore with employers how you can achieve a healthy life/work balance *and* deliver top-quality results for your employer.

Effects of Negative Self-Esteem and Fear. Negative self-image holds you back by promoting fear of failure. It prevents you from taking risks that can lead to growth and development. The result is stagnation, even regression, but not successful development. Have you ever avoided attempting a new activity or goal because you feared failure or rejection?

Sometimes you base your behavior on imagined fears, not on facts. You allow fear to limit your full potential. Following are tips for dealing constructively with fears and enhancing your success.

1. When working on a challenging goal, such as public speaking, avoid negative images. Concentrate on developing your skills and knowledge; then plan and act positively, and visualize your success in detail.

2. Assess the situation. Get training or additional information if necessary.

3. Seek support from those who motivate you.

4. Act with courage and conviction; be persistent.

Maintaining a Healthy Self-Esteem. Because you may experience changing levels of self-esteem resulting from life experiences, you need to work deliberately at strengthening and maintaining self-esteem. A few techniques for building self-esteem are as follows:

1. **Believe it can be done and make a commitment.** Remember how positive suggestion positively influences your subconscious!

2. **Identify your strengths** in writing, and dwell on past successes.

3. **Set written goals** for improvement and take action.

4. **Practice positive self-talk.**

5. **Visualize your success.**

6. **Make positive action a habit.**

7. **Surround yourself with a positive environment** (positive people and positive reading, viewing, and listening materials).

8. **Look good to feel good.** Looking your best boosts your confidence, and others respond positively to a good appearance.

9. **Stay fit.** Take care of your body, mind, and spirit. Exercise, eat properly, rest, and balance work with other life activities.

Develop Proactive Skills

In his world-acclaimed book 7 *Habits of Highly Successful People,* Stephen Covey emphasizes that the way people typically approach challenging situations and tasks is a major determinant of career success. Many choose either a proactive or reactive approach in dealing with difficulties or challenging tasks and situations. They may also fall into the habit of using one of the approaches predominantly. One of these approaches is a consistent career booster; the other, a guaranteed detriment.

Behaviors common to both approaches are outlined in Figure 1-3.

The Proactive Approach—A Synergy Booster. The proactive approach to dealing with challenges focuses on problem solution and positive action. Those who use this approach aim to resolve problems or master challenging tasks by taking full responsibility for their assignments and career growth. They actively seek resources for goal achievement. They also strive for win-win solutions that best meet the needs of all involved.

Proactive people also regularly practice the nine positive success strategies emphasized in this chapter. All of theses success strategies enhance your ability to take proactive steps that will boost your career success.

Typical Proactive Behaviors	Typical Reactive Behaviors
Focus on problem solution/personal growth	Focus on problems/difficulties of the situation (not on solutions) and have a generally negative attitude
Take responsibility for own behavior and for personal or team assignments and productivity	Blame others or circumstances for the difficulty or try to shift responsibility for solution to others
Seek synergistic solutions through productive relationships	Procrastinate in the face of a difficult task or problem
Employ personal motivation skills based on positive expectations	Don't seek resources for problem solution (networking, researching for useful information, and so on)
Encourage/assist others	Don't strive to motivate self or others to improve or excel
Network and strive to develop mutually beneficial relationships, share information and perspectives, get and give support	Diminish energy of others around them

Figure 1-3: Typical Proactive and Reactive Behaviors

Develop strong proactive habits and associate with other proactive people. The contagious synergy can mutually expand your potential immeasurably.

The Reactive Approach Is a Career Minimizer. The reactive approach focuses on problem avoidance and negative personal reactions. Those who fall into this habit focus on problems, not on solutions. Their habitually negative behaviors greatly diminish their career opportunities and, in some cases, can lead to depression.

Both Approaches Are Contagious. Have you noticed how enjoyable it is to be around people who are typically proactive? Their positive, supportive, and action-oriented behaviors are energizing and motivating—they "rub off" on those they work and interact with. They motivate others to perform at their best, and they infuse a healthy aura that encourages creativity and increases productivity.

Rewards of Proactive Behaviors Are Great. With practice, you will increase your ability to use proactive behavior as your predominant style and enjoy greater success throughout your career. Also, by associating with other proactive people, the contagious synergy can mutually expand your career potential. The following list summarizes the beneficial outcomes that result from developing good proactive skills.

- Enhance self-esteem/increase personal motivation
- Increase problem-solving skills
- Increase self-esteem and professional reputation
- Improve ability to correct personal errors and strengthen skills
- Build positive working relationships that boost career success potential for all
- Improve performance in all endeavors
- Gain skills under direction of mentors and in networking with others
- Increase knowledge and career resources
- Expand perspective

Complete Career Action 1-5

CAREER ACTION 1-5

Access the Internet and Develop a Proactive Success Action Plan

Directions: Launch your web browser and follow the steps below.

1. Access the *Your Career: How to Make It Happen* web site at www.levitt.swlearning.com. (You will be accessing this web site for numerous Career Actions, so bookmark this address in your web browser.)

2. Locate the **Proactive Success Action Plan** form.

3. Read the instructions and enter your answers on the form for the **Proactive Success Action Plan**.

4. Print your completed form and file it in your Career Management Files Binder.

APPLY THE NINE SUCCESS STRATEGIES

Use the nine success strategies emphasized in this chapter to reach your full career potential. Apply these success strategies regularly throughout your job search and career. Throughout your life, pursue your goals with an assertive belief in yourself and your rights and practice thinking and acting positively and proactively. Success is not a one-time destination; it's a lifelong journey.

✓ CHECKLIST:

Applying Nine Success Strategies

☐ Think and act positively.

☐ Visualize your positive performance.

☐ Use positive self-talk.

☐ Use affirmation statements.

☐ Write clear short-term and long-term goals, and revise them when necessary.

☐ Take regular action to achieve defined goals.

☐ Practice assertive behavior.

☐ Maintain self-esteem through positive thinking and actions.

☐ Develop proactive skills.

critical thinking *Questions*

1. Which of the nine success strategies are most useful for strengthening your career planning and job search success?

2. How can projecting enthusiasm and positive expectations help you in an interview?

3. What are the effects positive and negative thoughts, images, and self-talk have on performance?

4. Would you rate your own assertiveness skills as excellent, good, or needing improvement? If you need improvement, what specific actions can you take to strengthen them?

5. What should be compiled in your Career Management Files Binder? How will it be useful to you throughout your career?

chapter **2**

TAKE A LOOK AT YOURSELF

In this chapter, you will:

- Document your education, work experience, and other activities related to a potential career to use in your job search and career development.

- Identify the career-related skills you developed through your education and work experience.

- Identify your personal, school-related, and work-related accomplishments.

- Use the Internet to complete personal assessments for planning and confirming your career choices.

"What do you want out of your life and your career? If you're like most people, you answer those questions with words like 'success' and 'happiness.' But unless you stop to figure out exactly what those words mean to you, the odds are stacked against you ever achieving either.

So what's the best way to figure out your specific life and career goals? Formalize the process. Take out a pad and pen, and spend an afternoon really studying your life."

Eric Wilinski
Senior Manager of Content
WetFeet

In Chapter 2, you take a complete inventory of your education, training, experience, accomplishments, values, work preferences, and performance traits. This personal inventory is an essential tool for developing or confirming your career target and for conveying your qualifications to potential employers.

KNOWING YOURSELF—A MUST FOR YOUR CAREER SUCCESS

To achieve each step (your first job, a promotion, or a job or career change) throughout your career, you must sell the product—you. Just as successful salespeople must know their products, you must know your qualifications and be able to communicate them clearly to employers in a resume, in a cover letter, and in interviews.

To help ensure wise job and career choices, you need to clarify what values and work environment preferences are important to you. The Chapter 2 Career Actions help you thoroughly inventory your training, education, skills, and work experience and identify your values and work preferences.

> *"It's not what you've got, it's what you use that makes a difference."*
>
> Zig Ziglar

Your Personal Career Inventory

In this chapter, all the information you compile about yourself through the Career Action assignments will form your personal career inventory. This will be an important source of information when you develop your resumes, cover letters, job applications, and more. Employers may want this information when considering you for a job. Included in this compilation are basic personal data and information about the following:

- Education and professional training

- Work experience, skills, and accomplishments

- People you can use as references

Record Education, Training, and Organizational Activities

The first step in compiling your personal career inventory is to document your education and training, including dates, places, career-relevant courses and activities, skills, and accomplishments. You will also document your membership and achievements in professional and other organizations related to your job and career targets. This information will help you identify or confirm an appropriate career choice, develop resumes and cover letters, and prepare for job interviews.

Complete this section of your personal career inventory thoroughly and accurately. Put yourself under a microscope, and look at every detail carefully. Ask people who know you well to help you document your accomplishments. Consider scholarships, honors, and awards you have received and competitions in which you have participated. In describing accomplishments, be as specific as possible. For example:

- Won first place in school math competition.

- Voted president of the senior class.

When identifying the skills and accomplishments you developed through your education, training, and organizational activities, consider two kinds of skills (or competencies) that employers are seeking: job-specific skills and transferable competencies.

Job-Specific Skills. Job-specific skills are the technical abilities that relate *specifically* to a particular job. For example, in accounting, preparing a balance sheet by using accounting software customized for a client is a job-specific skill. Relining brakes on a vehicle is a job-specific skill for an auto mechanic. Operating medical diagnostic equipment is also a job-specific skill.

Transferable Competencies. Transferable competencies are abilities you have that can be applied in more than one work environment. For example, both accountants and auto mechanics are required to have such transferable competencies as the ability to read, write, use mathematics, and use computers. Other transferable competencies include working well with others, leading, organizing work and materials, solving problems, making decisions, and managing resources.

> Complete Career Action 2-1

CAREER ACTION 2-1

Education, Training, and Organizational Activities Inventory

Directions: Access Career Action 2-1 on your Learner's CD, or use the form on page 22 of your text. Complete each section of the form that applies to you. Be thorough in providing details.

List Experience and Skills

In Career Action 2-2, you will document all your work and other pertinent experience and include the dates and places of these experiences. You will also list the skills and knowledge you developed and any accomplishments, achievements, or recognition you received as part of these experiences. You want to include both job-specific skills and transferable competencies.

Experience should include paid or volunteer work (e.g., volunteering on community service projects and fund-raising), internships, or cooperative education experience. Be specific about the contributions you made. For example:

- Raised 20 percent more in contributions over previous year.

- Designed a web interface for LAN bandwidth usage tracking, improving network efficiency by 45 percent.

- Suggested new file management procedures that reduced filing error rate by 25 percent.

Complete Career Action 2-2

Identify Job References

The final step in completing your personal career inventory is to identify job references. A job reference is someone who can vouch for your capabilities, skills, and suitability for a job. References are typically people who have been your instructors and coaches in school or your supervisors or coworkers in volunteer and paid work environments. Therefore, you should review your inventory of education and work experience for potential job references.

Identify people who can *and are willing* to confirm (from firsthand observation) your good performance

> *"All our dreams can come true, if we have the courage to pursue them."*
>
> Walt Disney

CAREER ACTION 2-2

Experience and Skills Inventory

Directions: Access Career Action 2-2 on your Learner's CD, or use the form on page 26 of your text. Complete each section of the form that applies to you. Be as specific and thorough as possible.

Coaches make good job references since they have first-hand knowledge of your determination to achieve goals and your ability to work with others.

on the job, in school, or in other activities. Employers usually want at least three job references listed on application forms. Ideally, these references are supervisors, employers, or others who know your work well. Relatives or classmates are not appropriate references. The more references you have available, the better prepared you are for your current and future job campaign.

If you are qualified to work in two different fields, such as retail sales and accounting, you will get the best results by having one set of references targeted for each of the two fields, or a total of six references (three in the sales field and three in the accounting field). Some organizations ask for different types of references. For example, an employer may ask for personal as well as professional references.

Use Career Action 2-3 to identify people you can use as your references. Make note of how they know you and in what areas they can speak about your performance.

Complete Career Action 2-3

SELF-ASSESSMENT

Another important part of knowing yourself is having an accurate assessment of your personal values, work preferences, and job-related performance traits. Understanding the personal factors that influence your performance and job satisfaction will help you make good choices when setting job and career targets and when considering specific job offers.

Values

Webster's New World Dictionary defines *value* as "that which is desirable or worthy of esteem for its own sake; the social principles, goals, or standards held

CAREER ACTION 2-3

Develop a List of Potential Job References

 Directions: Access Career Action 2-3 on your Learner's CD, or use the form provided on page 28. Identify at least three (but as many as possible) potential job references from your education/training and experience/skills inventories. Also consider contacts at professional associations. Record the names of your references, their addresses, and other pertinent contact information. Plan to contact each reference and ask him or her to write you a letter of reference.

or accepted by an individual." By working in a job that matches your values, you greatly increase the chances of enjoying and succeeding in your job. Career Action 2-4 will help you identify and prioritize your values.

The right career is one that complements your skills, interest, values, and environmental preferences.

SUCCESS TIP

Identify your skills, abilities, work experience, values, and work preferences to achieve a good job match.

Work Environment

Most people spend a lot of time in their work environment. To maximize your success, identify the work environments you prefer and perform best in. For example, if you are an extrovert, you probably won't enjoy working in an isolated environment. Career Action 2-4 will help you clarify what is important to you in a work environment.

Complete Career Action 2-4

Personal Qualities and Work Performance Traits

To get the job you want, you must be able to sell your personal qualities, positive job performance traits, and enthusiasm to prospective employers. In Career Action 2-5, you will identify these qualities

and traits to help you find a suitable job target match.

Identifying your personal qualities and work performance traits will also help you decide what type of work you are best suited for.

Complete Career Action 2-5

CAREER ACTION 2-4

Values and Work Environment Preferences Inventory

 Directions: Career Action 2-4 will help you identify and prioritize the values that are important to you and will also help you clarify the kinds of work environments you prefer. Remember, there are no wrong answers in defining what's important to you. Access Career Action 2-4 on your Learner's CD, or use the form provided on page 30.

Personal Qualities and Work Performance Traits

 Directions: Access Career Action 2-5 on your Learner's CD, or use the form provided on page 33. Follow the directions to complete Career Action 2-5.

SELF-ASSESSMENT RESOURCES

Many self-assessment resources speed up the process of making and confirming a successful career choice. (Note that some services may have a fee attached to them.)

- **Your school career services staff and counselors.** These specialists can provide a wide variety of aptitude and interest tests.

- **The Internet.** You can find useful information on careers and jobs on the Internet. Many sites offer online tools to assess your career interests and values and to help match the results with appropriate careers and jobs.

- **Commercial software packages.** Some commercial software packages are available on the Internet and through school career offices.

Complete Career Action 2-6

 SUCCESS TIP

Complete self-assessments to help match your interests, values, and personality style to appropriate careers.

Online Self-Assessment Test

Directions: Use the Internet to locate and complete two or three career self-assessment tests that measure your interests, values, or personality style. Print the results for your Career Management Files Binder. Some versions of tests to search for include The Career Key, The mini-Myers Briggs Type Indicator quiz, and The Kiersey Temperament Sorter. Resources for this assignment include the following:

1. The *Your Career: How to Make It Happen* web site at www.levitt.swlearning.com. Access the Links page; then click on the Self-Assessment links category. From there, review the self-assessment links and select assessment tests you are most interested in completing.

   Also check out "Efficient web researching links" for more information on conducting Internet research.

2. Your favorite search engines

   Conduct a search using a search string such as *self-assessment*.

PERSONAL BEST
Professional Ethics

A code of ethics is a set of principles—written or unwritten—that guides your behavior. These principles are based on your personal values. For example, if you value honesty, honesty will be part of your ethical code.

How will your behavior in the workplace reflect your personal values and ethics? If everyone else plays computer games during work hours, will you? According to Kenneth Blanchard and Norman Vincent Peale, authors of *The Power of Ethical Management*, you should ask yourself three questions when faced with an ethical dilemma.

Is it legal? Will you be breaking any laws or company policies by engaging in this activity?

Is it balanced? Is it fair to all parties in the short term as well as the long term? Is this a win-win situation for all those involved?

Is it right? Does this action go against your conscience? How does this decision make you feel about yourself?

✓ CHECKLIST:
Self-Assessment

Check the actions you are currently taking to increase your career success:

☐ Identifying skills, abilities, work experience, values, and work preferences to achieve a good job match.

☐ Completing self-assessments to help match interests, values, or personality style to appropriate career and job targets.

critical thinking *Questions*

1. Why is it important in career planning and a job search to assess and document thoroughly your education, training, work experience, and accomplishments?

2. Why is it useful to identify your work performance traits and career-related personal qualities?

Education, Training, and Organizational Activities Inventory

Directions: This inventory of your education and training contains four sections: (1) High School Inventory; (2) Business, Career, or Technical Education Inventory; (3) College or University Inventory; and (4) Seminars and Workshops Inventory. Complete each section that applies to you. List information related to your career target. Be thorough in documenting your accomplishments and achievements.

HIGH SCHOOL INVENTORY

Name of School: _____

Address: _____

_____

Dates of Attendance: _____ to _____ Date of Diploma: _____

Grade Point Average: _____ GED (Date): _____

1. **Career-Related Courses.** List the career-related courses you completed.

   _____

   _____

2. **Career-Related and Organizational Activities.** Describe your involvement in school, extracurricular, community, and other activities (examples: clubs, sports, organizations, and volunteer work).

   _____

   _____

3. **Career-Related Skills.** List the skills you developed in high school and through other activities. Include both job-specific skills and transferable competencies (examples: operating a computer, calculating numbers, persuading others, using specific tools/equipment, leading others, and working in a team).

   _____

   _____

4. **Accomplishments, Achievements, and Recognition.** List all special accomplishments, achievements, and recognition you received in high school and through other activities (examples: selected to play lead in musical production, selected to serve on state debate team, and awarded first place in competition). List any scholarships or honors you earned. Also summarize praise received from instructors, peers, and others.

   _____

   _____

Continued on next page.

CAREER ACTION 2-1 (continued)

BUSINESS, CAREER, OR TECHNICAL EDUCATION INVENTORY

Directions: Complete one form for each school attended. Duplicate the form if you have attended more than one business, career, or technical school.

Name of School: _____

Address: _____

_____

Dates of Attendance: _____ to _____ Date of Diploma: _____

Grade Point Average: _____ GED (Date): _____

1. **Career-Related Courses.** List the career-related courses you completed.

   _____

   _____

2. **Career-Related and Organizational Activities.** Descibe your involvement in school or extracurricular activities, in professional or career and technical associations, in the community, and in other activities (examples: sports, clubs, voluteer work, and student organizations such as Business Professionals of America).

   _____

   _____

3. **Career-Related Skills.** List the skills you developed through your classes and other activities. Include both job-specific skills and transferable competencies (examples: operating a computer, using specific software, presenting and creating oral and written communication, calculating numbers, persuading others, operating specific equipment/machinery, using specific tools, organizing and leading others, working as a team member, studying, analyzing, and researching data).

   _____

   _____

4. **Accomplishments, Achievements, and Recognition.** List all special accomplishments, achievements, and recognition you received for school and other activities. List any scholarships or honors you earned (examples: awarded second place in state business education skills competition, earned service award, earned perfect attendance award, served as class officer, inducted into National Vocational-Technical Honor Society, and restored two-bedroom apartment).

   _____

   _____

Continued on next page.

COLLEGE OR UNIVERSITY INVENTORY

Directions: Complete one form for each school attended. Duplicate the form if you have attended more than one college or university.

Name of School: _____

Address: _____

_____

Dates of Attendance: _____ to _____ Date of Diploma: _____

Grade Point Average: _____ GED (Date): _____

1. **Career-Related Courses.** List the career-related courses you completed.

   _____

   _____

2. **Career-Related and Organizational Activities.** Describe your involvement in school and extracurricular activities, in professional or other associations or organizations, in community activities, in volunteer work, and in other activities (examples: clubs, offices held, volunteer work, and community projects or programs).

   _____

   _____

3. **Career-Related Skills.** List the skills you developed through your classes and other activities. Include both job-specific skills and transferable competencies (examples: supervising, marketing, finance, sales, teaching, accounting, computer operation or programming, nursing, care taking, physical fitness/therapy, specific software, electronic applications, oral and written communication, calculating numbers, persuading and leading others, working as a team member, and researching).

   _____

   _____

4. **Accomplishments, Achievements, and Recognition.** List all special accomplishments, achievements, and recognition you received for school activities. List any scholarships or honors you earned (examples: served as class officer, won scholarship, prepared lesson plans in student teaching that were used as model for campus, selected for only paid internship in business department, and won regional award).

   _____

   _____

Continued on next page.

CAREER ACTION 2-1 (continued)

SEMINARS AND WORKSHOPS INVENTORY

Directions: List the seminars or workshops you have attended. If necessary, add to the list of seminars and workshops by keying in the additional information if you are using a computer for this activity or by using additional paper if you are handwriting this activity.

Name of Seminar/Workshop: _____

Offered by: _____ Date(s): _____

Career-related concepts or skills I learned: _____

Name of Seminar/Workshop: _____

Offered by: _____ Date(s): _____

Career-related concepts or skills I learned: _____

Name of Seminar/Workshop: _____

Offered by: _____ Date(s): _____

Career-related concepts or skills I learned: _____

Name of Seminar/Workshop: _____

Offered by: _____ Date(s): _____

Career-related concepts or skills I learned: _____

Name of Seminar/Workshop: _____

Offered by: _____ Date(s): _____

Career-related concepts or skills I learned: _____

Experience and Skills Inventory

Directions: Complete one form for each position or project (cooperative work experience, internship, volunteer/paid work experience, military experience). Begin with the most recent experience, and continue in reverse chronological order. Two copies of the form are provided; duplicate the form for additional job experience.

POSITION TITLE: _____

Name of Organization: _____

Address: _____

Telephone Number: _____ Salary (if paid experience): _____

Circle Type of Experience: (1) Cooperative   (2) Volunteer   (3) Internship   (4) Paid Work

Dates of Employment or Involvement: _____

Supervisor Name/Title: _____

1. **Career-Related Skills.** List the job-specific skills, transferable competencies, and responsibilities you developed in this position.

   _____

   _____

2. **Accomplishments and Achievements.** List your accomplishments in this position, preferably in measurable terms (examples: increased sales by 20 percent, reduced order processing time by 15 percent by developing more efficient processing methods, named employee/volunteer of the month, and supervised evening shift of eight employees).

   _____

   _____

3. **Praise Received.** Summarize praise received from employers, coworkers, and customers.

   _____

   _____

Why did you leave? _____

Performance rating (circle one):   Excellent   Very Good   Good   Needs Improvement   Poor

Continued on next page.

CAREER ACTION 2-2 (continued)

POSITION TITLE: _____

Name of Organization: _____

Address: _____

Telephone Number: _____ Salary (if paid experience): _____

Circle Type of Experience: (1) Cooperative   (2) Volunteer   (3) Internship   (4) Paid Work

Dates of Employment or Involvement: _____

Supervisor Name/Title: _____

1. **Career-Related Skills.** List the job-specific skills, transferable competencies, and responsibilities you developed in this position.

   _____

   _____

2. **Accomplishments and Achievements.** List your accomplishments in this position, preferably in measurable terms (examples: increased sales by 20 percent, reduced order processing time by 15 percent by developing more efficient processing methods, named employee/volunteer of the month, and supervised evening shift of eight employees).

   _____

   _____

3. **Praise Received.** Summarize praise received from employers, coworkers, and customers.

   _____

   _____

Why did you leave? _____

Performance rating (circle one):   Excellent   Very Good   Good   Needs Improvement   Poor

Develop a List of Potential Job References

Directions: List at least three people who would recommend you to prospective employers. List more references if possible. Be sure to get permission to use their names as references during your job search.

Name: _____

Title and Organization: _____

Address: _____
                        Steet   City   State   ZIP Code

Telephone: _____
                       Home   Work   Fax

E-Mail Address: _____

How I know this reference: _____

Date permission received to use as a reference: _____

Date of reference letter on file: _____

Date of last personal contact: _____

Name: _____

Title and Organization: _____

Address: _____
                        Steet   City   State   ZIP Code

Telephone: _____
                       Home   Work   Fax

E-Mail Address: _____

How I know this reference: _____

Date permission received to use as a reference: _____

Date of reference letter on file: _____

Date of last personal contact: _____

Continued on next page.

CAREER ACTION 2-3 (continued)

Name: _____

Title and Organization: _____

Address: _____
        Steet   City   State   ZIP Code

Telephone: _____
        Home   Work   Fax

E-Mail Address: _____

How I know this reference: _____

Date permission received to use as a reference: _____

Date of reference letter on file: _____

Date of last personal contact: _____

Name: _____

Title and Organization: _____

Address: _____
        Steet   City   State   ZIP Code

Telephone: _____
        Home   Work   Fax

E-Mail Address: _____

How I know this reference: _____

Date permission received to use as a reference: _____

Date of reference letter on file: _____

Date of last personal contact: _____

Values and Work Environment Preferences Inventory

PART 1: VALUES

Directions: Review the values listed below, and rank the importance of each as it relates to your career and job goals (H = high, M = medium, and L = low).

Value	Ranking (H, M, L)
1. Adventure (risk taking, new challenges)	_____
2. Education/Learning/Wisdom	_____
3. Social Needs (need for relationships with people)	_____
4. Self-Respect/Integrity/Self-Discipline	_____
5. Helping/Serving	_____
6. Recognition/Respect From Others	_____
7. Freedom/Independence (working independently with minimal supervision)	_____
8. Security (job, family, national, financial)	_____
9. Spiritual Needs	_____
10. Expression (creative, artistic)	_____
11. Responsibility (reliability, dependability)	_____
12. Balance in Work and Personal Life	_____
13. Others (List other values below and rank each one.)	

_____   _____

_____   _____

_____   _____

_____   _____

_____   _____

_____   _____

_____   _____

_____   _____

Continued on next page.

CAREER ACTION 2-4 (continued)

PART 2: WORK ENVIRONMENT PREFERENCES

Directions: In the boxes to the right, place a check mark next to each work environment condition you prefer.

Work Environment	Check Those Preferred
1. Indoor work	☐
2. Outdoor work	☐
3. Industrial/manufacturing setting	☐
4. Office setting	☐
5. Working alone	☐
6. Working with people	☐
7. Working with things	☐
8. Working with data	☐
9. Working with ideas	☐
10. Challenging opportunities	☐
11. Predictable, orderly, structured work	☐
12. Pressures at work	☐
13. Problem solving	☐
14. Standing while working	☐
15. Sitting while working	☐
16. Busy surroundings	☐

Continued on next page.

Work Environment

Check Those Preferred

17. Quiet surroundings ☐

18. Exciting, adventurous conditions ☐

19. Safe working conditions/environment ☐

20. Creative environment ☐

21. Opportunities for professional development and ongoing training/education ☐

22. Flexibility in work structure ☐

23. Teamwork and work groups ☐

24. Opportunities to supervise, lead, advance ☐

25. Opportunities to make a meaningful difference ☐

26. Using cutting-edge technology or techniques ☐

27. Integrity and truth in work environment ☐

28. Stability and security ☐

29. High-level earnings potential ☐

30. Opportunities to participate in community affairs ☐

Others (List other conditions you are seeking in your job target.)

_____ ☐

_____ ☐

_____ ☐

_____ ☐

_____ ☐

_____ ☐

_____ ☐

CAREER ACTION 2-5

Personal Qualities and Work Performance Traits

Directions: Rate yourself on each of the personal qualities and work performance traits listed below by using a scale of high, average, or low (H, A, or L). For example, if you think you have a high degree of dependability, write H in the space to the right of *Dependability*. Be sure to list other qualities or traits that are important for success in your targeted career. In preparing your resume and preparing to interview well, you should be able to prove that you possess these traits by giving examples of how you have used them successfully. At the end of the form, write at least five brief positive examples of how you have used these qualities or traits.

Personal Quality or Work Performance Trait	Rating (H, A, L)
1. Initiative/Resourcefulness/Motivation	_____
2. Dependability	_____
3. Punctuality	_____
4. Flexibility	_____
5. Creativity	_____
6. Patience	_____
7. Perseverance	_____
8. Humor	_____
9. Diplomacy	_____
10. Intelligence	_____
11. High energy level	_____
12. Ability to work well with a team	_____
13. Ability to set and achieve goals	_____
14. Ability to plan, organize, prioritize work	_____
15. Outgoing personality	_____
16. Ability to handle conflict	_____
17. Optimistic attitude	_____
18. Realistic attitude	_____

Continued on next page.

Personal Quality or Work Performance Trait	Rating (H, A, L)
19. Enthusiastic attitude	_____
20. Willingness to work	_____
21. Orderliness of work	_____
22. Attention to detail	_____
23. Ability to manage time well	_____
24. Honesty and integrity	_____
25. Ability to multitask	_____

Others (List and rank other positive personal qualities or work performance traits.)

_____ _____

_____ _____

_____ _____

_____ _____

_____ _____

_____ _____

_____ _____

_____ _____

_____ _____

_____ _____

Examples: List at least five positive examples of how you have used some of these qualities and traits in the past.

_____

_____

_____

_____

_____

_____

chapter 3

WHAT DO EMPLOYERS WANT?

In this chapter, you will:

- Assess your skills and work attitudes from an employer's perspective.

 Use the Internet to enhance your self-assessment and career planning activities.

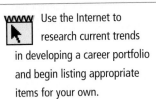 Use the Internet to research current trends in developing a career portfolio and begin listing appropriate items for your own.

- Set a career target.

"When hiring for any position, I look for people who have a grasp of computers and good communication skills. I also look for people who can work well with others, adapt easily to change, and be creative when looking for new ways to do things."

Debbie Bornholdt
Human Resource Project Manager
QVC, Electronic Retailer
West Chester, PA

Chapter 3 identifies the skills, work attitudes, and other qualifications that employers focus on in making hiring decisions. The chapter guides you through a self-assessment from the employer's perspective. The assessment will help you identify your most important qualifications so you will be ready to present them effectively to an employer during your job search. This chapter identifies excellent career and job-planning resources to help confirm appropriate goals. Chapter 3 also explains the importance of developing a career portfolio.

WHAT EMPLOYERS WANT

Employers want to hire people who will make their businesses more successful. The most desirable employees have the specific skills, transferable career competencies, work values, and personal qualities necessary to be successful in the employers' organizations. The more clearly you convey your skills as they relate to your job target, the greater your chance of landing your ideal job. Chapter 3 helps you identify these skills and qualities so you will be prepared to interview successfully.

Job-Specific Skills

Employers seek job-specific skills (skills and technical abilities that relate specifically to a particular job). Two examples of job-specific skills are using specialized tools and equipment and using a custom-designed software program.

Transferable Skills and Attitudes

Change is a constant in today's business world. Strong transferable career skills are the keys to success in managing your career through change. The most influential skills and attitudes are the abilities to:

- Work well with people.

- Plan and manage multiple tasks.

- Maintain a positive attitude.

- Show enthusiasm.

Employers need workers who have transferable career competencies—basic skills and attitudes that are important for all types of work. These skills make you highly marketable because they're needed for a wide variety of jobs and can be transferred from one task, job, or workplace to another. Examples include these:

- Planning skills

- Research skills

- Communication skills

- Human relations and interpersonal skills

- Critical thinking skills

- Management skills

Take, for example, a construction supervisor and an accountant. Both must work well with others, manage time, solve problems, read, and communicate effectively—all transferable competencies. They both must be competent in these areas even though framing a house and balancing a set of books (the job-specific skill for each field, respectively) are not related. In every occupation, transferable competencies are as important as technical expertise and job-specific skills.

Complete Career Action 3-1

CAREER ACTION 3-1

Skills and Competencies Profile

Directions: Access Career Action 3-1 on your Learner's CD, or use the form on page 43 to complete Career Action 3-1.

Assessing Yourself From an Employer's Perspective

In Chapter 2, you identified specific skills you developed in school, in work, and through other activities. This chapter has provided you with insights on how employers view skills and competencies. Now it's time to review your inventory and self-assessment from an employer's perspective. How would an employer categorize your skills and personal qualities?

Complete Career Action 3-2

CAREER PLANNING RESOURCES

Many convenient resources are available to speed and improve the processes of making and confirming your best career choice. Review the following resources and place a check mark next to those you could use to improve your career planning. (Note that comprehensive sources of job information are provided in Chapter 6. You may want to review those now because some of them can also be career planning resources.)

- **Your school career services staff and counselors.** These counselors specialize in assisting students with career planning. They provide aptitude and interest tests, as well as current resources for and information about the job market and occupational fields.

- **The Internet.** A wealth of career planning and job information is available through the Internet. Many sites offer online tools to assess your career interests and values and to help match the results with appropriate careers and jobs. The *Your Career: How to Make It Happen* web site links to many of these.

See your school career services office for recommendations for productive web sites, and check out the career center web sites of your local colleges or universities.

CAREER ACTION 3-2

Career Competencies Inventory

Part A: Access Career Action 3-2 on your Learner's CD, or use the form on page 47 to complete Career Action 3-2. As you read the summary of competencies, foundation skills, and personal qualities listed, think about and check each one you've developed.

Part B: Once you have completed Part A of this Career Action, do the following:

1. Write descriptions of at least three of the following activities in which you have carried out tasks on a regular basis:

   a. Current or past jobs

   b. Community, school, volunteer, or other activities

2. List as many examples as possible of both task- and job-specific skills and transferable competencies you used in each of the activities you described in number 1.

SUCCESS TIP

Identify your job-specific skills and transferable competencies to convince employers you fit the job.

- **Computerized career information systems.** With these systems, users complete a computerized questionnaire regarding their personal interests and abilities. The program then provides a list of occupations consistent with a user's answers. Other information provided may include job descriptions, hiring requirements, employment prospects, and education and training requirements. Check with your school career counselor or state department of education to locate the nearest computerized system.

- **City, county, state, and federal employment or human resources departments.** For information about government occupations, contact the employment or human resources department that manages employment in your target field.

- **Career planning publications.** Ask your school career services counselor or librarian for help in locating books, magazines, and articles about your field and current job target. (Many of these are now available online.)

- **People you know.** Contact people you have observed or known, people you admire, and people who have jobs just like the one you dream of. Ask them to help you explore your readiness for a similar job or career.

- **Volunteer work.** Volunteer experience can be a big asset when applying for the job you want. It demonstrates initiative and helps you get a feel for a job and a career. You can volunteer on a part-time or temporary basis or arrange an internship through your school.

PERSONAL BEST

Career Competencies

Your transferable career competencies or skills are every bit as important to your success in the workplace as your job-specific skills and training. The ability to identify, communicate, and demonstrate these skills in an interview could make the difference between you and other qualified job candidates.

The SCANS Report (Secretary's Commission on Achieving Necessary Skills), published by the U.S. Department of Labor, identified the transferable competencies essential for career and business success in the twenty-first century.

Workplace Competencies

1. **RESOURCES:** Identifies, organizes, plans, and manages resources.

2. **INTERPERSONAL:** Works well with others.

3. **INFORMATION:** Acquires, organizes, interprets, and uses information.

4. **SYSTEMS:** Understands complex social, organizational, and technological systems and interrelationships.

5. **TECHNOLOGY:** Works with a variety of technologies (tools, equipment, computers).

Foundation Skills and Personal Qualities

1. **BASIC SKILLS:** Reads, writes, and performs mathematical operations; listens; and speaks.

2. **THINKING SKILLS:** Thinks creatively, makes decisions, solves problems, visualizes, knows how to learn, and reasons.

3. **PERSONAL QUALITIES:** Displays responsibility, self-esteem, sociability, self-management, integrity, and honesty.

SUCCESSFUL CAREER PLANNING REQUIRES FLEXIBILITY

Changing technologies and a global economy cause some careers to become obsolete or vastly changed. Broaden your job options. Prepare to qualify for two closely related career goals, such as being a mathematician or a systems analyst, that require related education, training, and general capabilities. Which transferable career competencies do you have that qualify you for jobs within and between career clusters? Ask a knowledgeable career counselor to help you identify multicareer goals appropriate for your interests and abilities. Continually work at developing your career flexibility and pursuing lifelong learning.

> Complete Career Action 3-3

SET YOUR CAREER TARGET

The work you have completed in this chapter has prepared you to set your career target. You may want to use the visualization skills from Chapter 1 to help define your personal career objectives. Together with friends and associates, brainstorm appropriate careers. Think about work, hobbies, and volunteer experiences you have enjoyed in the past. What kind of work do you want to do? Where would you like to do this work? How much do you want to get paid for your work? What is the best career match for your unique skills, experiences, values, and interests? The form for Career Action 3-4 will help you organize your thoughts.

> Complete Career Action 3-4

CAREER ACTION 3-3

Internet Career Planning Resources

 Directions: Use several of the Internet resources below. Search for information regarding your career and job targets, including descriptions of your targeted fields and jobs, salary information, employment outlook projections, and more. Prepare a written summary of your findings, or print useful information you find.

- Bureau of Labor Statistics www.bls.gov
- America's Career InfoNet www.acinet.org/acinet
- JobStar www.jobstar.org (click on "Career Guides")
- Occupational Outlook Handbook www.bls.gov/oco
- collegeboard.com www.collegeboard.com/apps/careers/index
- O*Net OnLine http://online.onetcenter.org

My Career Target

Directions: Access Career Action 3-4 on your Learner's CD, or use the form on page 50 to complete Career Action 3-4.

SUCCESS TIP

Use a variety of career planning resources to help choose and validate appropriate career and job goals.

YOUR CAREER PORTFOLIO

A portfolio is a collection of documents and other items that demonstrate your skills, abilities, achievements, experience, and training. The purpose of a career portfolio is to organize relevant examples of skills and achievements you can present during interviews as proof of your qualifications. Developing and using a career portfolio provides tangible proof of your qualifications. It also demonstrates important skills that employers are seeking: critical thinking, analyzing, planning, and preparation.

Examples of appropriate portfolio items include the following:

- An official copy of your transcript(s)

- Your resume

- Exemplary samples of your work, such as business writing, graphic artwork, and printed samples from software presentations

> *"Formulate and stamp indelibly on your mind a mental picture of yourself succeeding. Hold this picture tenaciously. Never permit it to fade. Your mind will seek to develop this picture!"*
>
> Norman Vincent Peale

- Evidence of specialized computer usage, such as desktop publishing and web site creation

- Awards

- Work performance evaluations

- Letters of reference

A more comprehensive list of appropriate items and ideas for building your portfolio are contained in the "Career Portfolio" section of Appendix B, "Career Management and Marketing Tools." Additional activities are presented later in this text to help you in developing an effective portfolio.

Portfolio samples can be from paid or volunteer work, internships, cooperative education, clubs, community activities, and more. Begin considering what you have done or accomplished that best demonstrates your qualifications for the job you want. For example, to demonstrate your computer skills, you could include transcripts listing related coursework or a CD containing examples of multimedia presentations or programming code you have developed. To demonstrate a strong background in foreign languages, you could include transcripts listing appropriate coursework and a letter of recommendation from an instructor or employer familiar with your language skills.

For now, you can use a folder to store appropriate portfolio items that you identify for use later in your job search. Begin listing appropriate items in Career Action 3-5.

Complete Career Action 3-5

Assemble a portfolio of items that demonstrate your abilities and accomplishments.

SUCCESS TIP

Begin listing appropriate items for your career portfolio that demonstrate your job qualifications.

CAREER ACTION 3-5

List Appropriate Portfolio Items

Part A: To identify additional useful ideas for your own career portfolio, search the Internet for career portfolio information using two or more search engines. Also check other links available on the *Your Career: How to Make It Happen* web site.

Part B: Access Career Action 3-5 on your Learner's CD, or use separate paper to complete Career Action 3-5. Take a moment now to list items that seem appropriate to include in your Career Portfolio. As you progress through the upcoming chapters, add other items to your list. Later you will be instructed to complete assembly of your actual portfolio.

_____

_____

_____

_____

_____

_____

_____

Collect portfolio items that will demonstrate your qualifications for prospective employers.

✔ **CHECKLIST:**

Assessing Yourself From an Employer's Perspective

Check each of the actions you are currently taking to increase your career success:

☐ Identifying job-specific skills and transferable career competencies to convince employers of appropriateness for the job

☐ Using a variety of career planning resources to help in choosing and validating appropriate career and job goals

☐ Developing a career portfolio of items to demonstrate job qualifications for prospective employers

☐ Collecting items that will demonstrate job qualifications for prospective employers

critical thinking *Questions*

1. Why is it important to develop a broad career base that is flexible enough to encompass at least two fields?

2. What career planning resources will be most helpful in your job search and career planning activities? Why?

3. Why do employers value employees who have the career competencies and foundation skills identified in the SCANS report?

CAREER ACTION 3-1

Skills and Competencies Profile

Part 1: Job-Specific Skills

Directions: Review Career Actions 2-1 and 2-2 to refresh your memory regarding the job-specific skills and transferable career competencies you developed through your education, training, and experiences. Then identify and list below the ten most important job-specific skills related to your current career target (examples: using job-specific computer software; operating specific equipment or tools; and performing specific tasks, such as mixing dental adhesives).

My Most Important Job-Specific Skills Related to My Career Target

1. _____

2. _____

3. _____

4. _____

5. _____

6. _____

7. _____

8. _____

9. _____

10. _____

In Chapter 9 (resume development) and Chapter 11 (the interview), you will be asked to prove that you have these skills by documenting examples of times you used them—providing "proof by example." Employers ask for these examples, and you need to be prepared to give them.

Continued on next page.

Part 2: Basic Skills and Attitudes

Directions: Review the following skill categories and related transferable competencies. Check the boxes to the left of every skill category that applies to you in any way. Then circle each transferable competency you have developed (those listed after each skill category). Finally, list under *other* any additional transferable competencies you have that relate to each category.

Skill Category	Related Transferable Career Competencies
☐ **Art:**	Drawing, designing, painting, sculpting, computer graphics design Other: _____
☐ **Athletics:**	Physical strength, physical ability, physical coordination, coaching, physical development, agility, team sports, individual sports Other: _____
☐ **Communication:**	Explaining/persuading, strong grammar/vocabulary, organizing thoughts clearly, communicating logically, listening, speaking, good telephone/reception skills, writing, knowledge of foreign languages Other: _____
☐ **Computer Technology:**	Computer operation, researching, training, testing, workflow analysis, evaluating, writing instructions, programming Other: _____
☐ **Creativity:**	Innovative, imaginative, idea person, bold Other: _____

Continued on next page.

CAREER ACTION 3-1 (continued)

☐ **Engineering:**   Researching, testing, designing, constructing, analyzing, evaluating, controlling, electronic technology

Other: _____

☐ **Human Relations:**   Counseling, diplomacy, negotiating, patience, outgoing, teamwork ability, understanding, resolving conflict, handling complaints

Other: _____

☐ **Management:**   Analyzing data, directing, delegating, evaluating performance, organizing people/data/things, leading, making decisions, managing time, motivating self/others, planning, budgeting money/resources, solving problems, supervising, interviewing/hiring people, owning/operating a business

Other: _____

☐ **Manual/ Mechanical:**   Good manual dexterity, building, operating, maintaining/repairing, assembling, installing, carrying, loading, lifting, cooking, driving/operating vehicles, performing precision work, assessing spatial relationships, operating heavy equipment

Other: _____

☐ **Mathematical:**   Mathematical computations, accuracy, analyzing data, mathematical reasoning, statistical problem solving, analyzing cost effectiveness, budgeting, applying formulas, collecting money, calculating

Other: _____

☐ **Office:**   Keyboarding, data entry, computer operation, text processing, data processing, office equipment operation, filing/retrieving records, recording data, computing data, record keeping, telephone skills, business writing

Other: _____

Continued on next page.

☐ **Outdoor Activities:**

Animal care, farming, landscaping, grounds care, boating, navigating, oceanographic studies, forestry, logging, mining, fishing, horticulture

Other: _____

☐ **Performing:**

Speaking, acting, dancing, singing, musical ability, comedy, conducting

Other: _____

☐ **Sales/Promotion:**

Persuading, negotiating, promoting, influencing, selling, projecting enthusiasm, organizing, handling rejection, following up

Other: _____

☐ **Scientific Activities:**

Investigating, researching, analyzing, systematizing, observing, diagnosing

Other: _____

☐ **Service/General:**

Serving, referring, receiving, billing, handling complaints, good customer relations, good listening skills, patience, managing difficult people, helping others, relating to others

Other: _____

☐ **Service/Medical:**

Nursing, diagnosing, treating, rehabilitating, counseling, consoling, sympathizing, managing stress/emergencies, good interpersonal skills

Other: _____

☐ **Training/Teaching:**

Teaching skills/knowledge, tutoring, researching instructional content, organizing/developing content, explaining logically/clearly, demonstrating clearly, coaching others, evaluating learning, addressing all learning styles

Other: _____

CAREER ACTION 3-2

Career Competencies Inventory

Directions: Check the boxes to the left of each competency, skill, or quality you've developed, and circle the portions of the detailed descriptions of each item that apply to you.

PART 1: CAREER COMPETENCIES

RESOURCES: Identifies, organizes, plans, and allocates resources

☐ **Manages Time:** Selects relevant, goal-related activities; ranks activities in order of importance; allocates time to activities; and understands, prepares, and follows schedules

☐ **Manages Money:** Uses budgets, keeps records, and makes adjustments to meet objectives

☐ **Manages Material and Facilities:** Acquires, stores, allocates, and uses materials or space efficiently

☐ **Manages Human Resources:** Assesses skills and distributes work accordingly, uses coaching/mentoring skills with peers and subordinates, evaluates performance, and provides feedback

INTERPERSONAL: Works well with others

☐ **Participates as Team Member:** Contributes to group effort

☐ **Teaches Others New Skills**

☐ **Serves Clients/Customers:** Works to satisfy customers' expectations

☐ **Exercises Leadership:** Communicates ideas to justify position and persuades/convinces

☐ **Negotiates Decisions:** Works toward agreements involving exchange of resources and resolves divergent interests

☐ **Respects Cultural Diversity:** Works well with people from diverse backgrounds

INFORMATION: Acquires and uses information

☐ **Acquires/Evaluates Information**

☐ **Organizes/Maintains Information**

☐ **Interprets/Communicates Information**

☐ **Uses Computers to Process Information**

Continued on next page.

SYSTEMS: Understands complex social, organizational, and technological systems and interrelationships

☐ **Understands Systems:** Knows how social, organizational, and technological systems work and operates effectively with them

☐ **Monitors/Corrects Performance:** Distinguishes trends, predicts impacts on system operations, diagnoses deviations in systems' performance, and corrects malfunctions

☐ **Improves/Designs Systems:** Suggests modifications to existing systems and develops new or alternative systems to improve performance

TECHNOLOGY: Works with a variety of technologies

☐ **Selects Technology:** Chooses procedures, tools, or equipment, including computers and related technologies

☐ **Applies Technology to Task:** Understands overall intent and proper procedures for setup and operation of equipment

☐ **Maintains/Troubleshoots Technology:** Prevents, identifies, or solves problems with equipment, including computers and other technologies

PART 2: FOUNDATION SKILLS AND PERSONAL QUALITIES

BASIC SKILLS: Reads, writes, performs arithmetic/mathematical operations, listens, and speaks

☐ **Reading:** Locates, understands, and interprets written information, including material in documents such as manuals, graphs, and schedules

☐ **Writing:** Communicates thoughts, ideas, information, and messages in writing and creates documents such as letters, directions, manuals, reports, graphs, and flowcharts

☐ **Arithmetic/Mathematics:** Performs basic computations and approaches practical problems by choosing appropriately from a variety of mathematical techniques

☐ **Listening:** Receives, attends to, interprets, and responds to verbal messages and other cues

☐ **Speaking:** Organizes ideas and communicates orally

Continued on next page.

CAREER ACTION 3-2 (continued)

THINKING SKILLS: Thinks creatively, makes decisions, solves problems, visualizes, knows how to learn, and reasons

☐ **Creative Thinking:** Generates new ideas

☐ **Decision Making:** Specifies goals and constraints, generates alternatives, considers risks, facilitates group decision-making processes, and evaluates and chooses best alternative

☐ **Problem Solving:** Recognizes problems and devises and implements plan of action and facilitates problem solving and brainstorming discussions

☐ **Knowing How to Learn:** Uses efficient learning techniques to acquire and apply new knowledge and skills

☐ **Reasoning:** Discovers a rule or principle underlying the relationship between two or more objects and applies it when solving a problem

PERSONAL QUALITIES: Displays responsibility, self-esteem, sociability, self-management, integrity, and honesty

☐ **Responsibility:** Exerts a high level of effort, perseveres toward goal attainment, and multitasks effectively

☐ **Self-Esteem:** Believes in own self-worth and maintains a positive view of self

☐ **Sociability:** Demonstrates understanding, friendliness, adaptability, and empathy; manages conflict effectively; is polite

☐ **Self-Management:** Assesses self accurately, sets personal goals, monitors progress, works well under pressure, and exhibits self-control

☐ **Integrity/Honesty:** Chooses ethical courses

Fine-Tune Your Competencies List

Directions: Review the items you identified in Career Action 3-2. Then select the ten strongest of these transferable career competencies and basic skills related to your current job target. List them below.

1. _____   6. _____

2. _____   7. _____

3. _____   8. _____

4. _____   9. _____

5. _____   10. _____

NOTE: You will expand on this information in Chapters 9 and 11.

My Career Target

Directions: Answer the following questions about your current career target.

1. In what career field are you planning to seek employment? (Examples: accounting, office management, health care, teaching, administration, construction, and computer technology)

_____

_____

_____

_____

2. What are the specific job or jobs you are targeting in your employment search? (List every job you are qualified for and interested in pursuing. Maximize your options by listing jobs within and between career fields or clusters that require transferable competencies you have.)

_____

_____

_____

_____

3. What specific activities are you most interested in performing in your ideal job? What energizes and excites you most?

_____

_____

_____

_____

4. Are you willing to travel or relocate? Explain.

_____

_____

_____

_____

EXPLORE CONTEMPORARY WORKPLACE ISSUES

chapter **4**

In this chapter, you will:

- Integrate personal financial management into your career strategies.

- Identify what globalization means to your career.

- Prepare for the trends of the twenty-first century using the Internet and other resources.

- Learn how employers expect you to work responsibly with others.

"Today, without question, information is the most valuable commodity on the planet. The ability of my team to articulate, educate, and navigate through the changing communication channels of the future is a harbinger of the company's success."

Lee Duffey, President and Founder
Duffey Communications, Inc.
Atlanta, GA

Chapter 4 provides an overview of topics critical to success in the workplace of the twenty-first century. Managing personal finances well is one key to career success. Additionally, contemporary issues in globalization, technology, teamwork, diversity and workplace equity, and ethics all play a role in career development. Use this chapter to help plan for the future and to develop the competencies, skills, and resources that will best support your career success.

MANAGE YOUR PERSONAL FINANCES

Many goals require both personal effort and money: a home, a car, and an education. Managing money well is also essential for achieving career success. Often employers will not hire people with a history of poor money management, such as defaulting on school loans or other lines of credit. Keeping expense payments current provides many benefits: protecting credit status, avoiding disqualification for employment, and being accepted for future loans at favorable interest rates.

Balance Wants and Resources. Plan and control your money with a well-designed monthly budget. Required income varies with individual circumstances, and a budget will reveal the amount of money you need to survive. Knowing this figure is crucial for you to be able to negotiate salary offers realistically.

Track Income. Tracking your sources of year-round income will help you anticipate and plan for income changes or variations. For example, you may earn quite a bit of money over the summer months but find that during the school year, income is down and expenses are up.

Track Expenses. Where does your money go? To manage your finances successfully, you need to allocate money for all your needs, including living, school, and personal expenses. Categorize and budget your expenses. If your actual expenses exceed budgeted amounts, determine where expenses can be cut.

Set Up a Regular Savings Plan. Regular contributions to a savings plan will allow you to save money to pay back college or other loans. Keep in mind you must pay a minimum amount per month on a student loan regardless of the balance. Savings will also help you accumulate the extra cash you may need if you choose a job that involves reloca-

Learn to manage your personal finances, and keep your living expenses below your income.

tion expenses. Start-up expenses (such as deposits for rent, utilities, and telephone) can be costly.

Use Credit Wisely. Establishing and maintaining good credit is a must for successful career development. Opening a credit account and using it wisely helps you build a positive credit rating.

The rewards for budgeting your income and expenses, saving money, and investing wisely include the following:

- Earning a good credit rating

- Maintaining your employment competitiveness

- Negotiating realistic wages

- Keeping financial peace of mind

- Providing money to achieve financial goals (such as a car, a home, an education, retirement security, and travel).

Complete Career Action 4-1

CAREER ACTION 4-1

Prepare Your Monthly Budget

Access your Learner's CD, or turn to page 62 and complete the Monthly Budget Planner form.

UNDERSTAND WHAT GLOBALIZATION MEANS TO YOUR CAREER

For the first part of the twenty-first century, experts predict that global trade among nations will increase three to four times faster than individual national economies. Success in this larger, more competitive market requires quality products that are innovative, timely, and efficiently produced. To meet the upcoming challenges, many companies are restructuring as follows:

1. Distributing design, marketing, and customer service operations across the globe

2. Moving manufacturing plants to locations that offer the appropriate combination of education and low labor costs

3. Purchasing product components from outside suppliers

4. Reducing the number of permanent employees

5. Relying on specialized teams, often made up of short-term workers, to meet critical deadlines

6. Recruiting highly skilled workers worldwide

In short, globalization is increasing competitive pressures, blurring economic boundaries, and relocating well-educated workers.

Appreciate the Major Role of Quality Assurance Programs

In the early 1980s, the European economies lagged behind those of the United States and Japan. After realizing that their many different production stan-

dards made them less competitive, Europeans began requiring suppliers of regulated products to meet the quality assurance standards adopted by the International Organization of Standards (known as ISO). Companies worldwide are establishing Total Quality Management (TQM) programs to achieve ISO certification. Total Quality Management programs are also referred to as Continuous Quality Improvement (CQI) programs. ISO standards have varied goals; some represent product conformance to established requirements, while others strive to achieve sustained customer satisfaction. Reassure employers you understand the importance of quality by submitting well-prepared job search documents. Study the TQM and CQI literature, and know how the quality process applies to your industry. During job interviews, ask employers about quality programs.

To compete in today's markets, companies often assemble specialized teams to meet critical deadlines.

PERSONAL BEST
Use Credit Wisely

Using credit beyond what you can afford creates a destructive cycle of more and more charging and deeper and deeper debt. Below are six tips to help you use credit wisely and protect your personal finances:

1. Avoid using credit beyond what you can afford.

2. Shop around for a credit card with good terms (such as no annual fee, grace periods, and a low interest rate). Watch out for cards that offer low initial interest rates that eventually increase, sometimes significantly.

3. Use only one credit card and use it sparingly.

4. Pay your entire balance each month. Or at least pay more than the monthly minimum payment.

5. Make sure the credit card company receives your payment before the due date.

6. Never use credit to extend your paycheck.

Use good budgeting skills, make informed choices, and exercise common sense to avoid a financial fiasco that can tarnish your credit rating for a lifetime.

Provide Service for Two Kinds of Customers

TQM and CQI have taught companies that success in today's marketplace requires satisfying two kinds of customers—internal and external. Internal customers are employees who build on the work of coworkers and depend on receiving quality work to complete their own jobs successfully. External customers contribute to successful companies by purchasing the final products and services. In the worldwide market, customer service means delivering satisfactory results to both types of customers.

Identify the internal and external customers for any job you consider. Research your industry so you can speak knowledgeably about current customer service issues and can give examples of how you handle typical customer concerns in a positive way.

Develop a Worldwide Perspective

Meet the challenges of globalization by developing a worldwide perspective. Demonstrate an understanding of the global competitive factors of your industry, and show a willingness to learn about international cultures. Tell employers if you are willing to travel or if you speak more than one language. As trading opportunities expand, career possibilities will also broaden and require more skills and more world awareness.

SUCCESS TIP

For a successful career in a global economy, learn about the economic, political, social, and technological trends in the world and provide quality products and service to all your customers.

PREPARE FOR THE TRENDS OF THE TWENTY-FIRST CENTURY

From everyday transactions with stores and banks to sophisticated international operations, technology removes time zone and geographic barriers, revolutionizes tools, and changes the processes used in working and making decisions. Technology will continue to evolve and affect your life and career at an ever-increasing pace. Incorporate technology into your career by keeping current on technological trends; by frequently updating your skills; and by keeping a flexible, positive attitude.

Understand the Contemporary Work Environment

One of the fastest-growing trends worldwide is the virtual corporation or office. Individuals who participate in these work environments are referred to as virtual employees, teleworkers, or telecommuters. The common element of telework is the use of computers and telecommunications to change the accepted geography of work. Flexibility is the primary concept behind this type of work. Some companies are reducing permanently assigned desks and introducing workstations equipped with computers or computer hookups, telephones, and basic office supplies so employees who travel among company locations can plug their laptops into the company computer network and start working.

Another trend that has grown rapidly is "hoteling." As a result of companies reducing their workforce and individuals opting to work within a more flexible schedule, organizations with surplus space available have set up office cubicles that they rent out to individuals who do not have "permanent" office space from which to work. Develop your technical and organizational skills and remain flexible so you can work comfortably and productively in the virtual office environment.

"Once a new technology rolls over you, if you're not part of the steamroller, you're part of the road."

Stewart Brand

Use Telephone and Computer Networks

Networks, which use computer and communications technology to link resources, make it easy for people to find, send, and receive information. Voice and data networks can provide nearly instantaneous access to items as diverse as company records, public chat rooms, and unwanted viruses.

Provide Security for Network Systems. Anyone with a computer, a telephone line, and a modem can access the Internet. Like any other society, the Internet has its share of vandals. Small companies that use the Internet to send inter- and intra-company e-mail, to sponsor company web sites, or to conduct monetary transactions usually protect their computers with host-based security programs. These special programs are installed on each computer to protect it from unauthorized access and from viruses.

Create an Intranet. Although any business may use the public Internet, many companies are setting up private, closed computer networks—called intranets. These intranets are used for internal communications to protect business information from competitive spying or sabotage. Intranets often start with electronic mail, scheduling, and collaboration applications to create an organization that extends beyond the physical constraints of buildings and walls. Companies typically restrict and/or examine incoming or outgoing data to stop unauthorized transmission of information or access to information by company-owned, employee-operated computers. Some companies even prohibit remote access, but most issue passwords to allow employees who travel or telework to use the intranet via telephone lines and modems.

Use an Extranet. When a company or an organization expands its network to include customers, suppliers, and partners outside the company or organization, it has created a structure known as an extranet. This type of network rests on three technologies: the Internet, groupware applications, and firewalls. Why would an organization develop and implement an extranet? Quick communication with customers and partners is an advantage in today's ever-changing marketplace.

Companies often use firewall security systems to protect their intranets and extranets but allow their employees to access the Internet. Firewalls use special combinations of hardware and software to restrict the types of information that can enter or leave these network systems. Firewalls can also be configured to provide network managers with usage patterns, the number of attempts to breach the system, or other information. In addition to firewalls, extranets often use some form of user identification (such as digital certificates), encryption, and virtual private networks (VPN) that navigate through the public network.

Recognize Privacy Limitations on the Internet, Intranet, and Extranet. Network managers have full access to network information, including in-house e-mail. Even if both the sender and the receiver delete a message from their computers' memories, the message still exists in the backup files of the sending and receiving servers. Protect your privacy: Do not send private information over the Internet, and transmit only legal, ethical company business over intranets. Also use passwords to protect the confidentiality of company information or sensitive personnel records.

Technology increases the pace of work by eliminating communication barriers.

Adapt to an Increased Work Pace

Technology has increased the work pace by reducing distance and time as barriers to communication. In the past, the pressures of decision making and the demands of work processes were buffered by the time it took for information to travel from one point to another. No one expected business information to be available quickly to all workers or to be delivered routinely to people who were traveling, on vacation, or at home.

Expectations have changed. People expect quicker results and faster decisions because information is now available swiftly from almost any location to workers at any level. The current direction is toward larger, more complex workloads, which has led to an increased sense of urgency for employees and to a growing infringement of work on leisure time.

Function as a Team Player

The availability of management information to all employees, the rapid rate of technological advances, and the competitive pressures of globaliza-

tion have combined to result in unpredictable staffing needs and fundamental shifts in the working structures of companies. The shift is away from management-directed systems toward "flat" team-directed systems that increase each individual's responsibilities.

Companies are using a skilled core group of leaders to develop strategies and goals and to manage work teams that perform the design, production, marketing, and servicing tasks. Technology, instead of middle managers, now transfers information between core groups and work teams. Flatter, leaner organizations respond more efficiently to competitive pressures and create a need for flexible, problem-solving team leaders.

Working in teams results in benefits for both team members and the organization in which they work. Those benefits include:

- **Collaboration.** People want to work well together and to support one another because they identify with the team.

- **Communication.** Team members realize the importance of passing on the information members need to operate more effectively.

- **More efficient application of resources, talents, and strengths.** People are applying themselves willingly. When one member lacks certain knowledge or competence, another is there to fill the gap.

- **Sound decisions and solutions made simultaneously.** A team can generate more discussion, ideas, and solutions than a single individual.

- **Quality.** Team members feel pride in the team effort and ensure that each member gets what he or she needs from other team members to turn out the best possible work.

Determine Potential Employment Growth Areas

Globalization, advancing technology, and the aging of baby boomers (the 76 million people born between 1946 and 1964) are stimulating a long-term shift from a manufacturing-based economy to a service-based economy. The *Occupational Outlook Quarterly* has projected that nearly one-half of all job openings between 2000 and 2010 will be in service, professional, and related occupations. Service and retail trade will account for 76 percent of job growth. Four industry groups are expected to account for almost one-half of all wage and salary growth in the economy: health services, business services, education services, and engineering and management.

SUCCESS TIP

Sharpen your technological and team skills so you can work productively with the flatter, leaner organizations that use the latest in computer and communications technology. Show employers you adapt well to change by demonstrating flexibility and by focusing on problem solving.

Recognize the Impact of Baby Boomers' Retirements

Only 12 percent of the pre-baby boomer generation chose to remain in the workforce after the traditional retirement age of sixty-five. If global markets continue to expand and if boomers (who make up 52 percent of today's working population) retire at the same rate as their parents, employers could face a serious labor shortage and a rapid rise in recruitment, training, and benefit costs. Current projections, however, show that several factors will keep 75 to 80 percent of baby boomers working in some capacity after traditional retirement ages:

- **Lack of money.** Most baby boomers over age sixty-five will need to work to supplement Social Security, to combat the effects of inflation, to offset reduced or nonexistent pensions, to pay rising Medicare and medical rates, and to maintain their pre-age-sixty-five standard of living.

- **Healthier elderly and longer life spans.** In the 1950s, the average life expectancy was sixty-eight years; today it is eighty years.

- **Personal satisfaction.** The National Institute on Aging published a survey that showed 75 percent of older workers would prefer to phase down from full-time to part-time work instead of retiring abruptly.

Understand Tailored Benefits Packages

Employers offer a variety of benefits options today. Several examples of options available are explained in the following list:

- **Offer personalized benefits.** Approve fixed-amount employer contributions that employees use to pay for choices from a smorgasbord of benefits (such as child care; long-term care insurance; elder-care services; family-care leave of absence; work/life programs; domestic partner benefits; prepaid legal, auto, home, and funeral insurance; and convenience or "concierge" services).

- **Allow workers to pay for additional benefits at group rates.**

- **Offer flexible working schedules.**

- **Restructure jobs** into part-time (including shared jobs), temporary, teleworking, or contractual assignments.

- **Reorganize the compensation system** to reward people quickly for performance.

- **Expand compensation packages** to include extra training, exposure to key decision makers, and increased recognition.

SUCCESS TIP

Research the compensation and benefits plans offered by various-sized firms in your industry. Recognize that employers may offer attractive, unusual benefits packages to enhance wages.

WORK RESPONSIBLY WITH OTHERS

Working responsibly with others will be the hallmark of a successful career in the twenty-first century. Economic, legal, and social forces worldwide will make it increasingly important to respect and value cultural, gender, and physical diversity in coworkers. Successful companies will view employee differences as assets to the teamwork that ensures successful customer service in diverse markets.

"Government cannot make us equal; it can only recognize, respect, and protect us as equals before the law."

Clarence Thomas
U.S. Supreme Court Justice

Promote Workplace Equity

To meet competitive pressures today, employers are working to integrate diversity into their businesses. Companies that meet and exceed legal requirements for workplace equity have increased productivity because employees feel valued and respected for their contributions. Most businesses with more than 15 employees have an official diversity policy to ensure compliance with the four federal laws that set the tone for workplace equity in the United States:

1. **The (Revised) Fair Labor Standards Act (incorporates the Equal Pay Act),** which applies to almost all businesses and defines the 40-hour workweek, covers the federal minimum wage, sets requirements for overtime, places restrictions on child labor, and prohibits compensating men and women differently for doing the same job.

2. **The Age Discrimination in Employment Act** prohibits companies that employ 20 or more people from discriminating against employees who are age forty or older.

3. **The Americans with Disabilities Act** prohibits employers with 15 or more employees from discriminating against people with physical or mental disabilities. This act also requires employers to make "a reasonable accommodation" for the needs of disabled employees as long as the accommodation does not represent an undue hardship on the employer.

4. **Title VII of the Civil Rights Act** makes workplace discrimination with respect to race, color, sex, national origin, and religion illegal for companies that employ 15 or more people.

The most frequently reported type of discrimination covered under Title VII of the Civil Rights Act is sexual harassment. Sexual harassment occurs when one person makes continued and unwelcome sexual advances, requests sexual favors, and displays other verbal or physical conduct of a sexual nature to another person against the other person's wishes. According to the Equal Employment Opportunity Commission (EEOC), sexual harassment occurs "when submission to or rejection of this conduct explicitly or implicitly affects an individual's employment, unreasonably interferes with an individual's work performance or creates an intimidating, hostile or offensive work environment." This type of discrimination can occur in a variety of situations and should be thoroughly investigated once reported.

Keep the following facts in mind:

- Harassers and victims may be men or women, and the victim is not necessarily of the opposite sex.

- The harasser can be a coworker, a customer, a supervisor, or someone not connected to the employee's work. The victim is not just the target of the harassment, but anyone who observed or learned about the harassment and was affected by it.

- Sexual harassment can occur even if there is no demonstrable effect on economic injury or discharge of the victim.

Promote workplace equity by demonstrating respect for others and openness to different perspectives. Further your career by relating positively to others in regard to physical abilities, gender, race, culture, age, religion, or sexual orientation.

Respect Privacy and Confidentiality of Your Company, Coworkers, Customers, and Suppliers

Working responsibly with others includes respecting individual, company, and customer privacy. Coworkers do not like having their privacy violated, and employers dismiss and often sue employees who "leak" proprietary information, abuse the company's computer system, or violate a nondisclosure agreement. Customers and suppliers also are assertive in protecting their confidential business information. They may take legal action or refuse to do business with people who violate their trust.

Treat Coworkers As You Would Want to Be Treated.
The openness of most working environments makes true privacy impossible, but the expectation of privacy remains. If you develop a reputation for being discreet and courteous, you will learn more, progress further, and become a respected member of the team.

Guard Your Company's Business Information. By accepting employment, you agree to join your employer's team and help your company succeed. Divulging proprietary information could undermine the ability of your employer to compete in the marketplace. Therefore, you have a moral and legal obligation to protect product, marketing, and management information. Before discussing work-related information with your coworkers, make sure you are in an appropriate location. Take reasonable precautions to protect important business information.

Honor Confidentiality Agreements With Customers and Suppliers. Learn about your company's policies regarding confidentiality or nondisclosure agreements. These agreements state that your company's representatives will not disclose or use clients' or suppliers' business information except for the legitimate purposes detailed in the agreement. Make sure you know what customers or suppliers expect you to do with sensitive information before you accept it. If you have any doubts, check with appropriate management personnel.

SUCCESS TIP

Follow the lead of the most successful companies: Respect diversity, honor confidentiality, and maintain a high ethical standard.

Develop Conflict Resolution Skills

Conflict is a natural part of life. The only way to avoid it is to live in a vacuum. If you are to manage conflict and prevent it from escalating, you must develop strong interpersonal communication and problem-solving skills. Several skills are particularly critical to your success in navigating through conflict that can arise in the workplace. To be successful at conflict resolution:

- Be an active listener.

- Define and analyze a situation and/or problem objectively.

- Use "I" messages to communicate how you feel without assigning blame.

- Understand barriers that may be preventing a solution and causing resistance and tactfully start breaking them down.

- Brainstorm for solutions.

- Evaluate possible solutions to choose a win-win solution in which the needs of all parties are met.

- Maintain your integrity and professionalism.

Conflicts are most successfully resolved when communication flows well, assertive rather than aggressive behavior is used, and a collaborative method is used.

Practice Ethical Behavior in the Workplace

According to one dictionary, ethics means "the moral principles which determine the rightness or wrongness of particular acts or activities." Nothing will damage your career as drastically as losing

> "Reading about ethics is about as likely to improve one's behavior as reading about sports is to make one into an athlete."
>
> Mason Colley
> U.S. Aphorist

your reputation for ethical behavior! In general, members of the business community expect you to be honest, open, accurate, law-abiding, and trustworthy.

Make Ethical Decisions. Most people believe they know the difference between right and wrong, but applying one's principles and maintaining one's integrity in the business world can be challenging.

Refuse to Take Unethical Actions. If you know an action is wrong, refuse to do it. If you aren't sure what to do, ask. Most companies make personnel, management, and legal resources available to employees. You also have the right to consult with your own spiritual or legal advisers.

If you have any reservations about an action, don't let yourself be talked into it. If you take an unethical action, you are the one who will have to live with the resulting loss of reputation and with the personal and legal consequences. Protect your long-term career by upholding your personal principles and values.

Complete Career Action 4-2

CAREER ACTION 4-2

Use the Internet to Research Contemporary Workplace Issues

   Directions: Turn to page 64 and complete Career Action 4-2.

✓ CHECKLIST:

Exploring Contemporary Workplace Issues

Check each of the actions you are currently taking to increase your career success:

☐ Mastering money with common cent$ by using a monthly budget

☐ Using a two-pronged approach when preparing for a successful career in the global economy of the twenty-first century: (1) learning about the economic, political, social, and technological trends; (2) providing quality products and excellent service to customers

☐ Showing employers your ability to adapt to change by demonstrating flexibility, focusing on problem solving, and working well in teams

☐ Sharpening technological skills

☐ Researching the compensation and benefits plans offered by the various-sized firms in a target industry

☐ Respecting diversity, honoring confidentiality, and maintaining high ethical standards

critical thinking *Questions*

1. Why is it important to manage your personal finances well?

2. How is technology changing the way people work?

3. What are four skills you should possess to deal effectively with conflict?

4. Why should you practice high ethical standards in the workplace?

Prepare Your Monthly Budget

Directions: Follow the steps below using this sheet or an electronic spreadsheet to prepare a monthly budget.

1. Add your additional item names to Column B.

2. Put appropriate amounts in Columns C and D.

3. For each numbered item, subtract Column D from Column C; place the answer in Column E. Indicate differences that are over budget with a negative (−) sign and under budget with a positive (+) sign.

4. Subtotal each category in each column.

5. In Columns C and D, put the total for line 3 on line 32 and the total for line 31 on line 33.

6. Subtract line 33 from line 32, and put the answer on line 34.

MONTHLY BUDGET PLANNER FOR MONTH OF

A Category	B Item	C Budgeted	D Actual	E Over (−) or Under (+)
1. Income	Wages			
2.	Other			
3.	Total Income			
4. Expenses	Rent/Mortgage			
5.	Car Payment			
6.	Child Care			
7.	Insurance			
8.				
9.	Loans			
10.				
11.	Savings			
12.	Allowance			
13.	Food/Living Items			
14.	Home Utilities			
15.				
16.	Telephone(s)			
17.	Cable TV			

Continued on next page.

CAREER ACTION 4-1 (continued)

A Category	B Item	C Budgeted	D Actual	E Over (−) or Under (+)
18.	Transportation			
19.				
20.	School Expenses			
21.	Credit Cards			
22.				
23.	Medical Care			
24.	Clothes/Shoes			
25.	Hobbies/Sports			
26.	Entertainment			
27.	Charity			
28.	Gifts			
29.	Vacations			
30.	Other			
31.	Total Expenses			
32. Totals	Total Income			
33. (less)	Total Expenses			
34.	Difference*			

*If your expenses exceed your income, reassess your budget.

Use the Internet to Research Contemporary Workplace Issues

Directions: Use the Internet to research one or more of the contemporary issues listed below, or select a workplace issue that especially interests you. Use your favorite search engines or those linked from the *Your Career: How to Make It Happen* web site. Write a brief summary of your findings below, or use separate paper for your report.

1. **Global Perspective:** Try the search string *international and business.*

   Also check these web sites:

   a.   Michigan State University: http://globaledge.msu.edu

   b.   Business Week: www.businessweek.com (Click on "Global Business.")

   c.   United States Council for International Business: www.uscib.org (Click on "What's New.")

2. **The Workplace:** Try the following three search strings: *the workplace, computers and networking,* and *telecommuting and virtual and office.*

   Also check these web sites:

   a.   Reengineering Resource Center: www.reengineering.com/articles (Click on "The Virtual Office.")

   b.   Virginia Tech: http://filebox.vt.edu/users/vmirpuri

   c.   Webopedia: http://webopedia.com (Do a search using the keyword *telecommuting.*)

3. **Tailored Benefits Packages:** Try the following two search strings: *workplace and benefits* and *work and life and benefits.* Also check the Yahoo Web Directory site at www.Yahoo.com. (Click on "Business and Economy," then "Employment and Work," and then "Employment and Workplace Issues.")

   Also check these web sites.

   a.   Employers Council on Flexible Compensation: www.benefits.net

   b.   International Foundation of Employee Benefit Plans: www.ifebp.org

Summary of Internet Research Findings

_____

_____

_____

_____

_____

_____

_____

ORGANIZE YOUR WINNING NETWORK

chapter 5

In this chapter, you will:

- Develop a personal support system list of people who can motivate you in your job search and provide moral support.

- Prepare a job search network list of people who can help you find solid job leads and provide professional suggestions for enhancing your job search preparation.

Use the Internet to search for current job search networking tips.

"What a lot of people don't recognize, until they are faced with a job search, is that it pays to stay networked—particularly in good times when you don't feel the need as much to keep in touch. Staying networked on a regular basis will put you steps ahead of everyone else who has not remained connected when it comes time for a job search or getting the information or resources you need."

Rebecca Zucker
Career and Executive Coach
Career Transition and Managerial Effectiveness

Statistically the most effective resource for finding a job is networking. Chapter 5 explains how to build a powerful job-search network. This chapter guides you through development of two important support groups to help you achieve your career goals: a personal support system to motivate you and a network of people to help identify solid job leads.

NETWORKING OFFERS BIG BENEFITS

Because networking is the No. 1 source of finding a good job, smart job seekers put a concerted effort into networking (the process of developing relationships with people who can assist with job search strategies and in finding strong job leads). The benefits of networking are great and include the following:

- Tapping into jobs you would not have access to otherwise

- Gaining insider information about the industry, about trends, and about job search and hiring processes in your field

- Getting the chance to promote yourself

- Obtaining referrals to other people who may help you

SUCCESS TIP

Develop a personal support system of people who can motivate and encourage you; help with resumes, job search letters, and interview practice; and act as sounding boards for job search planning.

> *"There is no such thing as a self-made man. You will reach your goals only with the help of others."*
>
> George Shinn

Members of Your Support System Play Many Important Roles

One support member could help boost your commitment. Another could help soothe your ego after a job rejection. Still another support member who is skilled in writing might help you polish your resumes and cover letters. These people sustain and motivate you when you need a push and help you reach your full potential.

YOUR PERSONAL SUPPORT SYSTEM IS YOUR COACHING TEAM

What is a personal job search support system? Your *support system* is the group of people who can motivate, advise, and encourage you (like a personal coaching team) during your job search and throughout your career. Good choices for your personal support system include people willing to provide you with motivational and instructional support (such as family; friends; school, work, or social acquaintances; former or current employers; career services staff and counselors from school; and instructors).

Identify Your Support System Members Now!

Select your support system members for the following qualities:

1. Ability to motivate you

2. Ability to help develop or edit effective job search communications (people with good writing skills) and ability to help you practice for interviews

3. Ability to help with solid job leads, to provide job search advice, and/or to share similar experiences

Complete Career Action 5-1

CAREER ACTION 5-1

List Your Personal Support System Members

 Directions: People who boost your morale and encourage you to reach goals should be tops on your list! Review the three areas you should consider in selecting support members. Then list names of your personal support members below. These people will become part of your larger "job search network" (explained in the next section of this chapter).

_____

_____

_____

_____

_____

DEVELOP A LARGE NETWORK— THE NO. 1 SOURCE OF JOB LEADS

Did you know that 65 percent of jobs are identified through networking? Getting your ideal job is a numbers game; the more people you make aware of your search, the more solid leads you will obtain. The goals of your networking should be:

- To make as many people as possible aware of your job search.

- To make a good impression.

- To seek job leads and referrals to others who may help.

- To seek career and networking suggestions.

Networking is the top source of job leads because employers prefer to hire people referred to them personally (through networking). Therefore, the larger your network, the greater your odds are of finding someone who knows a viable prospective employer. So tap into this dynamic source, build your successful network, and get the word out now.

Networking Pays Off: A Case History

Consider this actual experience: After Roland completed a computer electronics training program, he sent resumes to all his prospects. Because he had overlooked a good source in his network, landing a job took him much longer than necessary. Six months into his job search, he was describing his job target to Helio, the owner of the print shop he frequented. From past experience, Helio knew that

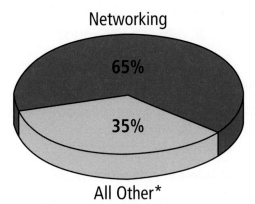

*Other includes employment agencies, ads, and miscellaneous sources.

Figure 5-1: Networking is the No. 1 source of job leads.

Roland's computer and technology abilities were good. A few days later the print shop owner mentioned this to another regular customer, Patsy, who had been looking for someone with Roland's skills for five months. Patsy called Roland for an interview; as a result, Roland landed an ideal job. However, he could have landed a job much sooner by including the print shop owner in his network from the start. Be sure you include absolutely everyone you know in your network.

Networking Sources

The network of people who can help you mushrooms exponentially with each new contact you make. People who know you personally are the most likely to help. Your network begins with people you know who link you to others, increasing your chances of discovering good job prospects. Review the list of networking sources below to help identify as many prospects as possible for your support network:

- Friends

- Relatives

- Current and former employers

- Colleagues or coworkers

- Instructors, trainers, coaches, counselors

- Career/job fairs

- Classmates and alums from your school

- People you serve or meet in your work or volunteer activities (clients, customers, others)

- People from your place of worship

- Neighbors

- Members, newsletters, membership directories, and web sites of your clubs, professional and trade associations, volunteer groups

- Web sites, bulletin boards, news/chat groups

- Professionals (physicians, dentists, accountants)

- People with whom you do business (salespeople, clerks, others)

Your personal network is larger than you think. Consider contacts where you work and play.

- People with whom you spend leisure time

- Service people (letter carriers, hairdressers or barbers, librarians, mechanics, clerks, others)

- People with whom your children or siblings associate (parents, teachers, club leaders, others)

- Who else do you know? (Don't overlook anyone!) Who do they know? Also consider spouses and family members of people you know. Someone could have a connection exactly where you need it.

Networking Expands Your Potential

You could easily have 100 to 500 acquaintances. Multiply that number by two (two referrals from each person), and the potential is astounding! This is why networking is the top source of job leads. The following guidelines will help you get the most from your networking efforts:

- **Ask Everyone for Advice.** In networking, getting job leads is important. Asking directly is not typically as productive as saying, "I'm looking for a _____ job. Do you have any advice for finding one in _____ (industry) (company) (city)?" This focuses on the word *advice* and makes your contacts more inclined to help. Be courteous. Also ask for names of referrals you could contact to seek additional information.

- **Put Career/Job Fairs High on Your List.** Career fairs are an excellent networking source because you can connect with many potential employers. Check with your school career center to find out what is offered in your area.

- **Participate Actively in Relevant Groups.** Join and be active in professional, trade, and other relevant associations or groups. They are a valuable resource for getting job leads and keeping informed of industry developments.

- **E-Network.** Search for and communicate with contacts via the Internet. Check sites in your field, news groups, message boards, chat groups, e-mail, and more. Seek career and job search advice and referrals from others who may be helpful. Share information and support with other job seekers.

- **Network for Life.** In today's changing work world, it is essential to build and maintain strong networking relationships throughout a career, not just during a job search. Networking regularly will help you remain informed and connected in your field and ready to make a successful job change when necessary.

- **Remember: It's a Numbers Game.** The more people who know about your job search goals and qualifications, the greater your chance of finding the ideal job! Networking is a tremendous force multiplier. Focus your energies on networking to expand your job search reach and to get the word out that you are looking for a job. By doing so, you will maximize your job and career development potential.

Complete Career Action 5-2

P E R S O N A L   B E S T

Networking Success Formula

To get the most from networking, take advantage of the following steps:

- Contact people who can help with your career preparation and job search.

- Treat every networking contact (whether a planned or spontaneous opportunity) with professional respect. Even if you don't believe the advice they offer is good, don't argue; just thank them for providing it. The impression you make can help or hinder the outcome.

- Discuss your job target with your contacts. In planned meetings, leave a copy of your resume and a brief outline of your job target and your qualifications. In spontaneous situations, follow up with this same information.

- Respect your contacts' time.

- Ask for the names of at least two other people you can contact to find job leads and information.

- Contact these two people; repeat the process.

- Follow up on every lead; be persistent.

- Within one day, send a thank-you note on quality stationery.

- Stay in touch throughout your search.

- Let your contacts know when you get a job.

Job Search Network List

Directions: Access Career Action 5-2 on your Learner's CD, or create a table like the one below on a separate sheet of paper. List the names of everyone you can think of for your job search network. Be sure to include the personal support members you listed in Career Action 5-1.

Then develop a Networking Organizer with spaces to record the following for each contact: person's name, mailing address, e-mail address, telephone number, dates of contact, and notes of needed follow-up.

Networking Organizer					
Name	**Mailing Address**	**E-Mail Address**	**Telephone Number**	**Dates of Contact**	**Notes/ Follow-Up**

SUCCESS TIP

Conduct organized networking meetings. Review your job target and qualifications, leave a resume, ask for referrals, get references, send thank-you letters, and follow up.

Update Your Network List. Update your job search network list periodically. Eliminate people who, over time, are reluctant or have too many other commitments that prevent their involvement.

Establish References. During your networking, seek influential references who are willing to vouch for your qualifications. These people should be able to attest to your strong performance at work, in school, or elsewhere and to your desirable character traits and values. They also should be willing to write letters recommending you to employers. Add their names to the list of references you recorded in Career Action 2-3. Also follow the guidelines below for developing references:

- Use only references who have given you permission to use their names, and thank them for allowing you to use them.

- Use only references who would recommend you highly from firsthand knowledge.

- Don't use relatives as references.

- Ask each reference to write a letter of reference for you that you can provide to employers.

- Keep copies of your reference letters in your Career Management Files Binder for use as needed during your job search.

- Let your references know when you will be using their names.

Maintain Active Communication

Communicate with your network members regularly to update them on your job search progress. Ask them to recommend additional job search strategies or job leads. It is best to contact the members of your network in person. Otherwise, use the telephone or e-mail to update them regarding your job search status and to get additional assistance and encouragement from them. Every job hunter can use regular encouragement. Someday you may be able to return the favor or extend it to another person who needs and deserves it.

Complete Career Action 5-3

Communicate with your network regularly to develop and refine your job search strategies.

CAREER ACTION 5-3

Use the Internet to Search for Current Job Search Networking Tips

Directions: Search for articles on tips for effective job search networking. You can use any of the web sites listed below, other sites you identify, or search engines. (Try using *job search networking* as keywords for your search.) Select at least two articles that interest you, and write a summary of each one.

1. CareerJournal.com   www.careerjournal.com

2. careermag.com   www.careermag.com

3. The Riley Guide   www.rileyguide.com

Members of your network should motivate you and help you with job search documents.

✓ **CHECKLIST:**

Organizing a Winning Network

Check each of the actions you are currently taking to increase your career success:

☐ Developing a support system: people who motivate and help with resumes and letters

☐ Developing a large job search network to help find job leads

☐ Conducting organized networking appointments: reviewing your job target and qualifications, leaving a resume, asking for referrals, getting references, sending thank-you letters, and following up

critical thinking *Questions*

1. What is networking?

2. What are the steps for effective networking?

3. Are neighbors and fellow club members as useful for networking as instructors or coworkers are? Explain your answer.

ENGINEER AN EFFICIENT JOB SEARCH

chapter **6**

In this chapter, you will:

www ▸ Use the Internet to research job listings and job trends information.

www ▸ Identify and use printed, human, Internet, and organizational sources of job information.

■ Use tools for organizing and conducting your job search efficiently.

"In planning your job search countless resources await you! Not only does your college guidance office offer assistance with skills testing and counseling, but we employers are offering internships, help with further college tuition, and great benefit packages to lure in the best applicants!"

Walter Boehm
ZF Corporation
Division of Ford Motor Company

This chapter identifies many solid resources to help you find jobs fast, including networking, direct employer contact, school career services centers, Internet sites, professional associations, and newspapers and other publications. The resources presented are based on extensive research with employment and placement counselors, with recent job seekers, and through the Internet. The more types of resources you use, the greater your job choices will be and the more quickly you will get optimum results. Chapter 6 also provides practical, efficient tools for organizing the job search to achieve your goals quickly.

SOURCES OF JOB LEADS

The following sources of job leads and related information will help you identify prospective employers. But don't limit yourself to the sources listed here. Use your imagination and some initiative. Many rewarding jobs are uncovered in personally creative ways. Your career objectives determine what sources are most useful to you.

Networking

Networking is the process of developing relationships with people who can assist with job search strategies and in finding strong job leads. Friends, relatives, and acquaintances (such as current and former employers, coworkers, and instructors) are statistically the best source of job leads for two reasons:

1. People who know you are more likely to be interested in your success. Therefore, they are most likely to help you in your job search.

2. A personal referral from a friend, a relative, or an acquaintance is highly influential with prospective employers if the employers know and respect the person referring you. Employers trust recommendations from people they know.

Since it's the most productive source, focus your efforts on networking (getting help from people you know) to identify prospective employers.

SUCCESS TIP

Focus your job search energy on networking—the No. 1 source of job leads.

Direct Employer Contact: Direct Bids and Information Surveys

Applicants trained in job search techniques often find jobs through direct employer contact because they are organized and professional in making con-

tacts by telephone, in writing, and in person. An effective method you can use to obtain solid job leads is arranging information interviews or surveys. These are meetings you arrange to obtain general career information and advice from prospective employers or from employees holding jobs similar to your job target. During such meetings, many job seekers obtain job leads as well as the career advice they request in scheduling the meeting. These meetings, known as career information surveys, are discussed further in Chapter 7.

SUCCESS TIP

Concentrate on direct telephone or face-to-face contact with employers. The most successful strategies involve direct contact with a hiring authority.

School Career Services Centers

School career services centers are valuable sources for obtaining job search information. Typically, these offices (a) maintain listings of local, regional, national, and global employers and listings of job openings; (b) assist with job search skills, interviewing, and resume and letter writing; (c) arrange and schedule on-campus interviews with students and prospective employers; (d) help research employer and salary information; and (e) provide career planning and job search counseling.

Internet and Job Information Web Sites

Many web sites serve as job bank connections for employers and applicants. Several of these sites are listed as part of Career Action 6-1. You can access these sites and several others under "Jobs Links" on the *Your Career: How to Make It Happen* web site. However, don't limit yourself to just these. Many web sites provide listings of job openings and opportunities to submit online resumes and offer useful career planning and job search information.

Additionally, the vast majority of employers have web sites today. Employer web sites typically provide information about the organization, information about available jobs, and instructions for submitting applications and resumes. Chapters 9 and 10 of this text provide more information about the electronic application and resume.

Publications of professional, technical, career, and trade associations as well as local newspapers are valuable sources of job openings and hiring trends.

Leaders in Your Occupational Field

Recognized leaders in your occupational field can be excellent sources of job leads. Successful people are usually knowledgeable about the employment needs of their peers and competitors. One of them may even consider hiring you after learning of your job target and qualifications. Be sure to include this valuable source in your job search. Ask instructors in your career field for names of leaders in your area who you might contact.

Professional, Technical, Career, and Trade Associations

Virtually every profession, vocation, and trade has one or more national associations to keep members informed of changing technology, methods, and trends. Such groups typically provide educational publications, workshops, and continuing education courses. They often announce job openings during meetings and in their publications.

The Internet and many libraries have information on professional, technical, and trade associations. For example, using both sources, you will find associations for information technology, accounting, writing, health care, teaching, and business management. Your career services staff and a reference librarian can help you identify organizations related to your interests and locate their web sites and publications. Check current and back issues of printed resources or Internet archives for help-wanted ads, and look for information about employment and job market trends.

Employment Directories

Directories listing employers in local areas and defined geographic regions are useful. Some employer specialty directories are also available in specific areas, such as manufacturing. To find such directories, check public, state, college, or university libraries; your school career counseling center; the Internet; and area chambers of commerce.

Want Ads (Newspapers, Other Print Media, and the Internet)

Check for job openings posted in a variety of ways:

- **Newspapers.** Look in the help-wanted section, the business section, and virtually all other sections of newspapers from locations that interest you. You can learn a lot about the hiring, expansion, downsizing, or start-up of organizations in an area. Many newspapers also post their classified ads on the Internet.

- **The Internet.** Check job listings and want ads on the Internet. The Internet allows quick, convenient access and linking to an enormous number of sources. Search on large job listing sites and small niche sites that focus only on your career field and/or specialty.

- **Journals and other publications.** Check the classified sections of both printed and online professional journals in your field, your school newspaper and bulletin boards, and other publications that target job seekers.

Learn About Job Market Trends. Get the most out of printed or Internet want ads. Use them to learn what kinds of employers are hiring and which appear to be expanding (indicated by several ads from the same organization). You can learn what experience, additional courses, and training you need for employment or advancement in your field.

Be alert for organizations that advertise actively— even for jobs that require more experience and education than you currently have. Active advertising indicates growth and job opportunities—and that other positions may be open.

Read Every Ad. Good opportunities are not always clearly evident. Be thorough; read every listing. Advertisements don't always appear under a logical job heading, and you may miss an important lead by looking only under the obvious heads.

If an advertised job differs slightly but is still related to your target, pursue the lead anyway. You could find yourself interviewing for an unadvertised job that fits your goals. Don't overlook the blind ads requesting that resumes be sent to an anonymous box

number. Some companies run blind ads to limit the number of individual contacts required to review applications. A well-prepared resume and cover letter can help you land a job this way.

Review Old Ads. Search the Internet and back issues of newspapers for ads that are 12 to 18 months old. If a company was hiring three months ago, it's a job lead for you. The company may not have found the right person, may have let the last person go, or may be expanding. Contact the firm and ask to schedule a career information survey. Your meeting could provide a good lead or even a job offer. (See Chapter 7 for survey details.)

Help-wanted advertisements are a limited resource for finding just the right job, but don't let a choice opportunity slip through your fingers for lack of attention. Perhaps family members or friends will help you with this daily task.

SUCCESS TIP

Don't limit your search to published job announcements. They represent only 15 to 20 percent of available jobs.

Don't Limit Job Search to Published Ads. As emphasized in Figure 6-1, published job openings represent only 15 to 20 percent of available jobs. Although these should not be overlooked and may lead to a good job, your odds are greatly increased if you use other job lead sources.

Small Businesses

According to the U.S. Department of Labor, approximately 55 percent of jobs in the United States are with small businesses, not large firms. This is a clear reason to research small businesses as an employment source. Information about openings with

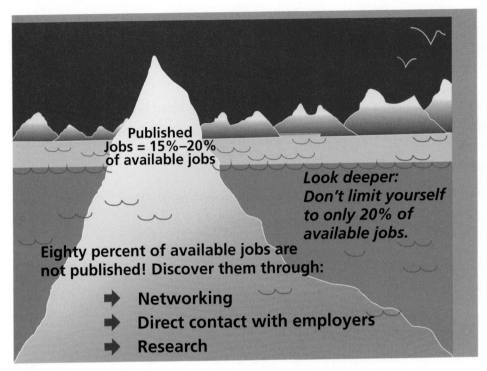

Figure 6-1: Published job openings: just the tip of the iceberg!
Source: U.S. Department of Labor

small businesses is available through chambers of commerce, your school career services center, employer directories, and help-wanted ads.

Complete Career Action 6-1

Private Contractors and Employment Agencies

Private contractors and employment or staffing firms can be useful sources for finding prospective employers, particularly if the one you select specializes in your field. The employment processes vary among these organizations. Some focus on connecting applicants with part-time jobs; others focus on full-time jobs.

Some of the employment firms connect employers and applicants to facilitate a full-time hire by the employer. Other employment firms actually serve as a permanent link between employer and employee,

and the employment firm handles all human resource functions. This relieves the employer of such activities as hiring, compensation, career development, and so on. Policies vary regarding who pays fees for securing a permanent job—the applicant or employer. Always try to negotiate in your favor. Before considering such a firm, research the following:

1. Does the firm have a good reputation? Ask the staff at your school career services center, employers who work with the agency to obtain employees, other job seekers, and the Better Business Bureau. Don't rely on one person's word. Also visit the agency you are considering.

2. How long has the employment firm been in business? What has happened to past clients?

3. Does the agency have expertise in placing people in your field? What employment firms are associated with ads for jobs you are targeting?

Use the Internet to Find Job Listings and Information

Directions: Use the Internet to access at least four of the sites listed below. (Also include any specialty sites in your field.) Browse through these sites, researching the following information. Prepare a written report of your findings.

1. Include the sites that had the most relevant information to your job target and field.

2. Summarize or print job listings you find for your field, and indicate the sources of the listings.

3. Summarize other useful job trends and job information you find in this search.

Web Sites

America's Job Bank	www.ajb.dni.us
The Black Collegian Online	www.black-collegian.com
CareerBuilder	www.careerbuilder.com
DirectEmployers	www.directemployers.com
EmploymentGuide.com	www.employmentguide.com
FlipDog.com	www.flipdog.com
Monster.com	www.monster.com
NationJob Network	www.nationjob.com
Net-Temps	www.net-temps.com
Saludos.com	www.saludos.com

4. If you would accept employment out of your local area, does the employment firm belong to a nationwide or regional system? Is it familiar with job opportunities, hiring trends, and salaries throughout the areas you would consider?

5. What services will the employment firm provide for you, and what would it expect you to do?

6. What are the costs to you? Get a written agreement spelling out every service you will receive, including how long counseling will take and how long you are entitled to the agency services.

7. Do you understand the contract? Read every word of it, and make certain you are willing to accept all the conditions. Ask the agency to clarify how it handles client dissatisfaction with job placement. Firms that guarantee a full refund are usually the most reputable.

Some employment firms focus on hiring applicants to perform contract work on a temporary or project basis. This is one of the most accessible means of reentering the job market and is a stepping stone from unemployment to employment. This arrangement offers two major benefits: (1) It gives the employer and the employee an opportunity to check for a "good fit" without the employee having to make a permanent commitment up front, and (2) the employment firm takes care of the administrative details. Many people find full-time jobs through this source by gaining experience in the temporary jobs.

To locate these companies, look in the Yellow Pages of your telephone directory or search on the Internet for *employment agencies, employment contractors, employment staffing agencies,* or *temporary-help agencies.* This job may not fit your career target perfectly, but it can provide some outstanding benefits, including those listed below:

- Reentry to the job market

- Experience you may lack

- References for work done well

- Additions to your list of solid job leads

- A possible full-time job

- On-the-job training and hands-on practical skill development

- Immediate income

State Employment Services

Through the U.S. Department of Labor, each state has an employment agency that includes a Job Service or Employment Services office. You can call the main state information number and ask for the number of the employment services office.

These offices provide such services as career counseling, job search techniques, training, referrals to upgrade training or education, and information on area job openings. Most offices maintain computerized data with up-to-the-minute information on job openings in the service regions. The job hunter is not charged a fee for this assistance.

Public Agencies: City, County, State, and Federal

City, county, and state agencies employ people in a wide variety of positions. Most agencies have a civil service system that requires application and pre-employment testing through a central human resources department. Consult your local telephone directory for the numbers of these agencies, and check with your school's career services office. You can also search online for links to jobs in states that interest you. Every state has its own employment agency and web site. Check America's Job Bank (www.ajb.dni.us). This site is a combined effort of all state employment offices, providing online listings of both private and public job openings.

Government employment agencies offer a number of employment services in addition to providing information about government jobs.

Federal agencies have a variety of positions, and many openings are projected to occur with the retirement of a large group of federal employees. Your local state employment office can refer you to the regional federal offices in areas that interest you. Check out USA Jobs (www.usajobs.opm.gov) for information about federal jobs. Also look for federal job information under *U.S. Government* in major area telephone directories. Request federal job information from your school career services center or your local state employment office.

Human Resources Departments in Private Industry

Contact human resources departments of private companies to learn about current job openings. If no openings are available, ask if you can leave your application and resume for future openings. If these are accepted, ask what action you need to take to keep your file open (for example, confirming your status every six months). Also ask about other job lead sources in your field. Some organizations offer telephone recordings of information about current job openings.

Career/Job Fairs

The primary reason employers go to community, industry, or school-sponsored career or job fairs is to find new talent, so go; you have to be there to be discovered! Career fairs are good sources of job leads and employer information. They are beneficial to employers and job seekers, allowing them to explore employment matches in a more relaxed, face-to-face format. These fairs are efficient ways to contact many employers in one day. Career fairs are also offered on the Internet; look for advertisements on job listing sites, and use search engines to locate online career fairs.

The following guidelines explain how to get the most out of on-site career fairs:

1. Take copies of your resume, your business cards (if you have them), and your business portfolio.

2. Set a goal to meet at least ten people at every career fair.

3. Plan your remarks. Present yourself professionally and confidently. Wear business-smart clothes. Shake hands, introduce yourself, summarize your qualifications briefly, and ask pertinent questions.

4. Before visiting your main employer targets, visit the less attractive firms to perfect your marketing pitch.

5. To your Job Search Network List (Career Action 5-2), add the names of everyone with whom you network and any needed follow-up.

Educational Institutions

For a teaching job, contact the human resources departments of school districts that interest you to find out about their application and hiring procedures. Also ask your school career services staff for help in locating jobs in education. Look in telephone directories for areas you would consider.

If no openings are currently available, request permission to leave your application and resume on file for future openings. Ask how you should follow up to keep your file updated and active. Also look into the possibility of being certified to do substitute teaching. This can be a good way to prove your abilities and possibly work into a regular teaching position.

Self-Employment

This form of employment continues to grow because of organizational downsizing and task/job outsourcing to control costs.

Learn Under Another Employer First. To succeed in your own business, adequate education, training, and knowledge are essential. In addition, you can significantly increase your chance of successful self-employment by first working for someone who has succeeded in the field. Learn the plusses and minuses as an employee, not as a new business owner.

Gaining experience and achieving solid accomplishments in the field first provide the credibility essential to landing work contracts on your own. Self-employment is worth considering particularly if you have related work experience and can get endorsements from people who are satisfied with your performance.

Research to Succeed. If you are seriously interested, interview people in your field who are successfully self-employed to learn what methods they have used. Also obtain and study self-employment information from published and Internet sources. Remember that you will need to earn enough to cover your insurance and other items provided by many employers as benefits; in some cases, this could require 30 percent more income. Finally, before starting your own business, plan carefully, develop a formal business plan, and check with the Small Business Administration for information on starting a business.

Networking Is Essential. To succeed in your own business, networking regularly with people in your field, with potential clients, and with customers is essential. Market yourself by being active in professional or trade associations and clubs related to your career field.

Start Small and Build. A smart way to begin self-employment is to do it part-time to develop a client base and essential references. Volunteer with groups to prove your skills. Start small; keep expenses at an absolute minimum; expand only with demand.

Success Tip

Consider self-employment if you have adequate experience; this is projected to be one of the largest sources of employment in the near future.

Volunteer work in nonprofit organizations can be a good source of work experience.

Nonprofit Organizations

Nonprofit organizations are good sources for jobs in public relations, solicitation, writing, management, health care, and other fields. They can offer growth opportunities, valuable work experience, and opportunities to demonstrate community service.

Examples of nonprofit organizations are the United Way, representing several organizations; the Red Cross; the March of Dimes; professional associations; federal grant support projects; Head Start programs; and health clinics for migrant workers. Look under *Associations* or *Social Services Organizations* in the Yellow Pages.

Classified Telephone Directories

Collect classified sections or Yellow Pages of telephone directories from areas you would consider for employment. Most of these directories are available on CD and the Internet (see www.superpages.com).

Look for employers in your field under all related headings (check the easy-reference indexes). This source provides comprehensive, readily available listings of current employers.

Library

Ask your local reference librarian for help in finding directories (business, product, company, and so on) related to your field of interest. These directories list names, addresses, telephone numbers, and general information about employers in your field. Also ask knowledgeable people in your field to suggest additional library job search resources.

Chambers of Commerce

Contact the local chamber of commerce in each of your geographic target areas. Chambers have complete, current lists of employers and often have names and telephone numbers of company executives. Most chambers also have information on new organizations that plan to locate in the area.

The Military

The military is a good source of employment and provides important training and experience. Talk with your career services staff and local recruiting officers to obtain information and to compare the offerings available.

Internships, Cooperative Education, and Volunteering

You can benefit from training internships, cooperative education programs, and volunteer work. You gain important experience and references who can verify your qualifications. You also demonstrate personal initiative and commitment (highly favorable attributes), enhancing your employability.

Reference Reading

Excellent publications are available to strengthen your career planning and job search in specific areas—particularly publications that specialize in your field. Ask your librarian and school career services staff for suggestions.

The Hidden Job Market

Numerous studies emphasize that 80 to 85 percent of job openings are never published and that personal search is required to uncover them. Many jobs are actually created by applicants; such jobs are part of the *hidden job market*. The first step to uncovering the hidden job market is to research your target employer thoroughly. Discover where you can provide a useful service or offer moneymaking or money-saving ideas. Then present your qualifications for this job or service so convincingly that the employer is motivated to create a job for you. The hidden job market is created through your own ingenuity. The hidden job market is further discussed in Chapter 12.

"Everyone who's ever taken a shower has an idea. It's the person who gets out of the shower, dries off, and does something about it that makes a difference."

Nolan Bushnell

PERSONAL AWARENESS OF MARKET TRENDS

Throughout your job search (and even before), look actively for job leads—from people, television, radio, newspapers, the Internet, books, and magazines and through personal awareness. Be aware of what is happening in your city and state, the nation, and the world. Notice how changing technology shapes new jobs and revises or eliminates traditional jobs. Through this awareness, you can identify emerging trends.

Major job market trends favor health care and fitness, information processing, electronics, computerization, robotics, energy development, services to the elderly, finance/accounting, engineering, education, and government, to name a few. Can you market your abilities in any of these areas? What other job market trends do you see emerging?

ORGANIZING AN EFFECTIVE JOB SEARCH

The energy you put into organizing your job search directly affects the speed and success of your search. The techniques that follow will help you maximize your efforts.

Compile Your List of Prospects

This chapter provides many excellent resources for identifying prospective employers. Use any of the suggestions that apply to your occupational field. Focus your job search efficiently by completing the following Career Action to identify the job lead sources most appropriate for your job target.

Complete Career Action 6-2

CAREER ACTION 6-2

Job Leads Source List

Directions: To focus your sources of job leads, access Career Action 6-2 on your Learner's CD or turn now to page 86 and review the directions for preparing your Job Leads Source List.

Develop Prospective Employer Records

To identify prospective employers to contact in your job search, research each source on your Job Leads Source List (Career Action 6-2). To best organize your job search, access the Prospective Employer Record on your Learner's CD or make copies of the form on page 87. File all your records in one folder, and use them to monitor your employer contacts and follow-up activities efficiently.

When it comes time to make calls or send your cover letters and resumes, you can search first for the records you marked as "Hot Prospects" to maximize your potential and your time in the job search. Use colored file tags to mark hot prospects.

Narrow Your List

After completing your Prospective Employer Records, concentrate on the employers who could best use your abilities. For now, eliminate the long shots, those who offer a slim chance for employment.

If you plan to do a direct mailing in your job search, narrowing your list of prospects is especially important. (A direct-mail job search consists of mailing cover letters with requests for interviews along with your resume to prospective employers.) Don't start this type of campaign until you have completed all the reading, assignments, and activities for Chapters 1 through 10 of this book. Note that a direct mailing of unsolicited resumes is statistically not a productive job search method unless you have high-demand skills.

The Job Market Is Not Always Organized—You Must Be!

Employers use a variety of hiring techniques. Their processes may be simple or complex, well or poorly organized, short or long. You, the job applicant, must be well organized—even if the job market is not. As you progress through this book, your store of job-seeking tools will increase. Use these tools to develop your own efficient, speedy, and successful job-seeking campaign.

PLANNING TIME FOR YOUR JOB SEARCH

If you are just finishing school, you will be competing with other new graduates for employment. The sooner you start your job search, the greater your advantage will be. Employers sometimes view a long delay between school or your last job and application for employment as a lack of initiative or a lack of employability.

Your Job Search: A Full-Time Job

A job search campaign should include daily activities and requires a minimum of 25 to 30 hours per week. If you're currently employed and seeking another position, you must look at your job search as a second job, which means you won't have as much time to devote to it.

PERSONAL BEST
Job Search Management

The following tips will help you manage your job search time effectively:

1. Set up an organized job search headquarters so you can easily lay your hands on anything you need and follow up on leads effectively. Use labeled file folders for your job search schedules, job lead lists, prospective employer records, and so on.

2. Prepare a weekly job search schedule. Use a monthly calendar to schedule your activities one or more weeks in advance. Record the hours to be spent each day on your search.

3. Prepare a daily job search plan. Plan your daily job search activities at least one day in advance. Use the Daily Job Search Organizer on your Learner's CD or the form on page 88 to help plan your daily goals.

4. If possible, begin your job search while still employed part- or full-time. (Employers consider employed applicants to be more employable than the unemployed. Why? Being employed is proof you can do a job well enough to keep it.)

5. If you aren't employed, begin your search the moment you know you need to get a job. If you graduate in June and will need a job then, start your search preparations in January—or before!

6. Report for work on your search as you would for a job. Procrastination is the job seeker's biggest enemy.

7. Never be late. Employers expect you to be punctual for all scheduled appointments.

8. Follow up every job lead immediately. Delays can cost you the job you are seeking.

SUCCESS TIP

Write out your job search schedule to increase your sense of commitment and to improve your organizational effectiveness.

Winning Job Search Routines

Establish a routine to help you stay focused and efficient. The following are appropriate daily activities:

- **Look the part every day.** Dress and groom yourself for success.

- **Organize your job search work area daily,** including your files, references, and related forms and materials. If possible, have a telephone and a computer in your work area.

- **Make telephone contacts** to arrange appointments, to communicate with your network, and so on.

- **Work on new leads.** Research, make telephone and written contacts, and arrange appointments.

- **Follow up.** Write thank-you letters, review leads, and take appropriate actions.

- **Arrange appointments** to network and gather information and for interviews.

SUCCESS TIP

Organize your job search to gain an advantage over those who don't plan an efficient search. Develop prospective employer records. Develop and follow a daily job search schedule. Be persistent. Follow up.

Your job search is a full-time job. Develop your own winning job search routine.

✓ CHECKLIST:

Organizing a Winning Job Search

Check each of the actions you are currently taking to increase your career success:

☐ Focusing job search energy on networking (the No. 1 job lead source)

☐ Concentrating on direct telephone or face-to-face contacts with employers

☐ Including the Internet as a job search tool

☐ Not limiting the search to published job announcements, which represent only 15 to 20 percent of available jobs

☐ Considering self-employment (with adequate experience)

☐ Allocating time in relation to the proven success rate of the top job search strategies: networking, advertisements, and employment agencies

☐ Planning and organizing the job search to gain an advantage over others and spending time on the job search every day

critical thinking *Questions*

1. Why should you make a conscious effort to tell everyone about your job search?

2. How can professional or trade associations help the job seeker?

3. How can you obtain employment information from organizations in private industry?

4. What sources do you think will be most useful for your job search?

Job Leads Source List

Directions: Review each of the sources of job information presented in this chapter, including the Internet sites you used in Career Action 6-1. Then list those sources you think would be effective in your job search. (Make additional copies of this form if necessary.)

Name of Source: _____

Address of Source: _____

Internet Address: _____ E-Mail Address: _____

Telephone Number: _____

Action Plans for Using This Source: _____

Name of Source: _____

Address of Source: _____

Internet Address: _____ E-Mail Address: _____

Telephone Number: _____

Action Plans for Using This Source: _____

Name of Source: _____

Address of Source: _____

Internet Address: _____ E-Mail Address: _____

Telephone Number: _____

Action Plans for Using This Source: _____

Name of Source: _____

Address of Source: _____

Internet Address: _____ E-Mail Address: _____

Telephone Number: _____

Action Plans for Using This Source: _____

Continued on next page.

CAREER ACTION 6-2 (continued)

PROSPECTIVE EMPLOYER RECORD

 Directions: Access this form on your Learner's CD or duplicate this page. Prepare one record for each employer you are targeting in your job search.

Name of Organization: _____

Address of Organization: _____

Internet Address: _____ E-Mail Address: _____

Telephone Number: _____ Fax Number: _____

Job Target Title: _____

Job Target Description: _____

_____

Person to Contact (name and title): _____

_____

Source of Information: _____

Referred by (person who will refer me): _____

Hiring Status: Position Open _____   No Position Currently Open _____

Other: _____

Potential: Hot Prospect _____   Possibility _____   Long Shot _____

Dates and Methods of Contact With Employer: _____

_____

_____

Date Resume and Cover Letter Sent: _____

Date of Interview: _____

Interview Follow-up: _____

_____

Comments: _____

_____

_____

_____

Daily Job Search Organizer

Directions: Access this form on your Learner's CD or duplicate this page. Record the name of the employer, the person you plan to contact, and the job target. Record the form of contact (personal visit, phone call, letter, or Internet contact) and the purpose of the contact. Summarize other job search goals you plan for the day. Complete the last three sections of the form at the end of the day, including a summary of your progress, a list of new job leads, and any necessary follow-up (sending a thank-you note or resume). Also note whether you achieved the purpose of each contact made.

Date: _____   Number of hours to be spent on job search: _____   From: _____   To: _____

Employer, Name of Contact, and Job Target	Form of Contact (personal visit, phone call, letter, Internet contact)	Purpose of Contact	Purpose Achieved (Yes/No)
1.			
2.			
3.			

Other Goals for Today (research, support system or network contact, schedule appointments, and so on): _____

Summary of Progress Made: _____

New Job Leads: _____

Follow-up/Next Steps: _____

chapter 7

INVESTIGATE JOB, APPLICATION, AND HIRING PROCEDURES

In this chapter, you will:

- Survey people holding jobs similar to the one you will be seeking to learn about the scope of their jobs and the hiring procedures used by their employers.

- Use the Internet to search for current information about application and hiring procedures.

- Prepare a Job Qualifications Profile to help in marketing your skills by identifying your current job target and by relating your qualifications directly to the target.

"We select the applicants for our branch of Microsoft from a corporate resume database. This database is made up of all of the resumes that are submitted online through our Microsoft Web site. I can run a query on the type of experience and job skills I am looking for, and the computer will do a search for me."

Carrie Fellhoelter
Senior Human Resource Administrator
Microsoft Corporation
Dallas, Texas

In this chapter, you learn more about existing jobs similar to the one you are targeting and about the application and hiring procedures typical in your field. You complete two surveys to obtain this information directly from people working in your career field. These will be your first outside Career Action assignments. You also use the Internet to locate additional tips regarding current hiring and job application procedures. The answers you obtain will help you land your ideal job. Finally, Chapter 7 guides you through the preparation of your Job Qualifications Profile, which will help you develop content for successful self-marketing in networking, resumes, cover letters, and interviews.

89

THE CAREER INFORMATION SURVEY

Through the Career Information Surveys in this chapter, you'll gain a decided advantage over your competition by meeting with people who hold jobs similar to your job target. Professionals in your field can provide valuable inside information and advice to help you realize your career goals. Through your meetings, you'll gain:

- **Practice:** You will go directly to the business community as you research and network. You will schedule appointments and practice communicating about your career and job targets—terrific preparation for actual interviews!

- **Information:** You will obtain important current information about the scope of jobs in your field and the hiring procedures. You may even get valuable job leads.

- **Competitive Edge:** You will have the edge over applicants who don't complete these activities.

To complete your Career Information Survey, you will contact two people holding jobs similar to your job target. You'll meet them at their work sites to learn about their jobs and the hiring procedures used by their employers. This will help prepare you for a successful job search in your field.

 SUCCESS TIP

Contact employees in your field to get current information about the scope of their jobs and hiring procedures.

Prepare Sample Questions for Career Information Survey

To prepare for your survey meetings, make a list of questions to ask your contacts. Following are some sample questions:

You can learn a lot about the workplace by watching how people interact. Be observant. Does the place you're visiting seem like a place you'd like to work?

A. Questions Regarding Job Scope and Career Development

1. Is the firm privately owned, a government agency, or a nonprofit organization? (Ask only if you don't already know.)

2. What are the main goals of the organization? Is it a product- or service-oriented firm? (Ask only if you don't know.)

3. What skills, education, experience, and knowledge are required to qualify for a position such as yours?

4. What personal qualities or traits are important in your work?

5. What are your specific duties?

6. What do you like most/least about your job?

7. What is the average starting salary range for a position such as yours?

8. What employee benefits are offered in this position (health insurance, retirement savings programs, others)?

9. What future changes do you anticipate in this field?

10. What additional or ongoing education or training do you need to achieve your career goals?

11. Does the employer offer on-the-job training for this position? If so, what does it involve?

12. Is continuing education for the position encouraged by the employer? If so, what kinds of programs are available or promoted and are fees paid by the employer?

13. Would it be possible to get a written description of your job if one is available?

14. What professional or other associations would you recommend for staying informed about this career field?

15. What publications would you recommend (books, journals, and so on)?

16. Could you suggest other people to help me with my research?

17. Do you have any advice for planning my career and job search?

B. Sample Questions Regarding Application, Interview, and Hiring Procedures

1. What are your general application procedures for positions such as the one I will be seeking?

2. Do you have an employment application form I could see, or could I a get a copy of one to review as a reference?

3. What are the interview procedures (one person interviewing the applicant, team interviewing, multiple interviews, typical length of interviews, testing)?

4. What types of questions are typically asked during interviews? Are applicants asked to give specific examples of how they have used the required job skills or how they have handled specific work situations?

5. What do you think is important to show in a resume for a position such as the one I will be seeking?

6. What advice do you have for preparing and interviewing successfully?

Study the Work Environment of Your Contacts

Through careful observation at the job site, you can learn about the working conditions for the type of job you want. So prior to the survey, also make a list of questions to consider about this environment. Following are some examples:

1. What type of work area does my contact have? Does my contact work at a desk, share office space, or have some other setup?

2. What equipment and software does my contact use?

3. Is the work environment appropriate for the type of work?

4. Is the environment quiet, noisy, slow-paced, or fast-paced?

5. Does my contact interact with others? If so, with whom and how often?

6. What type of dress is appropriate?

7. Is the atmosphere formal or informal?

8. Are work areas neat and clean or cluttered?

Spot a Top Place to Work

Be alert to the work atmosphere, and listen for comments from your contacts. Employees of desirable workplaces often mention freedom, trust, pride, teamwork, fair pay and benefits, opportunities for growth, recognition, and fairness in management. Ask about and watch for these characteristics during your meetings. Keep these qualities in mind as you select your actual job prospects.

Now prepare your own questions about the job and work environment.

Complete Career Action 7-1

Career Information Survey Worksheet

Directions: Prepare a Career Information Survey Worksheet by preparing two sets of questions:

1. Prepare the career information questions you will ask your contact during your survey meeting (those regarding the job, career development, and hiring procedures).

2. Prepare the work environment questions you want to answer for yourself through observation.

Some of the sample questions listed earlier may apply to your field, but also add additional questions necessary for your field. The goal is to clarify your understanding of the particular job, the occupational field, the typical work environment, and the hiring procedures. Leave adequate space after each question to record the information you obtain. Place these questions in a professional binder to use during your surveys; projecting a professional image is important in all outside assignments!

Make Your Appointment for a Survey Meeting

To make your appointment, contact at least two organizations employing people in your occupational field. Making the initial contact in person is preferable. If you can't do that, use the telephone, but first review the telephone techniques outlined in Chapter 12.

![Success Tip icon] SUCCESS TIP

Dress and act professionally in all outside assignments to project competence and to encourage job leads.

Ask to speak with a person whose job is similar to your job target. Emphasize that you are carrying out an assignment from your instructor or doing research in your field. Explain that you want to learn about your occupational field as part of your career planning research. *Do not say you're looking for a job.* Strangers are more likely to help you with career planning research than with getting a job. Follow the guidelines below when making your appointment:

1. **Be clean, neat, and properly dressed if you make your appointment in person.**

2. **Introduce yourself.**

3. **State your purpose**—completing an assignment from your instructor at (name your school). If you are using this book independently, state that you are conducting career research.

4. **Request an appointment** to ask a few questions about the person's job and the occupational field.

5. **Confirm the date and time.** If you're making your initial contact in person, the individual may offer to meet with you immediately. Be prepared by having your binder and questions with you!

6. **Thank the person for his or her time and assistance.**

Connect With Hard-to-Reach Employers

Some organizations are not as accessible for career survey meetings. If your target employer is such an organization, follow the guidelines below to identify people with whom you can meet for the survey.

1. **Turn to your network.** Ask everyone in your job search network (friends, family, school counselors, and so on) to help you identify people working in your targeted employment field—someone you can meet with to gather career information. Your network can provide opportunities that would not otherwise be available to you.

2. **Search the Internet.** Many firms have computerized hiring processes and provide application and hiring information through their company web sites or through third-party job bank/job-posting web sites. If your target employer uses this process, obtain the company or third-party Internet addresses, search for the application and hiring information, and print your findings or prepare a written summary to submit as your report for Career Action 7-2.

3. **Choose a closely related employer target.** If you are unable to schedule an appointment to meet with your preferred employer, schedule a meeting with a closely related organization. Face-to-face meetings give you the valuable business communication practice necessary to outdistance your competition.

SUCCESS TIP

Use the Internet to research job descriptions and hiring information of hard-to-reach employers.

Complete Career Action 7-2

CAREER ACTION 7-2

Internet Research of Hiring Procedures

Directions: Identify at least two major company or organizational web sites that offer information regarding employer application and/or hiring processes. When you reach your target sites, search for information about jobs, application processes, resume submission, and so on. Prepare a summary report of your findings.

Web resources for finding major employers:

- Search engines (accessible through the *Your Career: How to Make It Happen* web site at www.levitt.swlearning.com)

- Enter names of employer companies or organizations (private; nonprofit; or state, county, or city government) you are researching to find links to their web sites.

- USAJobs   www.usajobs.opm.gov (for information about federal jobs)

- WetFeet.com   www.wetfeet.com/asp/home.asp

- Wall Street Research Net   www.wsrn.com

PERSONAL BEST

Career Information Survey Meeting

Take your career information survey meetings seriously. If you make a strong first impression, you could gain job leads from the activities. Some people actually obtain job offers. Maximize your information-gathering sessions by following these tips:

- Dress and act professionally. (See Chapter 11 for appropriate grooming guidelines.)

- Be courteous, friendly, and professional.

- Arrive on time.

- Learn your contact's name. Use it when you first meet, when you leave, and in follow-up.

- Begin by restating your reason for being there.

- Ask well-prepared open-ended questions. Let your questions show you did your homework.

- Move quickly through your prepared questions and avoid wasting time.

- Take brief notes of your contact's answers. However, don't write out every answer completely. (Do this as soon as possible after the meeting.)

- Practice active listening skills.

- Pay attention to body language—both yours and the person's you are interviewing.

- Obtain the names of other individuals you can contact.

- Be alert for job leads and accept help enthusiastically. Do not make a direct bid for a job. (If you do, you risk offending your contact.) You asked to schedule a career information meeting, not an interview!

- Apply the nine success strategies. Conduct your career information survey meetings with energy, enthusiasm, and attention to detail.

Write thank-you letters promptly to the people who helped you with your career information survey meetings.

SUCCESS TIP

Throughout your career information survey, emphasize your interest in developing a career, not in "just getting a job." This shows you are serious about finding the best match between you and the employer so you both gain maximum results.

Complete Career Action 7-3

Follow Up the Meeting

Within one day of your survey meeting, write follow-up thank-you letters to the people who helped you with the assignment. Use good-quality stationery and handwrite or key the letters neatly. If a contact offers to help you with a job lead, hand deliver or mail a copy of your resume to your contact within a week. (This person could become a key part of your job search network!) If you don't already have a resume, prepare one following the guidelines in Chapter 9. If you have a resume prepared, compare it to the guidelines provided in Chapter 9.

CAREER ACTION 7-3

Participate in Career Information Survey Meeting

Directions: Schedule and conduct your career information survey meeting(s). Write the answers to your survey questions, and be prepared to discuss your findings in class.

- Schedule as many of these meetings as possible; the benefits of gaining current information and possible job leads are great.

- Also consider contacting people in your field who screen, interview, or hire job applicants to discuss the job hiring processes in particular. This could put you closer to a future job interview if you perform impressively during your information-gathering meeting.

- Small companies often have only a few employees; the company owner may also be the hiring authority.

JOB QUALIFICATIONS PROFILE: A SNAPSHOT TO PERSUADE EMPLOYERS

The Job Qualifications Profile organizes the qualifications information you summarized about yourself in Chapters 2 and 3. This profile gives you a solid description of your abilities and how they relate to your job target. This is exactly the information employers need in order to see evidence of a good match between the job and the applicant—you! Follow the steps below to start developing this summary and preparing yourself for a successful job search:

1. **Clearly identify your job target.** If you have not yet done this, a career counselor can help you. Also refer to the information in Chapter 3 to identify other sources of career planning information and assistance.

2. **Write a clear description of your targeted job.** Obtain job descriptions from prospective employers. If this isn't feasible, ask your school career counselor or librarian to help you locate a general description of your job target in the *Dictionary of Occupational*

> *"Act as if what you do makes a difference. It does."*
>
> William James

Titles, published by the U.S. Department of Labor. For more complete descriptions of major occupations, refer to the printed version of the *Occupational Outlook Handbook* or to the online version at www.bls.gov/oco.

3. **Refer to the information compiled in Chapters 2 and 3.** This information will help you complete the rest of the Job Qualifications Profile form outlining your abilities as they relate to your job target.

4. **Copy or print the profile form (Career Action 7-4) for multiple job targets.** If you're looking for employment in more than one field or area, prepare one Job Qualifications Profile for each target. Develop the broadest possible career planning base by including as many options as possible.

Your Job Qualifications Profile will serve as a valuable resource throughout your lifetime for writing your resume and letters and for preparing for interviews for each job you target. As you develop new skills and gain more experience, training, and education, your goals will change or expand. You can repeat the self-analysis exercises in this book at any time during your career. Your Job Qualifications Profile will result in a well-organized summary of those qualifications that relate directly to your current job target. This profile provides the snapshot of your qualifications necessary to persuade an employer to hire you for the job you want. Now access Career Action 7-4 on your Learner's CD, or follow the directions to complete the form on the following page.

Complete Career Action 7-4

SUCCESS TIP

Develop a Job Qualifications Profile to market yourself successfully to employers

✓ **CHECKLIST:**

Investigating the Job, Application, and Hiring Procedures

Check each of the actions you are currently taking to increase your career success:

☐ Contacting employees in the field to get current information about the scope of their jobs and hiring procedures

☐ Dressing and acting professionally in all outside assignments to project competence and to encourage job leads

☐ Using the Internet to research job descriptions and hiring information of hard-to-reach employers

☐ Developing a Job Qualifications Profile to help in successfully marketing yourself to employers

critical thinking *Questions*

1. What benefits can you gain by conducting career information survey meetings?

2. What is the most significant information you obtained from the outside assignment for this chapter?

3. How can you use your Job Qualifications Profile information in your job search and interviews?

CAREER ACTION 7-4

Job Qualifications Profile

Directions: Supply the information called for on this Job Qualifications Profile. Refer to your completed Career Actions from Chapters 2 and 3. Use a copy or printout of this form to develop a summary for each of your job targets.

1. Title of job target:

_____
_____
_____

2. Description of job:

_____
_____
_____

3. My education and training related to the job target:

_____
_____
_____

4. My work experience related to the job target:

_____
_____
_____

5. My accomplishments related to the job target:

_____
_____
_____

Continued on next page.

6. Praise or recognition I have received related to the job target:

_____

_____

_____

7. How my skills and transferable competencies relate to the job target:

_____

_____

_____

8. How my values relate to the job target:

_____

_____

_____

9. How my work environment preferences relate to the job target:

_____

_____

_____

10. How my personality traits relate to the job target:

_____

_____

_____

11. What appeals to me about this job:

_____

_____

_____

RESEARCH PROSPECTIVE EMPLOYERS

In this chapter, you will:

 Use Internet, printed, and people resources for research on prospective employers, your job target, and your career field.

- Expand your job search and career planning vocabulary through review of job descriptions, employment applications, job advertisements, and selected newspaper and journal articles.

"It is very likely I will ask applicants, 'Why do you want to work here?' If they are knowledgeable about our organization, applicants can answer this question effectively."

Caroline Carlson
Associate Staffing Manager
Kraft Foods

Chapter 8 explains how to gather current information about your field and about prospective employers so you can customize your job search communications and emphasize your related strengths and suitability for the job. Many resources for researching employers are presented, including research with recognized leaders in a field, career or job fairs, Internet sites, libraries, and professional or trade associations. Doing this research gives you a major advantage over candidates who don't conduct research.

COMPLETE INDUSTRY, EMPLOYER, AND JOB RESEARCH FOR BIG PAYOFFS!

Research gives applicants a big competitive edge. Employers nationwide say applicants who research employers well increase their employability as much as 25 percent! Figure 8.1 shows the competitive advantage you can gain over other applicants through employer research.

The advantages of researching your career field and employers affect the success of your job search in many ways:

- **Competitive Edge:** Employers view candidates who don't have solid knowledge of the employer's business and industry as weak choices. Many applicants don't bother to research employers. If you do, you have the competitive edge.

- **Better Career Decisions:** Having current knowledge of an employer, an industry, and a job target allows you to make informed career decisions about employers and to assess your interest in and qualifications for specific jobs.

- **Improved Ability to Market Your Skills and Get Hired:** Researching employers improves your ability to discuss specifically how your qualifications match the employer's purpose, goals, and needs. Employers are most willing to invest training resources in applicants who demonstrate initiative and commitment through their research of an employer and the industry.

- **Compensation for Lack of Experience:** Industry knowledge helps you compensate for lack of actual or extensive job experience.

- **Increased Confidence:** Being well informed helps you communicate more clearly, feel more confident, and project greater competence.

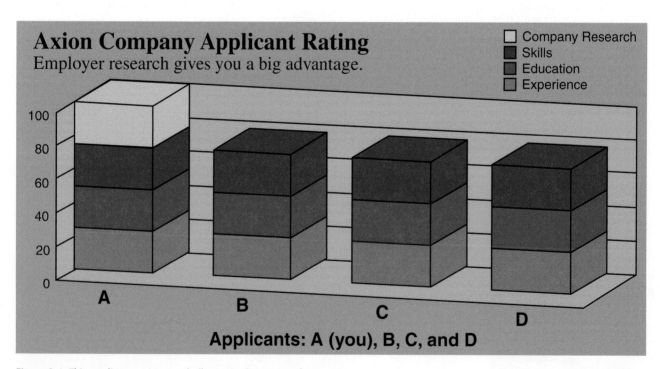

Figure 8-1: This applicant-rating graph illustrates the power of research.

Visiting a potential employer is a good way to get a personal perspective and gather information about the company.

Learn What You Should Know

Strengthen your employability by improving your knowledge in the following three areas:

1. **General Information About the Occupational Field.** Learn about the current and predicted industry trends, general educational requirements, job descriptions, growth outlook, and salary ranges in the industry.

2. **Information About Prospective Employers.** Learn whether the organization is publicly or privately owned. Verify company names, addresses, products or services (current and predicted, as well as trends); history; culture; reputation; performance; divisions and subsidiaries; locations (U.S. and global); predicted growth indicators; number of employees; company philosophies and procedures; predicted job openings; salary ranges; and listings of managers of your targeted department within the organization. Also learn about the competitors and customers.

3. **Information About Specific Jobs.** Obtain job descriptions; identify the required education and experience; and determine prevalent working conditions, salary, and fringe benefits.

Success Tip

Gain the competitive advantage by researching to learn about employers; they expect you to be knowledgeable about the job, the company, and the industry.

Use Many Sources of Information

This section identifies resources for industry, company, and job information.

People Resources

People are strong resources for learning about the character and function of an organization and for gathering general information about the industry. If your target employer is a small organization, people are typically the best research sources.

Employees of Your Target Employer. Current and previous employees know about hiring procedures; employee satisfaction levels; job descriptions and responsibilities; skills, education, and experience required for jobs; company objectives; salary information; and advancement opportunities. Don't rely only on opinion, however, particularly if it's extremely negative or overly positive.

Your Target Employer. When possible, visit target employers to get a personal perspective. Be sure to dress appropriately. Ask for literature about the organization, such as a brochure, mission statement, strategic plan, or stockholder's report. If appropriate and affordable, try the company's product or service to increase your knowledge.

Customers, Clients, or Patients. Ask customers, clients, or patients their opinions of the employer's service, reliability, products, and general reputation.

Competitors. Research competitors of your target employer to learn about the industry. Compare positions available, pay rates, and benefits as well as the education, skills, and experience required.

Instructors, Professors, and Counselors. These people are often knowledgeable about local employers and the industry. Since they may serve as job references for you, be professional, punctual, and reliable in dealing with them.

School Career Services Centers. School career services staff generally have comprehensive resources for learning about industries, specific companies, specific jobs, local employers, and more.

Recognized People in the Field. Successful people in your field are excellent resources for learning about the industry and prospective employers. Complete Career Action 8-1 to learn more about your career field through discussions with experienced leaders. It could lead you directly to the job you are hoping for!

> *"The next best thing to knowing something is knowing where to find it."*
>
> Samuel Johnson

Complete Career Action 8-1

Career/Job Fairs

As noted previously, career/job fairs offered by communities and schools and on the Internet are valuable sources of employer information. It would take hundreds of hours to reach the number of individual companies that you can access in one day at a career fair.

Use fairs to gather company literature and to find out directly what job skills and knowledge are required, to learn keywords you can emphasize in your resume, and to schedule interviews.

Libraries

Check out the reference sections of college, university, or public libraries for extensive employer and industry information available in printed, microfilm, and electronic format. Reference librarians can help you locate appropriate resources.

The following list of resources will help in completing your research and preparation:

- Company pamphlets, brochures, and annual reports
- *Dun & Bradstreet's Million Dollar Directories*
  - *Thomas Register of American Manufacturers*
  - *Standard and Poor's Stock Reports*
  - *Value Line Investment Survey*
  - *Moody's Manuals*
  - *Business Periodicals Index*
  - *Readers' Guide to Periodical Literature*
- *Job Choices*—excellent magazine of the National Association of Colleges and Employers; check school career services centers
- *Occupational Outlook Handbook*—published by the U.S. Department of Labor, Bureau of Labor Statistics; usually available in school career services centers
- Area telephone directories
- Newspaper and journal articles
- *Fortune* and *Forbes* magazines and *The Wall Street Journal*
- *Standard and Poor's Register of Corporations, Directors and Executives*

Also ask reference librarians for assistance in locating international business information if your target employer has international holdings or is based outside the United States.

CAREER ACTION 8-1

Contact Recognized People in Your Field

 Directions: Follow the five steps below for researching trends and information sources in your industry. In this activity, you will gather industry information so you can communicate well during your job search, making you a more persuasive candidate. The purposes of this meeting are to learn all you can about your career field and to identify methods of updating your industry information and skills.

Remember, do not ask for a job or an interview during this meeting.

Steps for Researching Trends and Information Sources in Your Industry

1. Contact at least two people working in your target industry who are recognized for their ability and accomplishments. Ask school career services staff, instructors, family, and friends to suggest people to contact.

2. Schedule a time, date, and place to meet. Call and ask whether your contact can meet with you to discuss career development questions.

3. Be well dressed and on time. Such meetings can lead to referrals or job offers.

4. Project professionalism. Take your neatly prepared survey questions in a professional binder. (Sample questions are listed below; add others of your own.)

5. Be prepared to discuss your findings in class, or submit a summary report.

Sample Questions for Career Action 8-1

1. What current trends do you think are most important in the industry? Where can I learn more about these trends?

2. To remain well informed about the industry:

   a. What publications (books, periodicals, and so on) do you recommend?

   b. What Internet web sites do you recommend?

   c. What professional or trade associations do you recommend?

3. What skills, education, and experience are necessary for my job target?

4. What new terminology or industry buzzwords do you suggest I know to be well prepared? (This information will be useful in Career Action 8-3.)

5. How did you succeed in the field? Would you recommend the same or a similar approach for me?

6. What other suggestions do you have to improve my employability in the field (further education, training, research, reading, and so on)?

PERSONAL BEST

Using the Internet for Research

The Internet is exploding with public and private web sites to research industries and employers. Use the Web to gather information about products and services, corporate history, recent trends, and more.

Researching Companies Online: This is an excellent site with multiple links and tips for online employer research: http://home.sprintmail.com/ ~debflanagan.

Search engines: Use search engines to conduct general searches for specific employers or specific career topics. Use these sites for recent news about your industry and target companies.

Financial sites: Use these sites to access sales and earnings information and recent news about public companies. Examples are listed below.

American Stock Exchange	www.amex.com
New York Stock Exchange	www.nyse.com
NASDAQ	www.nasdaq.com

Employer sites: Visit sites of employers that interest you. Always check out the "Jobs" or "Careers" and the "What's New" or "News" items to get current, updated information. Mine the entire site, searching for nuggets of information you can use during your job search to demonstrate your knowledge and Internet skills.

As you cruise the information highway, remember that while electronic information is valuable and sometimes the most up-to-date information source, many important facts vital to evaluating an employer can be found only in print sources. Often the Internet provides summaries of topical information; the full text is available through library research. In addition, employer web sites emphasize only their positive aspects; so don't rely on just this one source.

Use your library's historical and electronic resources to find articles and information on employers that interest you.

RESEARCH LOCAL AND SMALL FIRMS

If you want a job with a local or small firm, the following are good resources for research:

- People in the field
- The area chamber of commerce
- The area Better Business Bureau
- Local newspapers
- Telephone directories
- Local libraries

Also learn about the occupational field in general (local, national, and global trends; professional and trade associations; and so on).

Professional or Trade Associations

Nearly every industry has professional or trade associations that provide journals, newsletters, and reports of current industry information and related trends. Many have membership lists (good prospective employer resources). Employers are impressed with applicants who know about their industry associations and publications.

Enhance your employability by joining a well-known professional or trade association in your field and reading its publications. Many have student chapters or memberships. Such extra effort can give you the power to outdistance your competition. Check the *Encyclopedia of Associations* to locate major associations. Also check Yahoo.com for professional associations at http://dir.yahoo.com/Business_and_Economy/Organizations/Professional and for trade associations at http://dir.yahoo.com/Business_and_Economy/Organizations/Trade_Associations.

Complete Career Action 8-2

DEVELOP AND INCREASE YOUR CAREER-RELATED VOCABULARY

A strong career-related vocabulary projects competence. Employers view this as a good indicator of job- and industry-related knowledge. Therefore, continually increasing your job- and career-related vocabulary is important. Career Action 8-3 is designed to help you do this. Your vocabulary can help or hurt you in your career; start now to build a vocabulary that strengthens your career.

SUCCESS TIP

Develop and regularly increase your job/career-related vocabulary to demonstrate competence and knowledge.

Complete Career Action 8-3

CAREER ACTION 8-2

Printed, People, and Internet Resources for Employer Research

Directions: Use printed, people, and Internet resources to research at least two companies that interest you. Learn about company products or services, company objectives, company location, earnings information, trends, and other information that interests you. Prepare a written summary of your findings.

Resources:

1. *Your Career: How to Make It Happen* web site. From the main menu, select "Links." Then click on "Researching Companies Links."

2. For additional research and resource ideas, refer to the Printed, People, and Internet Resources for Employer Research form on your Learner's CD or on page 109 of this text.

Job Search and Career Development Vocabulary

Directions: To create a vocabulary list and use the terms to shine in your resumes, cover letters, interviews, and follow-up communications:

1. Obtain two general job descriptions for the type of job you are seeking. Get these directly from employers, from people currently working in similar jobs, from job postings, or from the Internet. If you can't find at least two written descriptions, obtain verbal descriptions from people working in your field and write them out. Also get one or more general job descriptions for your job target from the *Occupational Outlook Handbook*.

2. Obtain at least two application blanks for the type of job you are seeking. Note that some employers only provide applications online. Access these through their web sites and download them.

3. Obtain at least two advertisements for positions similar to your job target. Check newspapers, professional journals, the Internet, your career services center, and so on.

   a. Carefully read through the job target material you obtain. Underline all action verbs (for example: *compile, analyze, operate, supervise*) and all keywords or nouns used to describe required or related skills, education, and experience, including the specific names of software programs or computer-related knowledge (for example: *operator, operation, accounts receivable, instructor / instruction, writing, analyzing, designing, evaluation, management, computing, computations, Word, Excel, UNIX*). Underline vocabulary, abbreviations, special terminology, and buzzwords unique to your field.

   b. Make a list of these terms, spelling each word correctly, and include definitions. If you don't know the definition of a term, find it. Categorize the terms as follows: (a) action verbs, (b) keyword nouns, (c) specialized terminology, (d) abbreviations, and (e) industry buzzwords.

4. Keep this vocabulary list and add to it whenever possible.

SUCCESS TIP

Competing applicants with equal education, training, and experience are judged on their verbal and written command of industry vocabulary. Develop a strong vocabulary to help land your ideal job.

APPLY YOUR INDUSTRY, EMPLOYER, AND JOB RESEARCH

Apply the information you obtain from your research as you write your resumes and cover letters and as you interview. Complete all the Career Actions in Chapter 8 to gather this essential information.

Review the information from the Printed, People, and Internet Resources for Employer Research form in Career Action 8-2 or on your Learner's CD to identify resources for answering specific research questions. Don't limit yourself to the resources

A vast amount of career information is available from a number of sources. School career services staff and reference librarians can help you identify those sources.

Learn About the Interviewer *Before* You Are Interviewed

Get the interviewer's name from the company when you schedule an interview. If you know anyone who works or worked with the interviewer or who knows the interviewer personally, contact that person to learn as much as you can.

Know What to Research

In researching the interviewer, learn as much as you can about the following:

- The interviewer's special interests or activities

- The interviewer's work philosophy, goals and objectives, and achievements

- The general development of the interviewer's career

If possible, find out how the interviewer prefers to be contacted for a job (by letter, in person, by telephone, by e-mail). This information can help you approach the interviewer in his or her preferred style and can help you phrase your remarks to meet the interviewer's interests and needs.

In small organizations, people who know the interviewer are the best resources for obtaining information about him or her. Don't press an assistant, a receptionist, or another employee too hard for information about the interviewer, however. Word may get back to the interviewer! If you are courteous, you may learn some useful information, but tread lightly; avoid coming across as pushy.

listed in this textbook. Ask school career services staff and reference librarians to help you identify those resources most valuable for your career objectives. Ask members of your network for their help in obtaining the most current and useful employer information.

Refer to Chapter 9 to see how you can use the information you find in your research to prepare powerful targeted resumes.

RESEARCH INTERVIEWERS

Round out your research by trying to learn about the interviewer. This can strengthen your competitive position, providing you with information that helps you communicate comfortably and connect positively during your interview.

SUCCESS TIP

Research to learn all you can about the interviewer to help you communicate comfortably and connect positively during your interview.

✓ CHECKLIST:

Researching Prospective Employers

Check each of the actions you are currently taking to increase your career success:

☐ Gaining a competitive advantage by researching to learn about prospective employers, who expect you to be knowledgeable about the job, the company, and the industry

☐ Developing and regularly increasing job/career-related vocabulary to demonstrate competence and knowledge

☐ Researching to learn about the interviewer to help make a positive connection with him or her during the interview

In small organizations, someone who knows the interviewer is the best resource for learning about the interviewer before your interview.

critical thinking *Questions*

1. What are the advantages of researching your occupational field and your targeted job?

2. What should you try to learn about the interviewer?

3. What are at least two Internet web sites you have visited that provide useful information about employers? Give at least two examples of the types of information you have found at each site.

CAREER ACTION 8-2

Printed, People, and Internet Resources for Employer Research

Questions About the Industry

1. What is the general job description for your occupational career choice?

   References: (a) school career services staff, (b) *Occupational Outlook Handbook,* (c) reference library

   Internet: (a) school career services web sites, (b) U.S. Department of Labor's *Occupational Outlook Handbook* (www.bls.gov/oco/home.htm), (c) employer web site addresses

   _____

   _____

   _____

2. What is the occupational outlook projection for your field? (Will occupational opportunities grow, diminish, stay the same? By what percentage? Over what period of time?)

   References: (same as #1)

   Internet: (same as #1) and America's Career InfoNet (www.acinet.org)

   _____

   _____

   _____

3. What is the current general salary range for your occupational field and for your job target?

   References: (a) people in the field, (b) *Occupational Outlook Handbook,* (c) school career services staff

   Internet: (a) same as #1—in the Department of Labor's online *Occupational Outlook Handbook* (www.bls.gov/oco/home.htm), select the title of your occupational cluster, choose the title of your field (and a subtitle if necessary), and then click on "Earnings"; (b) JobStar Salary Surveys (www.jobstar.org), and then click on "Salary Info"; (c) Salary.com (www.salary.com)

   _____

   _____

4. What occupations are closely related to your first occupational choice?

   References: (a) *Occupational Outlook Handbook*, (b) school career services staff

   Internet: (same as #1)

   _____

   _____

Continued on next page.

Questions About Prospective Employers

1. What are the products or services of prospective employers you have identified?

   References: (a) people in the field, (b) *Dun & Bradstreet's Million Dollar Directories,* (c) annual reports of the employer, (d) *Moody's Manuals*

   Internet: (a) employer web sites—look for products, services, and annual reports; (b) Researching Companies Online (http://home.sprintmail.com/~debflanagan); (c) *Your Career: How to Make It Happen* web site (www.levitt.swlearning.com)—click on the "Links" button, and then select "Researching Companies Links"; (c) Monster.com (www.monster.com); (d) Hoover's Online (www.hoovers.com); (e) search engines

   _____

   _____

   _____

2. What is the size of the employer organization, number of employees, location, sales assets, stock market standing?

   References: (a) people, (b) *Dun & Bradstreet's Million Dollar Directories,* (c) *Standard and Poor's Buyers' Compendium of American Industry,* (d) annual company reports.

   Internet: (a) all sources listed in #1, (b) Wall Street Research Net (www.wsrn.com), financial information web sites

   _____

   _____

   _____

3. Has the company shown consistent and substantial growth? What is the financial and competitive position of the company in the industry?

   References: (a) people in the field, (b) company annual reports, (c) *Fortune* magazine, (d) *Forbes* magazine, (e) *The Wall Street Journal,* (f) *Value Line Investment Survey,* (g) *Dun & Bradstreet's Million Dollar Directories*

   Internet: (a) all sources listed in #1, (b) annual reports of the employer, (c) *Your Career: How to Make It Happen* web site (www.levitt.swlearning.com)—click on "Links" and then on "Financial Information Links"

   _____

   _____

   _____

Continued on next page.

CAREER ACTION 8-2 (continued)

4. Who are the competitors?

References: (a) people in the field, (b) *Dun & Bradstreet's Million Dollar Directories*, (c) telephone directory Yellow Pages, (d) chamber of commerce, (e) *Fortune* magazine, (f) *Forbes* magazine, (g) *The Wall Street Journal*

Internet: (a) Wall Street Research Net (www.wsrn.com), (b) Researching Companies Online (http://home .sprintmail.com/~debflanagan), (c) WetFeet.com (www.wetfeet.com), (d) Vault.com (www.vault.com), (e) SuperPages.com, a national online yellow pages directory (www.superpages.com)

_____

_____

_____

_____

5. What are the current trends in the industry, and are technological changes occurring or anticipated in the field?

References: (a) people in the field, (b) professional and trade associations, (c) publications in the field, (d) *The Wall Street Journal*

Internet: (a) employer web sites; (b) America's Career InfoNet (www.acinet.org); (c) Wall Street Research Net (www.wsrn.com); (d) web sites of professional, trade, and other associations in your field; (e) Internet search engines

_____

_____

_____

_____

_____

_____

_____

_____

_____

_____

_____

_____

_____

_____

Continued on next page.

Questions About the Job Itself

1. What is the title of the position you will be seeking?

   References: (a) the company or organization—check with the human resources department or the department or employer you are targeting, (b) people currently in the field and knowledgeable about your job target

   Internet: (a) employer web sites—check under *human resources, employment opportunities*, and so on), (b) other sites you found useful in the previous questions

   _____

   _____

   _____

2. What are the job description, duties, and responsibilities of the job and the required skills, education, and training?

   References: (a) the employer organization (many provide written job descriptions on request), (b) employees of the company or people working in similar jobs

   Internet: (a) employer web sites (check under *human resources, employment opportunities*, and so on), (b) other sites you found useful in the previous questions

   This question will help you identify the requirements of the position so you can relate your qualifications for the job in your search communications. Do your research carefully and be complete in your answer. You are the one who benefits!

   _____

   _____

   _____

   _____

   _____

   _____

   _____

   _____

   _____

9

PREPARE A WINNING RESUME

In this chapter, you will:

- Identify the elements of a winning resume.

- Identify critical differences among paper, electronic, and web resumes.

- List appropriate keywords to use in your resumes.

- Write a clear, appropriate job objective.

- Outline the content for your paper resume.

- Prepare and evaluate your paper resume draft, make corrections, and produce a final resume.

- Create an electronic resume.

 Use the Internet to access and research a job/resume-posting web site.

"I do an initial read through of all resumes to make sure they are clear and concise. If a resume is poorly written or has obvious typos, I will not read it a second time. A sloppy resume is not considered because it shows lack of effort and attention to detail. The second time I read a well-written resume, I look for specific skills and related experience that is pertinent to the position I am hiring for."

Tracy Bradshaw
Project Director
KRA Corporation

Chapter 9 shows you how to write and deliver resumes that get you interviews. A good resume is your key to getting interviews. Most employers choose candidates to interview based largely on their resumes. The employer's selection is based on a quick visual screening or computerized search of the resumes he or she receives. Employers look for a match between their needs and the applicants' qualifications. Your resume must be written so it passes this initial screening and a more detailed analysis. This chapter explains how to create resumes that will pass these tests.

WHAT IS A RESUME?

A resume is a short document detailing your qualifications for a particular job or job target. As a job applicant, you need at least two resume versions: a scannable paper resume and an electronic resume.

In some fields, having a web resume is also an asset. These three types of resumes are described in the following table, Figure 9-1, "Resume Types, Purposes, and Formats." Specific instructions for preparing each type of resume are presented later in this chapter.

Resume Type	Purpose	Format
Scannable paper resume	To hand or mail deliver	Visually attractive layout for human readers Word-processed and specifically formatted to scan cleanly into a database
Electronic resume	To transmit resume clearly electronically (by e-mail and in online resume builders or e-forms) For employer use in compiling, searching, and maintaining a resume database for staffing purposes	ASCII/text only
Web resume	To be posted as a web document designed to showcase applicant's HTML skills and may include a portfolio of artistic, specialized computer, and other abilities (for example, graphic art, CAD drawings, and video or musical performance clips)	HTML programming

Figure 9-1: Resume Types, Purposes, and Formats

Scannable Paper Resume

A scannable paper resume is a word-processed resume designed:

- To be visually appealing.

- To be delivered by regular mail, by hand, or by fax.

- To scan clearly into a database by computer software.

In the past, the traditional paper resume was an attractive and sometimes elaborately word-processed hard copy document. Today many employers electronically scan paper resumes into resume-tracking and search software. Because some word processing formatting elements don't scan well, paper resumes should now be made scannable by omitting word processing formatting that doesn't scan correctly. Instructions for accomplishing this are included later in this chapter.

Electronic Resume

An electronic resume is an ASCII text document designed to be delivered via e-mail or via an online e-form. This resume must be completely stripped of word processing codes and is, therefore, a plain-looking document. Electronic resumes must be specially formatted (explained later in this chapter) so they can be transmitted electronically to employers, be easily read on screen through an e-mail program, and be transmitted directly to a resume-tracking program for processing. Because electronic resumes save employers the scanning step, many employers prefer this format.

Web Resume

A web resume is formatted in HTML so it can be posted on the Internet as a web document. The web resume looks like an attractive paper resume. The difference is that it can contain more sophisticated graphics. It is designed to show-

Your resume may be circulated to managers within a company by e-mail or fax.

case the applicant's HTML skills and may also link to a web page portfolio of artistic, specialized computer, and other abilities (for example, graphic art, charts, CAD drawings, and video or musical performance clips).

WHAT MAKES A WINNING RESUME?

A winning resume is one that gets you a job interview. The following scenario explains how employers process resumes and what features help candidates land interviews:

- ABC Company receives your resume (along with many others) in response to a job advertisement. ABC Company electronically scans all resumes and stores the contents in an electronic database for easy distribution and retrieval.

- Since hiring managers don't have time to interview everyone who submits a resume, resumes are typically reviewed by a human resources staff member to select candidates who appear most qualified. This review and

> *"People often say that motivation doesn't last. Well, neither does bathing—that's why we recommend it daily."*
>
> Zig Ziglar
> American Sales Trainer, Author, Motivational Speaker

selection process may be done by a person or by software that searches resumes for *keywords*. These are words representing qualifications the company has instructed the software to search for.

- The selected resumes are reviewed again, and the resumes of candidates may be circulated (in hard copy format or online) to the hiring authorities. These people choose candidates who appear most qualified and are likely to work well with existing employees.

From that scenario, you can infer that a winning resume achieves four objectives:

1. Quickly shows that the candidate has the qualifications necessary for the job

2. Demonstrates that the candidate can meet the employer's needs

3. Suggests that the candidate is someone who is likable and works well with others

4. Appeals to both human and electronic reviewers

The table illustrated in Figure 9-2, "Four Keys to Writing a Winning Resume," provides quick guidelines for achieving these four key objectives in your resume. Review these guidelines to get a good sense of how to best focus the content of your resume to get positive results. The balance of this chapter walks you through all the stages of writing winning resumes.

PREPARE TO WRITE YOUR RESUME

Before you begin writing your resume, you should do the following:

- Complete a thorough inventory of your education and skills (see Chapters 2 and 3).

- Consider the kind of work environment in which you thrive.

- Set a career target (see Chapter 3).

- Complete research to identify specific companies or job titles that interest you.

If you haven't already completed Chapters 2 and 3 of this book, do so before beginning to write your resume.

SUCCESS TIP

Begin the resume-writing process by taking an inventory of your qualifications.

FOUR STEPS TO PREPARING YOUR RESUME

Writing a resume to get an interview typically does not happen on the first try. It requires completing these four carefully planned steps:

1. Decide on your job objective.

2. Choose the most appropriate resume layout.

3. Organize carefully and write forcefully.

4. Fine-tune each section of your resume.

Don't rush the process. If you skip or skimp on any of these steps, you will greatly diminish your chance of achieving the purpose of your resume: getting the interview and, ultimately, the job.

SUCCESS TIP

Write a clear, appropriate job objective to focus your entire resume.

FOUR KEYS TO WRITING A WINNING RESUME

KEY	WHY	HOW
1. Quickly show you have the qualifications for the job	The first cut in resume reviews takes only seconds. Your qualifications for a job must be quickly apparent.	Include a clear job objective. Include a qualifications or capabilities section at the top of your resume. List most pertinent data first.
2. Demonstrate you can meet the employer's needs	Once past the initial qualifications review, employers want to know if you can apply those skills to solving their problems.	Reflect your knowledge of the job and employer in your resume. Include examples of work-related accomplishments (for example, reduced errors, saved money, and increased sales/productivity).
3. Suggest that you are likable and work well with others	Employers want to work with people who have positive personal and performance traits.	Emphasize your enthusiasm, cooperation, and dependability. Stress activities, teamwork, and leadership in organizations. Include words such as *accurate, cooperative, creative, flexible, organized,* and *self-directed.*
4. Pass both human and electronic reviews	Many employers scan and process resumes electronically. Resumes are read and assessed only by humans in some organizations.	Include keywords throughout your resume to pass electronic reviews. Use action words to demonstrate accomplishments and to appeal to human readers. Format your resume for clear scannability.

Figure 9-2: Four Keys to Writing a Winning Resume

Step One: Decide on Your Job Objective

The first step in writing a successful resume is to specify a concise job objective that describes the job you are seeking. Your entire resume will be organized around this objective. A clear job objective, such as *medical technician*, will help you determine the best way to organize your resume, select appropriate keywords, and present your experience. Detailed instructions for writing an effective job objective are provided later in this chapter under "Step Four: Fine-Tune Each Section of Your Resume."

Step Two: Choose the Most Appropriate Resume Layout

The most common resume layouts are as follows:

- Reverse chronological
- Functional
- Combination

Review the following descriptions of these resume formats, and consider which one best meets your needs.

Reverse Chronological. Use this layout to show skills, work experience, and logical career progression directly related to the job target. Choose this layout to emphasize steady, related work experience without major employment gaps or numerous job changes. At the top of the resume, place the information category that best supports your job objective. List employment history in reverse chronological order with the most recent experience first, and stress the major accomplishments and responsibilities of each position. Avoid repeating details common to several positions. (See Figure 9-6 on page 139.)

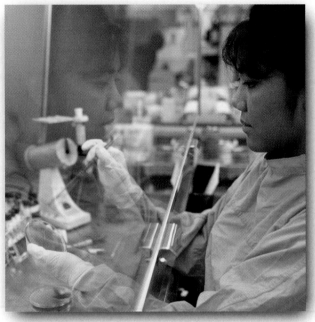

A clear job objective, such as *medical technician*, will help you determine the best way to organize your resume, select appropriate keywords, and present your experience.

Functional. Use the functional format if you lack work experience directly related to your job target. This format is also appropriate if you have gaps in employment; it emphasizes your capabilities related to the job target. Clearly emphasize your skills that relate to the job objective, and substantiate these with measurable accomplishments. Use separate paragraphs to emphasize each skill category. Arrange the paragraphs in order of importance to the objective, listing the most important skill first. (See Figure 9-7 on page 140.)

Combination. Capture employers' attention by immediately emphasizing the match between your skills and the position requirements. Consider this format if you want to emphasize your skills or if you have limited experience. List your skills just below the position objective. Then incorporate accomplishments in a reverse chronological list of job experiences. Add credibility by linking

> *"What we do for ourselves can get us by. What we do for others is what gets us ahead, whether in our profession, spiritual pursuits, or relationships."*
>
> Dr. Vincent Muli Wa Kituku

your achievements with specific employers and time periods. Place your education summary where it best supports your objective. If your education is more closely related to the skills required for your target job, place your educational information before your work experience information. (See Figure 9-8 on page 141.)

SUCCESS TIP

Choose the resume layout that best supports your job objective.

Step Three: Organize Carefully and Write Forcefully

Use the following general guidelines as you write and edit your resume.

Write Concisely and Clearly. Convey your qualifications as clearly and concisely as possible, but don't omit pertinent information that could cost you the interview. Use phrases, not complete sentences.

You can write more concisely if you avoid using clichés and dated expressions and overly complex terms. Some common examples and alternatives are shown below.

Clichés/Dated. . . . . Concise

at this point in time	now
ballpark figure	estimation
explore every avenue	explore the options
last but not least	finally
left no stone unturned	used every possible method

Complex/Wordy . . . . Concise

utilized	used
endeavor	try
equitable	fair
initiated	started

Use Numbers and Specific Examples of Accomplishments. Your resume will be clearer and more powerful if you use specific terms and examples to describe accomplishments. Notice the more forceful impact the specific examples have.

General/Vague. . . . . Specific

reduced costs significantly	reduced costs by 20 percent
the leading producer	top producer of 60 employees

The most persuasive resumes describe applicants' accomplishments with numbers, percentages, and dollar amounts to emphasize how the accomplishments could meet the prospective employer's needs. Use numbers whenever possible to enhance the credibility of your achievements.

Notice how the numbers in the second example below strengthen the accomplishment:

- Processed more orders than any other member of the work team.
- Processed **40 percent** more orders than any other member of the work team.

Try adding the word *that* to an accomplishment statement. If necessary, use an estimated measurement (*approximately, averaged, up to,* or *more than*).

- Developed a new filing system that reduced filing time by 25 percent.
- Developed stock procedures to reduce backorders by 50 percent.

SUCCESS TIP

Use numbers, percentages, and action verbs to describe your accomplishments forcefully.

PERSONAL BEST

Identify Marketable Assets

In hiring, employers look for applicants who have demonstrated accomplishments in skill and knowledge areas relevant to the job requirements. To identify your marketable assets, apply the following questions to your paid jobs, volunteer work or involvement in organizations, and classroom and other experiences.

1. How have I increased my skills and/or knowledge?

2. How have I solved problems or made decisions or recommendations? Were the results effective? Explain in measurable terms (numbers, percentages, and so on).

3. Have I organized or planned tasks, activities, and projects? Explain.

4. Did I work well under pressure and meet critical deadlines? Explain.

5. Have I used technology? How? Have I been innovative? How?

6. Have I cut costs or increased revenues? Explain clearly using measurable terms.

7. What equipment and software can I operate proficiently?

8. How can I measure the results of my work (numbers of customers served, percentage increase in production, percentage decrease in costs or errors, and so on)?

9. Did I work with a team? How did I contribute? Did I lead others? Explain.

10. What reports and documents have I written?

11. Have I helped train, develop, or motivate others? Explain.

12. Did I manage money for a group? Explain.

Emphasize your marketable assets that add value to an employer's organization.

Use Action Verbs and Omit *I* and *My*. To satisfy resume-search software, you need to include keywords, which are usually nouns that reflect employer needs. Ultimately, however, you want a person to view your resume, so you also need to include action statements that include verbs, which are persuasive to human readers.

When writing action statements, complete sentences are unnecessary. Employers want to find the important information quickly. Omit *I*, *me*, and *my* to increase conciseness and avoid sounding like a braggart. (Employers already assume the resume is about you.) Use action verbs and phrases to show that you take initiative and actively participate in problem-solving and decision-making processes (*wrote proposal, improved process, increased sales*). Notice how the specific action verbs in the second example convey a stronger image.

- My duties included reviewing marketing trends, analyzing statistical data, and preparing annual sales reports.

- **Conducted** extensive market research; **analyzed, diagrammed,** and **reported** results of sales data; and **wrote** annual sales reports.

Use a thesaurus to find just the right words to convey your qualifications accurately and clearly. Notice the use of more specific action verbs (*designed* and *implemented*) in the second example below. Specific verbs increase the clarity of the description and the scope of responsibility and also convey a greater sense of accomplishment.

- **Started up** the inventory-tracking system.

- **Designed** and **implemented** the inventory-tracking system.

- **Organized** and **trained** volunteers who solicited contributions and **raised $55,000** for citywide "elder-help" campaign.

- **Coordinated** school student-body elections and **reduced** final ballot processing time by **25 percent.**

Use Keywords Strategically. Keywords (the required skills, knowledge, and capabilities for a position) are those that employers search for in reviewing resumes visually or electronically. Think of keywords as the magnets that draw attention to your resume, and include as many appropriate keywords in the qualifications section as possible.

Keywords name attributes that qualified candidates must have. Resources for identifying appropriate keywords for your job target include industry terminology and specific words or short phrases gleaned from the employers' job descriptions and ads. Also review company web sites and publications and web sites in your industry and related professional associations. These words describe employer-valued qualifications. A list of sources follows to help you identify appropriate keywords.

- Job titles

- Skills/specialties

- Education, certifications, licenses, course work

- Work and volunteer experience

- Community and other clubs/activities

- Computer/software/hardware skills and specialized tools

- Relevant personal qualities

- Industries, buzzwords, jargon, acronyms

- Accomplishments

- Industry/professional organizations

- Awards

Include keywords throughout your resume and repeat critical keywords. The more keywords the software identifies, the more likely your resume will be selected and you will be called for interviews.

Also use synonyms for keywords; employers may use different terms as search criteria. For example, *budget* may be a synonym for *forecast*, *BA* for *Bachelor of Arts*, and *supervisor* for *manager*.

Computerized resume-search programs typically seek nouns. In searching for AutoCAD drafters, the computer looks for nouns (and noun synonyms) such as *CAD, engineer, AA degree, certified drafter, Computer-Aided Drafting, AutoCAD, wiring diagrams,* and *physics*.

Figure 9-3, "Keyword Search Samples," on page 122 illustrates examples of keywords resume-tracking software searches for in filling two different positions.

Complete Career Action 9-1

SUCCESS TIP

Keyword choices are critical. An employer may not read your resume unless it first gets several hits in a computer search. Getting a hit means the computer matches a word (keyword) in your resume to one it is seeking.

Position Title	Sample Keywords
Accountant	CPA, audit, accounting, accounts receivable/payable, statistics, spreadsheet, finance, systems training, computer, database, team player, B.B.A. Accounting, accurate, project leader, customer relations, accounting database
Web Specialist	HTML, Web development, web hosting, web design, Perl, Java, SQL, Dreamweaver, Flash, database management, server administration, security, firewalls, FTP, Internet imaging, web design internship, American WebMaster's Association, Western Regional Graphics Award

Figure 9-3: Keyword Search Samples

CAREER ACTION 9-1

Identify Appropriate Keywords

  Directions: Access your Learner's CD or use a separate sheet of paper to write your responses.

1. Prepare a comprehensive list of appropriate keywords to use in your resumes (industry terms; acronyms; and terms describing job positions, experience, education, skills, and so on).

2. Use the Internet as a primary resource in your research. Also use any of the resources listed below to help identify keywords.

3. Print a report that includes your list of keywords and a list of the resources you used to identify them.

4. File your summary report in your Career Management Files Binder for future reference.

Resources for Identifying Keywords for Your Resume:

- The *Your Career: How to Make It Happen* web site at www.levitt.swlearning.com (see *search engines* and *job search/career planning* links to research resume and keyword information)

- Job advertisements and descriptions for positions you are considering (online or written publications)

- Web sites of employers you are considering

- Government publications such as *The Occupational Outlook Handbook* (search online too)

- Professional associations in your field (check web sites, publications, meetings)

- Internet search engines to search for job descriptions

- Online encyclopedias and dictionaries

Tailor Your Resume to Specific Openings.

Employers expect resumes to be tailored for specific positions. Use word processing software to tailor your resumes to specific job titles, job advertisements, and employers. The targeted approach is 100 percent more effective than the one-size-fits-all resume. Here are ways you can tailor your resume:

- Use capabilities and keywords in your job objective and within your resume that match those in the job ad.

- Identify the name of the company, organization, or industry.

- Use appropriate industry terminology.

SUCCESS TIP

Tailor your resume to meet the needs of the employer. Match your resume to the job description. Use specific industry and job-related terms.

Limit Your Resume to One or Two Pages. Keep your scannable paper resume to one page unless you have extensive work experience; in that case, two pages are acceptable. Employers prefer brief paper resumes. Make every word count and emphasize how you meet employers' needs. Electronic resumes are often longer for reasons discussed later in this chapter. The content, however, should be as concise as possible.

Step Four: Fine-Tune Each Section of Your Resume

As you write your resume, apply the writing guidelines provided earlier. Include the sections most appropriate for your resume, and present them in the order that best fits your job target needs.

Contact Information. Provide your name, mailing address, telephone number (including message phone), e-mail and web addresses (if appropriate), and fax number. Place all your contact details at the top of the resume.

Note that many employers are turned off by applicants who use unprofessional e-mail or web address names. To avoid losing a job opportunity, be sure your address names are professional, not cutesy or crude.

Job Objective. The job objective is a statement of your employment goal. Place your job objective directly after your contact information. The job objective:

- Should be stated as a job title or type of work desired.

- Should reflect the needs of the employer based on your research.

- Can also include one or more of your most important job-relevant skills and areas of specialization.

This helps employers match you to appropriate openings. If you have more than one job objective, write separate resumes for each job objective.

- **Job Objective:** Waiter in an exclusive restaurant where knowledge of international cuisine is an added value.

Tailor your objective as specifically as possible. The general objective above could be tailored to an advertisement for a waiter in a French restaurant:

- **Job Objective:** Waiter in a four-star French restaurant where knowledge of the French language and cuisine are added values.

Complete Career Action 9-2

123

Write Your Job Objective

Directions: Write a job objective for your targeted job. You may want to use one of the job descriptions you collected earlier as a reference for this assignment. Reflect the needs stated in the job description you are referencing.

Qualifications Section and Keyword Emphasis. The qualifications section should highlight why you are the candidate for the job. Because the qualifications section is a focal point for employers, emphasize specific, relevant skills and capabilities and related accomplishments. Include examples such as:

- Skills and knowledge of software/hardware.

- Years of experience in a specialized field or knowledge of specialized skills.

- Relevant credentials and degrees.

- Relevant accomplishments in work or volunteer experiences, community involvement, and other activities.

Review the Career Actions you completed in Chapters 2 and 3 to extract qualifications, skills, desirable personal traits, and other abilities you can list as keywords that best match your job target. Present these in order of importance as they relate to your position objective under the qualifications section. Format the qualifications section as a bulleted list to draw attention to each item; for example:

- Graphic and multimedia design including streaming audio/video, analysis graphs, and custom web graphics

- General ledger, inventory control, accounts receivable and accounts payable experience

- Proven team-player skills demonstrated in three successful internship projects

In the body of your resume (under the appropriate section, such as work experience, education, or re-

lated activities), provide proof of the qualifications you list in the qualifications section.

If you don't have strong work experience related to your job objective, use the functional resume layout and the qualifications summary to emphasize your accomplishments and skills in areas other than paid work experience.

SUCCESS TIP

Choose the right words. Use a thesaurus to find the best words to describe your capabilities and accomplishments.

Work Experience. For a reverse chronological layout, list your most recent job first, ending with the earliest job you held. (For the functional and combination resumes, review Figures 9-7 and 9-8 on pages 140 and 141 to see how work experience is presented.) For each job, list the dates of employment; the employer's name, city and state; the job title; and a brief results-oriented description of the job. In your descriptions, give specific examples of accomplishments, such as increased sales, decreased costs, and reduced errors. Quantify where possible (by percentage, by a specific dollar figure, by a number of items produced or sold, and so on).

> *"Use the right word, not its second cousin."*
>
> Mark Twain

If you have held increasingly more responsible jobs with one employer, show this to demonstrate reliability and the ability to learn and achieve on the job. List only new responsibilities and accomplishments for each promotion. Continuing job duties will be assumed by the reader. (See Figures 9-15a and 9-15b on pages 154-155 for an example.)

If you have little work experience, list part-time and summer work, internships, school projects, volunteer work, and community involvement. Emphasize all accomplishments and skills developed in these experiences—even if they don't relate directly to your job target. For example, if you just graduated and you worked throughout your schooling, one accomplishment might read as follows: Earned 65 percent of school expenses working part-time during school year and full-time during summers.

This demonstrates positive working ability, initiative, and potential for learning. Employers consider these qualities real pluses, particularly in entry-level applicants.

If you have limited relevant work experience, list internships and school, community, and educational activities and achievements on your resume.

SUCCESS TIP

Tailor your resume to best support your objective.

Other Experience. Use this section to bring out other experience pertinent to your job objective. Include activities such as membership, leadership (offices held), and awards earned in professional or trade associations; honorary groups; and social, service, and school organizations. All these activities show that you are well rounded and able to work with others.

Instead of the heading "Other Experience," consider options that may be more appropriate for you, such as "Awards and Honors," "Volunteer Work," "Community Service," "Certificates Earned," "Activities," and "Professional Associations."

Education. List your education in reverse chronological order. List the names of technical schools, colleges, and universities you have attended; the years of attendance; and the degree(s) or certificates earned. Include relevant certifications, specialized training, and seminars.

If you are (or will be) a recent graduate with limited work experience, highlight school activities, internships, and achievements in the education section. Support your job objective by listing related major(s), minor(s), and courses. A liberal arts student with courses in business will benefit from listing business courses when applying for a business job.

If you have several years of work experience pertinent to your job objective, emphasize and list your work experience first. Then condense the education section of your resume.

Research your target employer to find out whether you should list your GPA on the resume. If your accumulated GPA is low but your GPA in your major is high, list your major GPA only. If your overall GPA is high and you graduated with honors, put it on your resume. It won't hurt.

Military Service. Include on your resume any military experience relevant to your job objective, emphasizing pertinent training, responsibilities, and accomplishments. Emphasize rapid progressions, significant promotion(s), and special commendations. Usually, military service is listed in the experience section. If you have an exemplary record, however, you can emphasize it under a separate heading. Don't use military jargon; use civilian terms.

Personal Data. Omit information about height, weight, age, gender, marital status, race, religion, and so on, from your resume. Fair employment laws prohibit employers from requesting such information. Do not include a photograph of yourself. In an effort to avoid discrimination, many employers will not consider a resume with a photo included or attached.

References. Generally, omit references on your resume. Research to learn whether your target employer wants you to submit references (names of people who can attest to your work abilities and personal qualities). Employers expect applicants to have references but differ in their preferences regarding when and how they want to see a reference list. Have a reference sheet prepared that includes names, titles, addresses, and contact information for each reference. Then you are ready to provide it to employees when they request it. A model reference sheet is provided on your Learner's CD.

> Complete Career Action 9-3

Outline Your Resume

Directions: Now that you have reviewed the resume-writing guidelines, you are ready to develop your own resume. Access Career Action 9-3 on your Learner's CD or use the Resume Outline form on page 159 to create your outline. Gather the following forms to help you with this activity:

- The documentation of your education and training, skills, and so on (Career Actions 2-1, 2-2, 2-3, 2-4, and 2-5)

- Your Job Qualifications Profile (Career Action 7-4)

Prepare an outline of your resume. Use the assignment form provided on page 159 to outline your resume, or create your draft in a word processing program, using the form as a reference.

Once you've completed the form, number the sections of the outline, ranking them in order of importance and relevance to your job objective. Present the material in your final resume in this order. For example, if your education is more relevant to your job objective than your work experience, place the education information before the work experience information.

FORMAT YOUR RESUME CORRECTLY

The next step in creating a resume is to use your outline as a reference in drafting and formatting the actual resume. As noted early in this chapter, you should prepare at least two versions of your resume—a scannable paper resume and an electronic resume.

Format Your Paper Resume

The scannable paper resume is designed to be delivered by mail, by fax, or in person. Produce your scannable paper resume using your word processing program (such as MS Word or Corel WordPerfect).

Customize Your Resume. Tailor your paper resume for individual employers by using terminology and descriptions that address the needs stated in their notices and advertisements of job openings. Also customize your resume for employers who specifically request your resume.

Make Your Paper Resume Easy to Scan. Since some companies scan hard copy resumes and convert them to ASCII documents for storage and processing, you need to make your paper resume scannable by using formatting that is both attractive to the eye and easy for computers to scan.

Make sure your paper resume is scannable. Avoid formatting that does not scan clearly.

A scannable paper resume must be stripped of certain word processing codes that scanners may not read clearly. If characters touch each other, they don't scan well. The following "do's and don'ts" explain how to format your resume so it will scan clearly and keep you in the running for an interview.

DO:

1. Do use a clean overall format. Visual legibility is extremely important.

2. Do use a simple, standard font such as Times Roman. Keep the font size between 11 and 14 points. The ideal font size is 12 point for body text and 14 point for headings.

3. Do add a space before and after slashes (for example, HTML / XMTL).

4. Do use acceptable character enhancements and codes such as bolding, centering commands, solid bullets, and regular and indent tabs.

5. Do print your resume on a laser or inkjet printer in black ink on one side of white or light-colored 8 1/2-inch by 11-inch paper. Standard copy machines don't produce a copy of high enough quality to ensure scannability.

DON'T:

1. Don't use a highly formatted style such as a newsletter layout or columns. Scanner software assumes that the text reads conventionally from left to right across the page in one column.

2. Don't use special justification (adjustable spacing between characters). Use the standard left-margin alignment so each letter is clearly visible.

3. Don't use underlining, italics, shadows, white letters on a black background, or colored text. These can blur or corrupt the scanned message.

4. Don't use parentheses; use a hyphen following telephone number area codes.

5. Don't include graphic images and avoid vertical and horizontal lines and boxes. (You can use one horizontal line if you leave adequate white space above and below it so the line doesn't touch and blur any letters.)

6. Don't fold or staple the resume. (Creases and staple marks can cause scanning errors.)

Examples of scannable paper resumes are shown in Figures 9-6, 9-7, 9-8, 9-9, 9-10, 9-13, 9-15a and 9-15b, and 9-16.

Use an Attractive, Appropriate Design. The general design of your paper resume provides employers with their first impression of you. Give your resume a professional look.

- Omit the heading RESUME at the top of your document.

- Single-space the body of your resume, and double-space or triple-space between sections or items in the resume. (Remember, your final resume should be only one page in length unless you have extensive work experience.)

- Use white or light-colored 8 1/2-inch by 11-inch paper.

- Frame your resume attractively. Ideally, use one-inch margins on all sides.

- Use white space effectively. Areas of white space draw attention to important parts of your resume, giving it an organized, uncrowded look.

- Format headings in all capital letters and bold, and indent text to emphasize resume parts. (Don't overdo this.)

Sample resumes (Figures 9-6 through 9-16) on pages 139-157 provide models to help you prepare your own winning resume. Examine the content and format of each resume and the summaries provided. Carefully mark the examples that are most useful for your needs.

Complete Career Action 9-4

CAREER ACTION 9-4

Draft Your Paper Resume

Directions: Review the resumes on pages 139-157. Mark the sections of these models that are useful to you. Resumes typically should contain all the standard resume sections listed below. The optional sections should be included when they support your main job objective or when an employer requests them.

Standard Resume Sections:

- Name and Contact Information
- Job Objective
- Work Experience

- Qualifications or Capabilities Section
- Education
- Other Experience or Activities

Optional Resume Sections:

- Military Service
- References (rarely needed)
- Personal Information

Prepare a written draft of your scannable paper resume using your resume outline as a reference. Be selective about the quality and quantity of information you include. Make every word count. Emphasize your qualifications and measurable accomplishments and include appropriate keywords.

Revise the Content. After you have drafted your resume, review it giving careful attention to every detail and marking areas that could be improved.

Once you have reviewed your draft, rewrite your resume, strengthening each area you marked. Eliminate unnecessary words; substitute stronger, clearer terms for weak ones. Your goal is to answer "yes" to all the resume questions in Figure 9-4.

After reviewing your draft, check the writing guidelines presented earlier in this chapter. Then complete Career Action 9-5, "Critique Two Resumes," and Career Action 9-6, "Complete Your Paper Resume."

> **Complete Career Action 9-5**

> **Complete Career Action 9-6**

Resume Checklist

Objective

✔ Does the objective include the job title or required abilities specified by the employer?

Qualifications

✔ Do your qualifications contain keywords that name requirements for the job?

✔ Are the qualifications relevant to your stated job objective? Are all your major strengths included?

Education

✔ If your education supports your job objective better than your work experience, have you placed the education segment first or vice versa?

✔ Have you emphasized courses, internships, degrees, certificates, and so on, that best support your objective?

✔ If your GPA is impressive, have you included it (overall or minor/major related to objective)?

Work Experience

✔ Does each job listing contain the employer's name and address (city and state) and your job title?

✔ Does each job listing describe your responsibilities and specific accomplishments?

✔ Are your job descriptions written using specific action verbs and keyword nouns that support your job objective?

✔ If your work experience is limited, have you included relevant paid and nonpaid internships and volunteer or other pertinent activities?

Related Activities

✔ Have you included professional and other organizations that support your job objective?

✔ Have you included relevant awards, achievements, and offices held?

The Big Picture

✔ Is the overall design appealing?

✔ Is the content correct (grammar, spelling, and punctuation)?

✔ Is the content logically organized and presented in order of importance to your objective?

Figure 9-4: Resume Checklist

Critique Two Resumes

 Directions: Assume you're evaluating candidates for an entry-level job as an accountant for a major accounting firm.

You are to write a summary comparing and evaluating the resumes of two top applicants—Alex Valenzuela and Ralph Greenwood. Their qualifications are almost identical. However, one has documented his qualifications more convincingly than the other.

Read their resumes (Figures 9-16 and 9-17 on pages 157 and 158). Determine which resume is more effective, and explain why in your summary. Be thorough, keeping in mind that your resume will be scrutinized this same way during your job search.

Complete Your Paper Resume

 Directions: Use a word processor to prepare your final paper resume. If you hire an expert to prepare your resume, also be sure to request an electronic file so you have the file for future revisions or updates.

Proofread and edit the content until the resume is perfect.

If you want more ideas for your resume, check out the "Links" page on the *Your Career: How to Make It Happen* web site. Check under the "Career Planning and Job Search Information" category. (Look for those that have the "Resume" indication to the right of the web site address.) Also check with your campus Career Center, typically an excellent resource for developing your resume.

Evaluate Your Resume. Once you have edited your resume, proceed to the critical evaluation step. Careful proofreading and evaluation is essential.

Recruit help from one or two objective members of your support system who have good writing and proofreading skills. Ask these people to review and critique your resume carefully. This assistance is vital to developing a successful resume.

SUCCESS TIP

Prepare and evaluate your resume draft; make corrections; develop a final perfect resume.

PREPARE AND FORMAT YOUR ELECTRONIC RESUME

Some employers request that candidates submit electronic resumes. The features of electronic resumes are described below.

Larger organizations and high-tech companies are more likely to require electronic resumes than smaller organizations. As a job applicant, you need to clarify with employers exactly which resume format they prefer: a paper resume that is delivered by hand or by mail or that is sent as an e-mail attachment or an electronic resume submitted at a web site or in the body of an e-mail message. Then provide that type.

ASCII Text Format. The primary difference between a paper and electronic resume concerns the formatting. Electronic resumes are relatively plain and unattractive because they must be ASCII (also called .txt or Text Only) documents. These are stripped of all word processing codes so they transmit correctly in the body of an e-mail message or so they can be processed by the employer through a resume-tracking program.

Keyword Emphasis. Using appropriate keywords throughout your electronic resume is important because these resumes are often electronically searched for keywords. Design your electronic resume to generate the largest possible number of keyword hits from automated-search software.

Keyword choices are critical. Review the information about keywords presented earlier in this chapter under the heading "Step Three: Organize Carefully and Write Forcefully."

Format your electronic resume carefully to ensure that the receiver views a clean-looking resume. Include relevant keywords to generate as many hits as possible by resume-tracking search programs.

Important Tips for Electronic Resumes. As you prepare your electronic resume, keep the following tips in mind:

1. **Use standard section headings.** Use standard headings like those in a paper resume; for example, Objectives, Qualifications, Experience, Education, and Related Activities.

2. **Use keywords throughout.** Using appropriate keywords throughout your electronic resume is essential. Spell these correctly. (Search software will not generate positive hits on your resume if the terms aren't spelled correctly.)

3. **Emphasize nouns.** Include noun forms of industry-specific terms, such as *accountant* rather than *accounting*. Also use nouns that describe strong interpersonal skills, such as *team player*. Search software frequently looks for noun forms.

4. **Back up your files.** Using a new filename, save your resume in ASCII format (on your hard drive and a disk or CD) so you can customize your electronic resume for specific employers.

SUCCESS TIP

Use appropriate keywords in all resumes to highlight critical skills for potential employers.

5. **Keep up to date on electronic resume technology.** Technology changes quickly; keep your knowledge of scanning and electronic resume technology current by verifying employer preferences and updating your knowledge. Check out the Internet resources listed in this chapter and on the *Your Career: How to Make It Happen* web site.

6. **Contact potential employers.** Ask whether you should fax or mail a scannable resume or attach one to an e-mail message as a backup to your electronic resume. Find out who should receive this resume, and address your cover letter (see Chapter 10) to that individual. Sending a backup scannable resume creates an opportunity to sell your qualifications in a visually appealing format.

Electronic Resume Formatting Guidelines. Get the edge on the competition by formatting your electronic resume correctly. Demonstrate superior knowledge and preparation. Use correct formatting so employers do not receive documents with wildly erratic line lengths and unreadable text.

Since all word processing codes are stripped out of electronic resumes, be sure to format your resume to compensate for the loss of bold text, bullets, and other formatting capabilities. Follow the instructions below to be sure your resume meets the employer's electronic expectations. The instructions assume your scannable paper resume was created with word processing software.

1. **Follow employer directions.** Obtain and read all employer instructions for creating and sending an electronic resume. If you have questions, send an e-mail message or call to request clarification.

2. **In your word processor, open the file containing your scannable paper resume.**

   a. Highlight the text and change the font to Courier 12 point. This monospaced font is the most reliable one for accurate e-mail transmission.

   b. Eliminate multiple columns.

   c. Limit line lengths to 65 characters by setting the left margin to 1.0 and the right margin to 1.25. Longer line lengths often transmit unevenly.

   d. Clean up the formatting:

   - Replace bullets with asterisks or hyphens.

   - Use all caps for headings.

   - Add blank line spaces between sections to make the content more readable.

   - Eliminate special characters, such as the copyright symbol (©), the ampersand (&), and mathematical symbols.

   e. Use the Save As command to give this document a new name and to save it as "Text Only with Line Breaks."

   f. Close the file and exit the word processing program.

3. **IMPORTANT: Open the document in your standard text-editing program, such as Windows Notepad (not in your word processing program).** This standard text-editing program creates the cleanest electronic resume.

   a. Place your name on the first line with no other text. (Resume-search programs look only for a name on this line.)

   b. Start all lines at the left margin.

   c. Use uppercase letters for headings, but use standard upper- and lowercase mix throughout the body of the document.

Format electronic resumes carefully to ensure clear transmission to and receipt by employers.

d. Place each telephone number on a separate line. Label each one, such as "home phone," "work phone," or "message phone."

e. Consider length. The specialized formatting may cause your electronic resume to become two or three pages long in your standard text editor program. Don't worry about keeping the resume to one page in this program; however, try to limit the document to two pages.

f. Save your resume again as a .txt document. Leave the file open.

4. Open your e-mail program and create a new message.

5. To ensure clean transmission, make sure your format is set to Plain Text format (not HTML).

6. Return to your standard text editor (Notepad), and select all (highlight) the resume text. Then copy and paste it into your e-mail message window. Or paste the text into the resume field at employer or recruitment web sites.

7. In the e-mail subject line, include the job title and/or reference number of the position for which you are applying.

8. Insert your electronic cover letter (see Chapter 10). In the e-mail message window containing your electronic resume, place the cursor above your electronic resume and paste in a copy of your electronic cover letter. Do not send a resume without a cover letter or a short message indicating that your resume is included.

9. Key a line of asterisks underneath your electronic cover letter to mark the end of your cover message and the beginning of your resume.

10. Clean up any odd spacing or other formatting problems. (See "Transmitting Your Electronic Resume" on page 134 for distribution instructions.)

Review the sample electronic resumes (Figure 9-11 on page 146 and Figure 9-12 on page 148) to see how these resume guidelines are applied.

Develop a Winning Web Resume

A web resume is one created in HTML format and published to the Internet. This format adds flexibility because it supports more sophisticated elements, such as animated graphics as well as sound and video clips. It is a good tool for displaying your expertise in computer technology (HTML, web site and graphic design, and more). Web resumes can also be creative sales tools for people who want or need to display their artistic abilities (for example, photographers, artists, singers, models, architects, and graphics and computer specialists).

Use of web resumes is most common in the high-tech industry, but they are also used in other fields. Research to determine whether a web resume is appropriate in your career field. Also note that a web resume should be used in addition to, not as a substitute for, your paper and electronic resumes.

Complete guidelines describing the purposes and benefits; tips for content; and publishing, verification, and distribution of web resumes are provided on the *Your Career How to Make It Happen* web site and on your Learner's CD. Also see the web resume (Figure 9-14) on page 152.

Make sure your resume (paper, electronic, or web) has no misspelled words, keyboarding mistakes, or formatting errors. Any of these flaws can cause your resume to be rejected immediately.

Distributing Your Resume

After developing your resume professionally, you'll want to distribute it effectively to meet the preferences of employers and achieve your ultimate goal: getting interviews.

Providing Your Resume to Your Network and to Employers

Provide your resume to your job search network members in the format they prefer (electronic, word-processed e-mail attachment, or hand-delivered paper resume). Providing your resume to your network members gives them information they need to help you find prospective employers.

Follow an employer's instructions for the preferred resume format and the preferred method of delivery: standard or overnight mail, fax or electronic transmission, or hand delivery.

Follow the employer's instructions for the preferred resume format and the preferred method of delivery (standard or overnight mail, fax or electronic transmission, or hand delivery).

Transmitting Your Electronic Resume

After you have created your electronic resume and placed it in your e-mail message window with an electronic cover message, practicing transmission of the message is essential. Send your electronic resume and cover letter or e-mail introduction to a friend and to yourself to see how well the documents survive the cyberspace transfer before you actually send them to an employer. You may need to tweak the spacing and format a bit. If necessary, find someone with more experience in creating and sending electronic resumes to help you tweak your resume until it formats and transmits cleanly.

If Asked to Send Your Resume as an E-Mail Attachment

Some employers ask applicants to send a scannable word-processed resume as an e-mail attachment so they can print and provide a hard copy for hiring specialists. If you are requested to do this, ask what word processing software and operating system (Windows or Mac, for example) is preferred.

Follow the requirements exactly to be sure the receiver can download your resume in a readable form. In your e-mail message, explain which word processing software and operating system you used.

Posting Electronic Resumes Correctly

Follow the guidelines below for posting electronic resumes to the Internet (through the web site of an employer or a recruitment company that lists jobs and accepts online resumes from applicants):

1. Follow the web site instructions exactly.

2. If the web site provides an open block for your resume, highlight and copy your electronic resume and paste it into the block.

3. If the web site provides a fill-in-the-blanks online resume form, copy and paste appropriate sections of your electronic resume into the form. If you need to key in new text, proofread carefully before sending it.

Also see page 184 of Chapter 10, Figure 10-10.

> Complete Career Action 9-7

CAREER ACTION 9-7

Create and Post Your Electronic Resume

Part A: Following the formatting guidelines presented, convert the resume you created in Career Action 9-6 to an electronic resume. Be sure to give your electronic resume a different name so you still have the original file for your paper resume.

Part B: Research and practice online resume posting. Access the *Your Career: How to Make It Happen* web site at www.levitt.swlearning.com and click on the "Links" button. Locate the "Jobs Links" category, and choose one or more resume-posting web sites (such as Monster.com, America's Job Bank, The Black Collegian Online, and Saludos.com) to review the instructions for creating and posting an online resume. Also review each employer's web site, and follow the instructions regarding resume preparation and submission. If you prefer, use other resume-posting sites for this exercise. Practice completing an online fill-in-the-blanks resume form or pasting your electronic resume into an open resume block. Print your resume and other pertinent pages before you submit your resume, and bring examples to share with your class.

Reinforce Your Resume With A Call

Don't rely on resumes alone to get interviews. It's a mistake to send out several copies of your resume and then wait for the telephone to ring. Two to three days after sending your resume, follow up with a call to make sure your resume was received. If you mail your resume, wait about a week to call. Your call reminds the receiver about you, demonstrates initiative, and increases your name recognition.

SPECIAL RESUME REMINDERS

To ensure your resume gets the best possible results, follow these reminders.

Be honest. An untrue statement could eliminate you from further consideration for a job. Employers pass on such information. Do not volunteer negative information about yourself, however. If you were fired from a job, don't list this on your resume. Discuss this during an interview, if necessary.

Omit references to salary. Reserve discussion of salary until after you've had adequate opportunity to discuss your qualifications in the interview. Presenting salary expectations in your resume weakens your negotiating position. If employers require your salary expectation, use broad numbers, such as "the mid-thirty thousands."

CAREER CHANGE RESUME TIPS

You will probably make more than one career change in your lifetime. This will require you to revise your resume to fit the new career objective. A realistic new career target is one for which you have already developed relevant, related skills. (You'll learn more about making a career change in Chapter 20.) To revise a resume to be used for a new career, refer to the following tips:

1. Make a list of all your work skills, knowledge, and experience.

2. Use a colored pen to place a check mark in front of each item on your list that matches or closely matches the needs of your new career target.

3. If necessary, change the wording of the items you checked to better fit your new career target. Use a thesaurus and your new career research to help identify appropriate terms. For example, when changing from a classroom teacher to an industry trainer, the terms *trainer*, *facilitator*, and *presenter* are more appropriate than *teacher*.

4. Create new resume skill and experience headings by grouping related items from your updated skills list into categories. Create a heading to describe each category.

5. Now that you have appropriate content, begin drafting and refining your new career resume. In other words, once you have completed this exercise of identifying appropriate content for a new job objective, you can now begin revising your existing resume to match your new job objective. See the excerpts from "before" and "after" resumes shown in Figure 9-5 below. (Complete resume models for these two "before" and "after" examples are provided on your Learner's CD.)

Excerpts From "Before" Resume

Job Objective: Service manager in multiline dealership

Auto Repair Customer Service
Scheduled appointments, performed preinspections, achieved upgrade sales on 95 percent of accounts, quoted estimates, wrote work orders, performed post-repair inspections, and explained statements to customers. Increased referrals from customers by 43 percent.

Parts Management
Managed ordering and stocking of mechanical and auto-body parts inventories, selected suppliers and negotiated vendor discounts that averaged 25 to 30 percent below wholesale, reconciled shipping invoices to billing statements, and approved payments.

Excerpts From "After" Resume

Job Objective: Insurance adjuster in automotive collision repair industry

Claims Management
Scheduled client appointments, determined mechanical and auto-body damages within 45 minutes, negotiated repairs with clients and insurance companies, prepared job documentation (pictures, work orders, billing), performed postrepair inspection, and explained statements.

Cost Containment
Obtained clients' agreement to use appropriate after-market and/or rebuilt parts on 98.7 percent of jobs; located replacement parts; negotiated price, delivery, and discounts, averaging 25 to 30 percent below wholesale; returned unused parts for credit; reconciled billing discrepancies; approved payments.

Figure 9-5, Compare Excerpts From "Before" and "After" Career Change Resumes

INTERNET RESOURCES FOR RESUME INFORMATION

The Internet is a rich resource for finding useful resume-writing and formatting suggestions. You can use your favorite search engine to research specific questions you may have. Also check out online resumes in your field for content ideas that may be appropriate for your resume. Quality sites offering useful resume development advice include the following:

- Rebecca Smith's eResumes & Resources www.eresumes.com

- eResumeIQ.com (web resumes) www.eresumeiq.com

- Quintessential Careers www.quintcareers.com

- The Resume Guide www.susanireland.com

- The Riley Guide www.rileyguide.com

- Monster.com www.monster.com

Harness the power of the Internet to locate useful information on resume trends and techniques and to review other online resumes for content ideas that may be appropriate for your own resume.

SUCCESS TIP

Use the Internet to locate current resume preparation tips and as a means for delivering your electronic resume.

✓ CHECKLIST:

Preparing a Winning Resume

Check each of the actions you are currently taking to increase your career success:

☐ Writing a clear, appropriate job objective to focus the entire resume

☐ Tailoring the resume to support the objective effectively

☐ Choosing the most appropriate layout for the resume to best support the objective

☐ Using numbers and action verbs to describe accomplishments

☐ Tailoring the resume to meet the needs of the employer; matching the resume to the job description by using specific terms and industry terminology

☐ Preparing and evaluating the resume draft; making corrections by applying effective writing techniques; developing a final perfect resume

☐ Using appropriate keywords

☐ Formatting electronic resumes carefully to ensure clear transmission to and receipt by the employer

☐ Using the Internet to locate current resume preparation tips and to deliver an electronic resume

critical thinking *Questions*

1. When should an applicant use separate objectives or resumes?

2. In what order should you present your resume data to best support your job objective?

3. Why is it effective to list a job objective followed immediately by a listing of related capabilities?

4. How is the electronic resume transmitted to employers?

KIMI R. OKASAKI
148 Barrister Avenue, Tucson, AZ 85726
• 520-555-0136   • kokasaki@provider.net

OBJECTIVE

Administrative Assistant for MegaMall Property Management Company

EDUCATION

Associate of Applied Science, 2003, Westfield Community College, Tucson, AZ
• Major: Administrative Office Technology, GPA 3.6

Related Courses and Skills
- Advanced Word Processing (Word, WordPerfect)
- Keyboarding at 75 words per minute
- Spreadsheet (Excel, Quattro Pro) and Database Management (Access)
- Records Management
- Bookkeeping I and Computerized Bookkeeping (QuickBooks Pro)
- Ten-key at 250 strokes per minute
- Presentation Software (PowerPoint, Presentations)
- Office Management
- Internet Software (Explorer, Netscape)

EXPERIENCE

Community Volunteer, Tucson, AZ   **December 1999-2002**
- **Humane Society:** Developed and customized spreadsheet report to track results of three fund-raising activities, reducing reporting time by 50 percent. Used Excel.
- **Secretary-Treasurer, Valley Elementary School Parent-Teacher Organization:** Published electronic newsletters, answered e-mail, maintained correspondence, maintained books for two years, and satisfied yearly CPA audits. Used Word and QuickBooks Pro.
- **Meals on Wheels:** Using Access, designed and maintained information database to enable Meals on Wheels to study the participation of 1,200 people.

Katz Department Store, Tucson, AZ   **March 1997-December 1998**
- Sales Supervisor, Part-time: Supervised four sales clerks; trained new sales employees. Computed daily cash receipts, balanced two registers, attained highest part-time sales volume, and had fewest sales returned.

Value Variety, Tucson, AZ   **Summers 1995, 1996**
- Sales Clerk, Floater: Provided complete customer service in sales and returns; coordinated weekly inventory deliveries.

Figure 9-6: Reverse Chronological Resume Sample (Job Objective—Administrative Assistant)

KIMI R. OKASAKI

148 Barrister Avenue, Tucson, AZ 85726   520-555-0136   kokasaki@provider.net

---

OBJECTIVE

Administrative Assistant for MegaMall Property Management Company

EDUCATION

Associate of Applied Science, 2003, Westfield Community College, Tucson, AZ
• Major: Administrative Office Technology, GPA 3.6

PROFESSIONAL SKILLS

Document Preparation: Expert using Word, WordPerfect, PowerPoint, and Presentations. Enter text at 75 words per minute. Integrate tabular data and graphics into documents using Access, Excel, and Quattro Pro. Write, format, and proofread printed and electronic business correspondence, reports, and newsletters. Research topics on the Internet (Netscape, Explorer).
  • Published electronic newsletters and maintained correspondence for Valley Elementary School Parent-Teacher Organization (VES-PTO) for two years.

Spreadsheet Management: Develop and maintain Excel and Quattro Pro spreadsheets.
  • Developed spreadsheet to track results of three fund-raising activities for the Humane Society that reduced reporting time by 50 percent.

Database Management: Configure, maintain, and generate reports with Access.
  • Designed and maintained an information database to enable Meals on Wheels to study the participation of 1,200 people.

Bookkeeping: Perform manual (ten-key at 250 strokes per minute) or computerized (QuickBooks Pro) bookkeeping functions from journal entry to end-of-period reports.
  • Maintained books for VES-PTO for two years and satisfied yearly CPA audits.
  • Computed daily cash receipts and balanced two registers as part-time sales supervisor of a department store.

Human Relations: Successfully cooperate with store managers, representatives of delivery companies and community organizations, and the general public.
  • Held positions of responsibility in three community organizations over the last three years.
  • Worked in two department stores: promoted to supervisor, trained new sales clerks, coordinated weekly inventory deliveries, provided customer service in sales and returns, attained highest part-time sales volume, and had fewest sales returned.

EXPERIENCE

Community Volunteer, Tucson, AZ	December 1999-2002
Katz Department Store, Tucson, AZ	March 1997-December 1998
Value Variety, Tucson, AZ	Summers 1995, 1996

Figure 9-7: Functional Resume Sample (Job Objective—Administrative Assistant)

KIMI R. OKASAKI

148 Barrister Avenue, Tucson, AZ 85726

520-555-0136   kokasaki@provider.net

OBJECTIVE

Administrative Assistant for MegaMall Property Management Company

RELATED QUALIFICATIONS

- Word processing in Word and WordPerfect
- Spreadsheet generation with Excel and Quattro Pro
- Database design and maintenance using Access
- Keyboarding at 75 words per minute
- Write and proofread printed and electronic business correspondence, reports, newsletters
- Presentation preparation using PowerPoint and Presentations software
- Internet research and e-mail correspondence using Netscape or Explorer
- Bookkeeping using QuickBooks Pro and ten-key at 250 strokes per minute
- Proven ability to work successfully with store managers, delivery companies, community organizations, and the general public

EDUCATION

Associate of Applied Science, 2003, Westfield Community College , Tucson, AZ
- Major: Administrative Office Technology, GPA 3.6

EXPERIENCE

Community Volunteer, Tucson, AZ   **December 1999-2002**
- **Humane Society:** Developed and customized spreadsheet report to track results of three fund-raising activities, reducing reporting time by 50 percent. Used Excel.
- **Secretary-Treasurer, Valley Elementary School Parent-Teacher Organization:** Published electronic newsletters, answered e-mail, maintained correspondence, maintained books for two years, and satisfied yearly CPA audits. Used Word and QuickBooks Pro.
- **Meals on Wheels:** Using Access, designed and maintained information database to enable Meals on Wheels to study the participation of 1,200 people.

Katz Department Store, Tucson, AZ   **March 1997-December 1998**
- Sales Supervisor, Part-time: Supervised four sales clerks; trained new sales employees. Computed daily cash receipts, balanced two registers, attained highest part-time sales volume, and had fewest sales returned.

Value Variety, Tucson, AZ   **Summers 1995, 1996**
- Sales Clerk, Floater: Provided complete customer service in sales and returns; coordinated weekly inventory deliveries.

Figure 9-8: Combination Resume Sample (Job Objective—Administrative Assistant)

SONYA REED
2332 Clovis Boulevard • Savannah, GA 31401
912-555-0109 • sreed@provider.net

OBJECTIVE

Health Information Technician position requiring the ability to perform detailed tasks, to change priorities quickly, and to communicate well

QUALIFICATIONS

- Registered Health Information Technician, 2003
- Family practice receptionist, 1.5 years: awarded Superior Service Certificate twice
- Five-month internship as assistant to Health Information Technician, Community Hospital
- Associate of Science, 2003

EDUCATION

Associate of Science, 2003, Savannah College of Georgia, Savannah, GA
    Major: Health Information Technology   GPA 3.6
    Related Courses and Skills
      • Medical Terminology • Clinical Classification Systems • Health Information Management
      • Health Delivery Systems • Health Data • Introduction to Health Law and Ethics
      • Human Disease Mechanisms • Word • Excel • Access • PowerPoint • Explorer

CERTIFICATION

Registered Health Information Technician, 2003

EXPERIENCE

- **Community Hospital, Savannah, GA**   **January 2003-May 2003**
  Clinical Internship. Under the direction of the Health Information Director, assisted Health Information Technician in reviewing and assigning diagnosis codes and DRGs. Abstracted appropriate information and retrieved medical records. Assisted chiefly with Medicare/Medicaid coding for three months. Checked charts into and out of records department.

- **Family Practice Partnership, Savannah, GA**   **July 2001-December 2002**
  Evening Receptionist. Answered telephone, scheduled appointments, and kept waiting room neat. Checked in patients, obtained insurance and billing information, and pulled charts for nurses. Copied requested records for transport to other medical offices. Provided cheerful, efficient service to patients; awarded Superior Service Certificate in 2001 and 2002.

ASSOCIATIONS

Community Hospital Volunteer, 2001 to Present
American Health Information Management Association, 2001 to Present

Figure 9-9: Scannable Paper Resume (Job Objective—Health Information Technician)

SUMMARY OF INFORMATION EMPHASIZED ON FIGURE 9-9: REED

1. **Objective**

Sonya uses an industry-standard job title to state her job objective concisely. To capture the attention of employers and to advertise her work characteristics, she includes job-related competencies that her targeted employers list in job postings.

2. **Qualifications**

Sonya includes several terms that both humans and resume search programs typically search for in filling a health information technician position. She emphasizes her Registered Health Information Technician certification first because it is a primary requirement for the job she is seeking. She also highlights her relevant work experience and her hospital internship assisting a health information technician. She includes her associate of science degree because this is a keyword that is also likely to be included in an electronic search of her resume.

3. **Education**

Sonya also puts her degree near the top of the resume to reinforce her job qualifications. She worked evenings during the two years she was in school and still earned a respectable GPA, so she includes this information on her resume. In addition, she lists classes from her major that are especially pertinent to employers and includes the computer programs she knows.

4. **Certification**

Since Sonya just graduated and has limited work experience, she places her national certification near the top of the resume to emphasize her qualifications and to show that she takes her profession seriously.

5. **Experience**

Sonya's internship through Savannah College of Georgia allowed her to work and learn at a local hospital. Because her internship lasted five months, provided hands-on experience, and is pertinent to her job objective, Sonya places it in the Experience section of her resume. Notice how Sonya describes her activities in industry-specific terminology.

Although Sonya's job at the family practice clinic was at a medical facility, she did not have any responsibilities that are directly applicable to her current job objective. She puts her award for superior service at the end of her job description to demonstrate that her job performance is above average.

6. **Associations**

The association on Sonya's resume reinforces her interest in the medical field. She adds her volunteer work because she knows her targeted employers value and promote community service.

DONITA SILVA

1247 Madison Road, Columbus, OH 43216   614-555-0100   dsilva@mail.com

---

OBJECTIVE

Computerized Accounting Systems Auditor I

QUALIFICATIONS SUMMARY

- Education in accounting practices and computer systems
- Programming competence in COBOL, C++, and Visual Basic
- Practical experience in EDP accounting applications
- Proficient in Word, Excel, Access, and Windows
- Proven interpersonal skills in an auditing environment
- Experienced in AS/400, PC, IBM OS/390, and Novell LAN operations

EDUCATION

Bachelor of Business Administration, 2003   • Renton College, Columbus, OH
• Major: Computer Information Systems   • Minor: Internal Auditing

Relevant Courses of Study:
• Analysis, Design, and Auditing of Accounting Information Systems
• Internal Auditing • Information Systems Auditing • Accounting Applications
• Database Management • Advanced Corporate Finance • Cost Accounting

Senior Internship: American Interstate Bank
Under the supervision of the managing field auditor of American Interstate Bank, performed
internal audits on the safety-deposit box operations of five local branches. Reviewed the audit
findings with the branch managers. Compiled final report and presented it to the managers.

EXPERIENCE

Alexander & Swartz, Columbus, OH   **9/02 to Present**
Part-time Assistant Staff Auditor. Assist in audits of cash, accounts receivable, and accounts
payable for midsized firms that use AS/400s. Interface with clients and write audit reports as
member of the Business Services Assurance and Advisory team.

Micronomics Company, Columbus, OH   **6/99-9/02**
Part-time Programmer's Assistant. Designed, documented, coded, and tested COBOL program
subroutines for order-entry system on Novell PC network. Achieved a 95 percent average program-
accuracy rate on test runs. Cataloged and filed new programs and program patches for the
company's software library.

Renton College, Columbus, OH   **9/97-6/99**
Computer Operator Aide. Using OS/390 system, copied files for backup. Verified accuracy of
reports and scheduled print sequences. Recommended schedule changes that improved efficiency of
backup procedures by 28.5 percent.

ASSOCIATIONS

Information Technology Management Association, 1998 to Present
Columbus Computer Club, 1997 to Present

Figure 9-10: Scannable Paper Resume (Job Objective—Computerized Accounting Systems Auditor I)

SUMMARY OF INFORMATION
EMPHASIZED ON FIGURE 9-10: SILVA

Note: Figures 9-10 and 9-11 illustrate how to tailor a resume for two different job objectives. Because this employer prefers it, Donita uses a one-page scannable resume.

1.	**Objective**	The title Computerized Accounting Systems Auditor I is clearly understood in the field.
2.	**Qualifications**	Donita incorporates keywords in this section to highlight the education, specialized knowledge, and practical experience she possesses that relate directly to the Computerized Accounting Systems Auditor I job objective. She shows she can be productive immediately.
3.	**Education**	Because the job Donita wants requires expertise in two fields—computer systems and accounting systems—she emphasizes the courses she took that combine the skills from both areas. She addresses the requirements of her job objective by stressing the auditing experience she obtained through the class project. She also emphasizes proven interpersonal skills—critical to acquiring and retaining clients.
4.	**Experience**	*Alexander & Swartz.* Donita provides proof of her interpersonal and on-the-job auditing skills in computerized accounting. She supports the most important qualifications needed for her job objective.
		Micronomics Company. By stating a measurable accomplishment, Donita shows she gets results.
		Renton College. The addition of another concrete accomplishment strengthens her credibility as an achiever.
5.	**Associations**	Membership in professional organizations related to the job objective demonstrates a commitment to remaining current with trends in the field—something employers value highly.

DONITA SILVA
1247 Madison Road
Columbus, OH 43216
(614) 555-0100
dsilva@mail.com

OBJECTIVE

Information Systems Analyst I position in a financial environment requiring
system design, programming, investigation, reporting skills

QUALIFICATIONS SUMMARY

*   Education in computer systems and in accounting practices
*   Proven interpersonal skills and team skills in a financial setting
*   Programming competence in COBOL, C++, Visual Basic
*   Practical experience in EDP accounting applications
*   Proficient in Excel, Word, Access, and Windows
*   Experienced in AS/400, PC, IBM OS/390, and Novell LAN operations

EDUCATION

Bachelor of Business Administration, Renton College, Columbus, OH, 2003
* Major: Computer Information Systems, *Minor: Internal Auditing

*Relevant Courses of Study: System Analysis and Design, Systems Development,
Quantitative Analysis, Advanced Programming, Data Communications, Database
Systems, Advanced Corporate Finance, Information Systems Auditing,
Statistical Techniques

*Senior Internship: J. Kemp Marketing Associates
Installed a five-PC Novell LAN, three printers, and associated software
(MS Office) for a small marketing services business. Assisted the consulting
systems analyst in customizing proprietary statistical program for marketing
research applications.

EXPERIENCE

Alexander & Swartz, Columbus, OH   9/02 to Present
Part-time Assistant Staff Auditor: Assist in audits of cash, accounts
receivable, and accounts payable for midsized firms that use AS/400s.
Interface with clients and write audit reports as member of the Business
Services Assurance and Advisory team.

Micronomics Company, Columbus, OH   6/99-9/02
Part-time Programmer's Assistant: Designed, documented, coded, and tested
COBOL program subroutines for order-entry system on Novell PC network.
Achieved a 95 percent average program-accuracy rate on test runs. Cataloged
and filed new programs and program patches for the company's software
library.

Renton College, Columbus, OH   9/97-6/99
Computer Operator Aide: Using OS/390 system, copied files for backup.
Verified accuracy of reports and scheduled print sequences. Recommended
schedule changes that improved efficiency of backup by 28.5 percent.

ASSOCIATIONS

Information Technology Management Association, 1998 to Present
Columbus Computer Club, 1997 to Present

Figure 9-11: Electronic Resume (Job Objective—Information Systems Analyst I)

Summary of Information
Emphasized on Figure 9-11: Silva

1. **Objective**

    The title Information Systems Analyst I is clearly understood in Donita's field, specifies the level of expertise and authority she is qualified to handle, and clarifies her area of interest and expertise. She highlights pertinent skills, implying flexibility, thoroughness, and responsibility.

2. **Qualifications**

    Since computer systems and accounting practices are primary skills required in financial work, Donita highlights these skills to meet the Information Systems Analyst I job objective. Accenting mainframe languages and hardware, microcomputer software, and experience in order entry and accounting applications stresses her flexibility. She emphasizes the names of hardware, operating systems, and program languages in which she is experienced to demonstrate her ability to use these skills immediately.

3. **Education**

    Donita highlights the courses she took that best support this job objective. Practical experience gained in a directly related internship demonstrates her scope of knowledge and dependability. She omits her moderate GPA.

4. **Experience**

    Alexander & Swartz. Donita uses action verbs and highlights her responsibilities and knowledge. She backs up her claim to have "proven interpersonal skills and team skills in a financial setting."

    Micronomics Company. Her claim to skill in program design and coding is supported with a measurable achievement.

    Renton College. Donita reinforces her image for getting results by stressing another accomplishment (28.5 percent increase in efficiency).

5. **Associations**

    Her memberships demonstrate continued professional growth.

```
DANIELLE RYAN
1205 Koch Lane
Seattle, WA 98115
(206) 555-0124
dryan@provider.net

OBJECTIVE

Network Support Technician for multilocation network

QUALIFICATIONS SUMMARY

* Education in network support technology
* Competent with peer-to-peer networks, UNIX operating system and command
line utilities, TCP/IP, LAN, WAN, and Network utilities
* Familiar with menu utilities, system backups, ANSI C fundamentals,
V Standards, and VNC (Virtual Network Computing)
* Practical experience with Word, Access, Excel, Windows NT4/2000/XP, and
Novell
* Experienced in building token-ring networks and intranet and extranet
technology
* Proven ability to work successfully in teams
* Excellent communication and interpersonal skills
* Highly skilled in multitasking, flexible, and adaptable


EDUCATION

Associate of Applied Science, Computer Network Support Technology Seattle
Technology College, Seattle, WA, May 2003
 Related Courses and Skills
  * Peer-to-Peer Networking Structures * WAN
  * TCP/IP LAN Transport System * UNIX * ANSI C * Linux
  * Remote Computing * Network System Administration
  * Networking Technologies * Client/Server Architecture
  * Interpersonal Communications * Technical Report Writing

Internship,TechNet, Inc., Seattle, WA                    January-May 2003
Technician Internship: Assisted technicians in installing and reconfiguring
multilocation wireless extranets.


EXPERIENCE

**ComputerStop SuperStore, Seattle, WA                    May 2001-Present
Installation and Repair Technician, Part-time: Assemble computers, install
hardware and software upgrades, provide in-store and on-site repairs to
computers and peripherals. Named "Employee of the Month" three times in 18
months.

**Seattle Technology College                    September 2001-January 2003
Computer Lab Technician, Part-time: Assisted faculty and students with
hardware- and software-related problems. Assembled, installed, and added PCs
to the network throughout campus. Answered 95 percent of trouble calls
within 90 minutes.


ASSOCIATIONS

Tech CORPS, Volunteer, 2001-present
PC Users Club, 1998-present
```

Figure 9-12: Electronic Resume (Job Objective—Computer Network Support Technician)

Summary of Information
Emphasized on Figure 9-12: Ryan

Danielle wants a job in a medium- or large-sized firm that has an extensive network. Many of the firms she would like to work for recruit IT (Information Technology) employees through Internet posting sites, so Danielle prepares a cyberfriendly electronic resume. She pays particular attention to formatting:

a. Using no word processing codes.

b. Using only standard characters available on the keyboard.

c. Using a 12-point Courier font.

d. Using a 6.5-inch line length.

e. Saving the resume as an ASCII file for easy transmission.

1. **Objective**	Danielle has researched the job market and knows the types of positions open to people with her skills. She writes a concise, targeted job objective. Employers reviewing resumes can immediately identify what jobs match her qualifications.
2. **Qualifications**	Because Danielle knows that electronic resumes are often sorted and selected by resume-search programs, she loads her Qualifications section with keywords emphasizing hardware/software knowledge and experience as well as strong interpersonal qualities. She wants any resume-search program to mark her resume for further evaluation, so she includes industry-specific terms that will increase the number of hits on her resume.
3. **Education**	In addition to her degree, Danielle includes courses she has taken. Because the course names are long, she separates them with asterisks and spaces. The course listings also use industry terminology to support knowledge claims in her Qualifications section and add other opportunities for search programs to choose her resume.
	Danielle puts her internship experience in the Education section. Her exposure to a networking configuration different from the traditional wired configuration is important because it expands her capabilities in employers' eyes.
4. **Experience**	Danielle's experience is complementary to her job objective. Notice how she uses measurable accomplishments that are meaningful to employers. She knows employers want to hire people who meet deadlines and who produce quality results.
5. **Associations**	Tech CORPS is made up of individuals and businesses that donate and/or install computers, software, and networks in schools and other educational institutions. Danielle's community service relates directly to her job target, shows her commitment to her community, and helps her keep current in her field.

Mike Banta
415 S. 23rd #43
Fresno, CA 93701
209-555-0152   mbanta@azm.com

OBJECTIVE   Seeking a receptionist position for a reliable person who has a strong work ethic

QUALIFICATIONS
- Windows, Word (Advanced), Outlook
- Keying at 45 words per minute
- Ten-key at 245 strokes per minute
- Excel and Access data entry
- Formatting business correspondence
- Filing: alphabetic, numeric, geographic
- Operating high-speed collating copy machine
- Multiline telephones

EDUCATION   State University, Fresno, CA
                      Office Occupations, Certificate, August 2003

                      McCaine Adult Education Center, Clovis, CA
                      MS Word: Levels I & II, June 2002

WORK EXPERIENCE   Fruitland West, Fresno, CA   Summer 2002
                      Cherry Sorter
                      Received a raise the second day for being one of the three fastest workers. Always arrived on time; promoted to Head Sorter.

                      Trail Mushroom, Clovis, CA   1997 to 2001
                      Crew Leader
                      Promoted to Crew Leader in 1998. Calculated weekly time cards and posted daily attendance records for 16 to 20 people. Left when company closed.

                      Picker
                      Picked and sorted mushrooms 35 percent faster than the company average.

Figure 9-13: Scannable Paper Resume (Job Objective—Receptionist)

Summary of Information
Emphasized on Figure 9-13: Banta

Note: Figure 9-13 illustrates Mike's excellent job of translating personal attributes—strong work ethic and reliability—into measurable benefits for an employer.

1. **Objective**

   Mike states a clear objective and stresses the strong personal attributes that enhance his job performance.

2. **Qualifications**

   Mike positions his skills at the top of his resume to assure the prospective employer that he is qualified for the entry-level job stated in his objective. Notice how the keying and ten-key skills are measured in terms meaningful to an employer.

3. **Education**

   Mike lists his most current schooling first. Mike's educational information explains where he learned the skills related to the job objective on his resume.

4. **Work Experience**

   Since his work experience is limited and not directly transferable to the receptionist position he is seeking, Mike emphasizes on-the-job accomplishments that demonstrate his value to the employer:

   "Received a raise the second day for being one of the three fastest workers. Always arrived on time; promoted to Head Sorter."

   "Promoted to Crew Leader in 1998. Calculated weekly time cards and posted daily attendance records for 16 to 20 people."

   "Picked and sorted mushrooms 35 percent faster than the company average."

John Chang

jchang@college.edu

6487 West Street
Davis, CA 56915
(649) 555-0177

Objective
Qualifications
Education
Experience
Associations

Objective

Web Specialist

Qualifications Summary

- Comprehensive web site development
- Web site hosting and registration; server administration
- SQL and Access database management
- Graphic and multimedia design, including streaming audio/video, analysis graphs, maps, and custom web graphics
- Network administration in Windows XP/2000/NT, UNIX, Linux, and Solaris

Computer Qualifications

Internet/Web Applications	Programming	Multimedia
Microsoft IIS	HTML	Adobe Photoshop
Security and Firewalls	SQL	MPEG Video Encoding
Adobe Acrobat	Coldfusion	Real Media Encoding
Netscape Composer	ASP	ArcView Mapping
Macromedia Dreamweaver	PHP	DivX Video Encoding
HTTP and FTP servers	Java	MP3 Compression
Multi Router Traffic Graphing	Perl	Adobe Illustrator
	Macromedia Flash	

Education/Certification

Associate of Applied Science in Internet Information Systems Technology, 2003
Twin Peaks Technical College, Twin Peaks, CA
Relevant Courses Completed: Extensive programming courses, server design, database management, network security, Internet imaging

- **Microsoft Certified Database Administrator (MCDBA)**

Work Experience

Please see web portfolio for examples of my work.

National Geographic Information Center, Boise, ID
Assistant Webmaster, Summer 2001 and Summer 2002
Updated the main databases and maintained a public Internet interface using Macromedia Dreamweaver and Active Server Pages (ASP). Created and more efficiently redesigned several branched sites, including photo galleries, statistics tables, and pdf document posting areas and archives. Produced geologic prediction analysis graphs using information gathered from remote automated geology stations. Designed a web interface for LAN bandwidth usage tracking, improving network efficiency by 45%.

- **On-the-Spot Award** received for extra effort, Geographic Festival, 2002

Perez Construction and Development, Boise, ID
Web Design Project, Summer 2002
Created entire web site for a small business in construction and land development training, which included setup, design, site registration, and site hosting.

Associations

American Webmasters' Association, 2000-Present
ASP Programmers Club, 2001-Present

Other formats of this resume: Printable: (pdf) (doc)   Electronic text: (ASCII)

Figure 9-14: Web Resume (Job Objective—Web Specialist)

SUMMARY OF INFORMATION
EMPHASIZED ON FIGURE 9-14: CHANG

1. **Objective**

   The title Web Specialist is commonly understood in John's career field.

2. **Qualifications**

   John summarizes industry-specific qualifications in a bulleted list immediately following the job objective. To capture the attention of employers, he also uses an eye-catching table and graphic logos of key software programs to emphasize the large number of programs relevant to his job objective that he is qualified to operate.

   Keywords emphasized. The names of these programs also serve as relevant keywords that are included in the downloadable electronic version of John's resume, likely generating hits in resume-tracking programs.

3. **Education**

   John's recent degree in Internet Information Systems Technology implies currency in the requisite knowledge base and satisfies the basic educational requirements for the position.

4. **Experience**

   To demonstrate application of his qualifications claims, in his work experience descriptions, John repeats important keywords and uses synonyms for keywords he listed in the qualifications section. Examples include the following: database, Dreamweaver, ASP, web site development/site registration, site hosting, web graphics/analysis graphs.

   Measurable accomplishments. John also includes a strong measurable accomplishment in the National Geographic Information Center description: "Designed a web interface for LAN bandwidth usage tracking, improving network efficiency by 45%." He also includes the On-the-Spot Award for extra effort awarded to him by the Geographic Festival.

5. **Associations**

   Membership in two nationally recognized professional organizations relevant to the job objective demonstrates John's active involvement in remaining up to date in the fast-changing high-tech career field. Employers are interested in this quality when hiring for a web specialist position.

LAURENT CHACON

1015 Cambridge Way, Houston, TX 77001
409-555-0191   Fax 409-555-0192   lchacon@provider.com

OBJECTIVE

Marketing Product Line Manager for wireless data communications company

QUALIFICATIONS

- Managerial and technical education: BSEE, MBA
- Strong skills in marketing strategies development and implementation
- Remote conferencing technology, Windows NetMeeting, videoconferencing
- Knowledgeable and professional interaction with customers, sales force, engineers, and manufacturing personnel
- Team leader for product line introduction
- Proven project management skills, PERT and Gantt charts, Microsoft Project
- Proficient with LANs (wired and wireless), WAN hardware and protocols, T1 Carrier networks, analog and digital telecommunications transmissions, UNIX, C++, Visual Basic, Linux, real-time embedded software
- Skilled presenter and proficient in PowerPoint development and delivery
- Experienced in RFP and RFQ processes
- Skilled in use of Word, Excel, Access, wireless technology, Novell certification

PROFESSIONAL EXPERIENCE

NETLINK INC, Dallas, TX   **1995-Present**

- **Marketing Manager, Southwest Division**   **2001-Present**

    Manage marketing operations in Texas, Nevada, Arizona, and New Mexico. Supervise a sales and service force that has an average annual growth rate of 50 percent and participate in executive-level strategic planning meetings. Direct the development and implementation of marketing plan for a banking application of LAN/WAN products; results so far include sales to 50 percent of the Southwest Division customer base. Led team whose 2002 sales strategies have doubled NETLINK's market share in the finance industry and expanded the customer base in hospitals by 80 percent.

- **Sales and Service Manager, Southwest District**   **1998-2001**

    Supervised account executives and increased district sales 150 percent in two years. Directed on-time, underbudget openings of offices in Houston and Dallas. Improved customer satisfaction 100 percent through systems-support teams that provide four-hour turnaround on service calls. Analyzed competitive forces in the Southwest and reported findings at quarterly planning meetings with upper management.

Figure 9-15a: Scannable Paper Resume (Job Objective—Marketing Product Line Manager)

- **Engineering Product Development Coordinator**   **1995-1998**

  Member of company start-up team developing ultra fast, self-contained, secure, low-power wireless transmission technologies. Coordinated hardware and firmware integration. Supervised component testing, provided engineering support for component production, and assisted in real-time embedded software development. Acted as marketing interface during technical presentations to customers.

University of South Texas, Houston, TX
Small Business Development Center   **1993-1995**

- **Intern: Technical Industries**
  Guided by the Center Director, assisted small businesses specializing in technical products to establish vendor sources, design and implement testing procedures, solve production problems, and train workers in manufacturing techniques.

EDUCATION

- University of South Texas, Houston, TX   MBA, 1995
- Mid-State College, Austin, TX, cum laude   BSEE, 1993

ASSOCIATIONS

- National Association of Consulting Engineers, 1998-Present
- Information Technology Management Association, 2003-Present; President, 2002
- American Society for Quality Control, 2000-Present
- Member, Board of Directors, Texas Red Cross, 1996-Present

Figure 9-15b: Scannable Paper Resume (Job Objective—Marketing Product Line Manager, page 2)

Summary of Information
Emphasized on Figures 9-15a and 9-15b: Chacon

Note: Laurent's extensive experience justifies a two-page resume.

1. **Objective**

   The focused objective reflects Laurent's ability to state goals clearly.

2. **Qualifications**

   The managerial, leadership, and technical capabilities that make Laurent an effective and productive leader in this field are summarized here, including his managerial and technical degrees, strong marketing skills, presentation skills, telecommunications and computer skills, and project-management skills.

3. **Professional Experience**

   NETLINK INC: *Marketing Manager.* Laurent emphasizes measurable achievements because this field is very results-oriented. Laurent proves competencies claimed in the Qualifications section.

   Sales and Service Manager. Laurent documents leadership, marketing strategies, and customer service achievements. Referring to the management level of the business-planning team emphasizes the responsible scope of his job as well as the respect he has earned.

   Engineering Product Development Coordinator. This position is vital to Laurent's success because it gives him credibility with technically knowledgeable customers and with the engineering and manufacturing elements in an organization.

   University of South Texas, Small Business Development Center: *Intern.* This internship is valuable because it reassures employers that Laurent understands the structure and scope of the entire business process.

4. **Education**

   Laurent has credible, impressive professional experience and does not need to emphasize specific courses taken. He places the educational background near the end of the resume because, at this point in his career, employers are more interested in accomplishments than education.

5. **Associations**

   Membership in related professional organizations demonstrates a commitment to remaining current with field trends—a quality respected by employers. Employees who contribute to the business community enhance the organizational image.

ALEX VALENZUELA

2440 Windom Way, Apt. 34   Los Angeles, CA 90063   213-555- 0165   avalenzuela@mail.com

---

OBJECTIVE

Staff Accountant, Audit Division

QUALIFICATIONS

- Experienced in invoicing, accounts receivable, accounts payable, general ledger, inventory control
- Self-starter, team player, goal-oriented, willing to travel
- Attention to detail, accuracy, and deadlines
- Strong communication, problem-solving, and customer service skills
- Proficient in Word, Excel, Access, Windows, QuickBooks Pro
- Work with PC network in client-server environment

EDUCATION

Bachelor of Business Administration, Accounting, 2003
University of Los Angeles, Los Angeles, CA   GPA 3.5
Relevant courses of study:
- Analysis and Design of Accounting Information Systems
- Information Systems Auditing • Managerial Accounting
- Cost Accounting • Tax Accounting • Financial Accounting
- Intermediate Accounting I, II, III • Commercial Law

Senior Internship, 12/02 to 4/03
Project Leader: Coordinated student team analyzing inventory system of a small trailer manufacturing company. The recommended just-in-time ordering and improved parts control systems reduced yearly carrying costs by 55 percent.

EXPERIENCE

O'Keefe and Associates, Los Angeles, CA   **9/01 to Present**
Part-time Bookkeeper: Use Quickbooks Pro to invoice clients, post income and expenses, process accounts payable, reconcile general ledger accounts, and prepare monthly balance sheets and P&L statements. Update expense-tracking spreadsheets for each client. Using Excel, reconcile monthly bank statement. Initiated shorter invoicing cycle and introduced discounts for prompt invoice payment; reduced A/R cycle to 35 days.

Rand and Company, Los Angeles, CA   **6/99 - 8/01**
Part-time Retail Sales Clerk: Sold 175 percent of quota.
Awarded "2000 Outstanding Employee/Customer Relations" certificate.

ACTIVITIES

Vice President, Beta Alpha Psi Accounting, 2003
Member, Information Science Association, 2000-Present
Member, Debate Team, 1999-2001

Figure 9-16: Scannable Paper Resume (Job Objective—Staff Accountant, Audit Division)

Ralph Greenwood
6780 Greenbriar Street,   Los Angeles, CA 90067

Education:
University of Los Angeles, Los Angeles, CA
B.B.A., Accounting, June 2003
Grade Point Average: 3.5

Major Courses of Study:
Commercial Law, Cost Accounting, Economics, Principles/Management, Auditing, Statistical Techniques, Programming Systems, Principles/Finance, Managerial Accounting, Systems Analysis & Design, and Intermediate Accounting I, II, III

Experience:
January to May 2003
Department of Accounting, University of Los Angeles, Senior Internship: Coordinator of student team. Analyzed inventory system of a small retail store. Recommendations to adopt just-in-time ordering and improved stock control saved company a significant amount of time and money.

2001-Present
Westworth and Company, Los Angeles. Part-time Bookkeeper. Responsibilities include: invoicing customers, posting income and expenses, handling accounts receivable and payable; preparing income statements and balance sheets, operating PC computer in client-server network with Microsoft software and Quickbooks Pro; reconciling bank statements; and updating client expense-tracking spreadsheets. Shortened time needed to invoice clients and to receive payments.

1999-2001
Tueller's Men's Shop, Los Angeles. Part-time sales. Duties included: making retail sales; maintaining merchandise displays; assisting with inventory; assisting with cashing out; maintaining orderly stockroom.

June 1997-February 1999
Woodland General Nursery, Los Angeles. Stock maintenance staff. Duties included: unloading new merchandise; arranging merchandise in assigned locations; maintaining orderly and clean grounds; carrying and loading purchases for customers; dispensing with disposable containers and other waste. Assisting with watering, feeding, spraying, and general care of nursery items.

Other Activities:
Beta Alpha Psi—Accounting, officer; Member, *University of Los Angeles Student Center*—2001-2002; *University of Los Angeles Swim Team*, member, 1999-2001.
Hobbies: Swimming, reading, piano, travel.

Reference:
University of Los Angeles Career/Placement Center, 1300 J Street, Los Angeles, CA 90063

Figure 9-17: Scannable Paper Resume (Job Objective—Staff Accountant, Audit Division)

CAREER ACTION 9-3

Resume Outline

Name: _____

Address:_____

_____

E-Mail Address: _____

Telephone Number: _____

Pager/Message Number:_____

Fax Number: _____

Web Site Address: _____

JOB OBJECTIVE: *(Refer to the sample job descriptions you were instructed to collect earlier.)*

_____

_____

_____

_____

RELATED QUALIFICATIONS: *(Use terms and keywords related to your target job to describe your capabilities and accomplishments.)*

_____

_____

_____

_____

_____

_____

_____

_____

Continued on next page.

WORK EXPERIENCE: *(Emphasize accomplishments stated in measurable terms, if possible. Start with the most recent job first, listing each job in reverse chronological order, ending with the earliest experience.)*

Dates Employed: From _____ To _____

Company Name: _____

City: _____ State: _____ ZIP Code: _____

Job Title and Description: _____

_____

_____

Dates Employed: From _____ To _____

Company Name: _____

City: _____ State: _____ ZIP Code: _____

Job Title and Description: _____

_____

_____

Dates Employed: From _____ To _____

Company Name: _____

City: _____ State: _____ ZIP Code: _____

Job Title and Description: _____

_____

_____

Continued on next page.

CAREER ACTION 9-3 (continued)

EDUCATION: *(List in reverse chronological order, most recent first, if you have attended more than one school. Do not list high school if you have higher-level schooling unless the high school is considered highly prestigious.)*

Name of School	City, State	Degree(s)/Certificate(s)	Years Attended
_____	_____	_____	_____
_____	_____	_____	_____

(For students with little or no work experience, expand the education section.)

Major(s): _____

Minor(s): _____

GPA: _____

Relevant Courses of Study: _____

_____

SCHOOL-RELATED ACTIVITIES: *(Organizations, clubs, tutorial experience, class projects, honor groups, internships, leadership, and so on)*

_____

_____

_____

OTHER RELATED ACTIVITIES/EXPERIENCE: *(Internships, volunteer work, membership or leadership in professional or trade associations, community organizations, social organizations, service clubs, and so on. List the name of the program or organization. Include a brief summary of your experience, accomplishments, and activities and the dates you were involved.)*

_____

_____

_____

MILITARY SERVICE: *(If applicable, list the branch of service, your highest rank, training received, areas of specialization, major duties, skills and knowledge developed, and location of service.)*

_____

_____

_____

Continued on next page.

INTERESTS: *(List interests related to your job target that demonstrate well-rounded abilities, including interaction with people, manual dexterity, intellectual pursuits, artistic ability, physical fitness, strength, continuing education, and personal/professional development.)*

_____

_____

_____

REFERENCES: *(Besides listing your references here, also have a list prepared and available should a prospective employer request one.)*

Name and Title: _____

Company Name and Address (including city and state):_____

_____

Telephone:_____

E-Mail Address: _____

Description of affiliation with this reference: _____

_____

Name and Title: _____

Company Name and Address (including city and state):_____

_____

Telephone:_____

E-Mail Address: _____

Description of affiliation with this reference: _____

_____

Name and Title: _____

Company Name and Address (including city and state):_____

_____

Telephone:_____

E-Mail Address: _____

Description of affiliation with this reference: _____

_____

PERFECT THE APPLICATION AND COVER LETTER

chapter **10**

In this chapter, you will:

- Discuss and practice effectively completing an application for employment.

- **WWW** Use the Internet to search for additional cover letter strategies that may be useful to you.

- Write an effective cover letter that includes a request for an interview.

"Through their resumes and cover letters, applicants should project the qualities of focus on total customer satisfaction, quality, and neatness, which are essential in the luxury hospitality industry. Employees are hired based on a selection process to ensure each person's philosophies are in line with those of The Ritz-Carlton."

Anand Rao
Corporate Director of Organizational Development
The Ritz-Carlton Hotel Company, L.L.C.

You will be screened into or out of an interview (and the job) on the basis of your job search package: resume, cover letter, and employment application. If you carefully completed the activities for Chapter 9, your resume should be top-notch. This chapter presents tips and activities for preparing winning employment applications and cover letters. Remember, the qualified job applicant who does only an average job of preparing these documents is screened out; applicants with equal qualifications who prepare these documents well remain in the running for the job. Chapter 10 explains how you can stay in the running by completing the application correctly, writing a results-oriented cover letter, and using the Internet to search for additional useful tips in these areas.

PREPARING THE EMPLOYMENT APPLICATION

In this section, you will learn how to complete an employment application correctly and professionally. This will help ensure that your application passes the screening process so you can stay in the running for the job.

How Important Is It?

Many job applicants greatly underestimate the importance of the employment application. Employers use the application to obtain standard information from all applicants. Many job seekers think of the application as something to get through quickly so they can get on with the interview. Wrong! This idea can be fatal to your job search. Employers consider application forms, cover letters, and resumes carefully. They use these documents to select interviewees and to weed out people who don't look qualified on paper.

Visit a company you are interested in, and ask for a job application form. Take it home to study and complete.

SUCCESS TIP

Follow the instructions on the application exactly, and make your application perfect. It's a primary screening tool.

Recognize Differences in Application Forms

Employers design their application forms to obtain the information they consider most important to making hiring decisions. This includes some information that applicants might omit from cover letters or resumes. By obtaining the same information from all applicants, employers can more fairly compare their backgrounds and qualifications. The cover letter and resume expand on applicants' qualifications and either improve or lessen their chances of getting interviews. The application is another essential tool for screening candidates.

Many employers computerize applicant information, scanning applications and filing the information electronically. Some have applicants fill out and submit computerized applications. Applications are searched electronically for specific categories of information (job objective, educational background, work experience, and so on). Employers use these categories of information to compare applicants. If you omit important information, your application may be passed over. One of the most important requirements in preparing an employment application is to **follow the instructions exactly!**

Both the length and complexity of application forms vary greatly. Some are relatively simple; others are lengthy. Often technical jobs require comprehensive application information.

Some organizations use long, complex applications with questions requiring detailed information. These are designed to test applicants' endurance (a desirable employee trait). Additionally, some organizations include questions that require applicants to summarize their philosophies of the job or occupational field, thus testing the knowledge and personal values of the applicants.

As you prepare applications for employment, treat every question seriously and completely. Even if an application is long, maintain high quality in all your answers. Those who don't are the first to be eliminated in this screening process. If the application is extremely long, complete it at home. Take two or three days to work out the best possible answers.

Get an Application Ahead of Time

Whenever possible, don't fill out the application in the employer's office. Why? Because you need to practice fitting your answers into the spaces provided on the form. (Often space is limited and you have to abbreviate information.) You also need time to word your answers well. Employers judge applications on neatness, completeness, and accuracy, as well as on the quality of the answers. It usually takes more than one try to achieve the wording and effect you want.

Keep the following tips in mind when completing your application:

- Read and follow directions. Prepare each section carefully.

- Make your application neat and legible.

- Use the correct lines or spaces for your answers.

- Practice on a copy of the application, squeeze in as much positive information about yourself as possible, and abbreviate to fit information in the spaces provided.

- Answer every question. Use N/A (not applicable) if the question does not pertain to you. This shows that you did not overlook the question or skip it purposely.

- Use correct spelling, grammar, and punctuation. Use specialized terminology correctly. (You never get a second chance to make a good first impression!)

- Include a second telephone number of a person who is readily available and willing to take messages for you. You can't afford to miss calls from prospective employers!

- Make certain all information is accurate (dates, addresses, telephone and fax numbers, names, and so on).

- Be honest. Employers check the facts and immediately eliminate a candidate who has supplied false information.

- Date and sign the application. Some organizations invalidate an application if it is not signed and dated.

> *"The closest to perfection a person ever comes is when he fills out a job application form."*
>
> Stanley J. Randall

Copy the Application and Use It as a Draft. Get the application ahead of time, make a copy of the original, and use the copy as a working draft. Ask the employer to mail an application to you or access the company web site to see if you can download and print an application. If you can't get an application ahead of time, get one from a competitor or a closely related organization and practice filling it out. Then you can use it as a guide if you are required to fill one out in your target employer's office.

Read the Directions First! By reading through the entire application, from the beginning to the end, you can see how requests for information may be interrelated, which helps you determine which items require more or less detailed answers. You will also avoid duplicating information, ensure that you write information in the right places, and learn what other information you might need before completing the application.

As you read your practice copy, use a colored pen to mark all special directions so you don't overlook or misunderstand any of these while completing your application. If you don't fully understand a portion of the application or if you do not know exactly what type of information the employer is seeking, call and ask. Following directions is important to employers. Be sure to demonstrate this quality when you apply for a job!

Complete Each Section of the Application Carefully

Suggestions for effectively completing the major parts of a typical application are presented in this section.

Personal Information. Look at the first part of the sample application shown in Figure 10-1 and notice the following:

- The last name is to be listed first, followed by the first name, and then the middle name or initial. Most applications are designed this way. Don't make a bad first impression (immediately demonstrating that you can't follow directions) by listing your name in the wrong order.

- This application asks only for a permanent address. Some applications call for a current address and then a permanent address. If your application calls for both, as a courtesy, you should repeat your current address under the permanent address section rather than leave it blank.

- The applicant listed a second telephone number where messages can be received. (Good! If you are out pounding the pavement for a job, you can still get the call for an interview this way.)

- Because the applicant had never applied to or been employed by the company, neither box was checked in the last portion of the personal section of the application. The applicant wrote N/A in the box labeled "Where and when?"

- The applicant indicated with a check in the "No" box that no relatives were employed by the organization. If check boxes were not an option, the applicant could have put N/A (not applicable) next to the request to list the names of any relatives employed by the organization.

- The e-mail address provided by the applicant allows the prospective employer to contact the applicant immedi-

ately. E-mail addresses are requested on applications because they provide a timely way to reach the applicant without playing "telephone tag."

As an alternative to using N/A for questions that do not apply, type or use a black ink ballpoint pen and a ruler to draw a line through the response area.

SUCCESS TIP

Do a top-notch job of preparing your application. The application is a primary applicant-screening tool.

Position Objective. Figure 10-2 shows the position information section of a job application form. Note the following tips for filling out this section:

- Be sure to list a definite position objective, position title, or position number. (A number is frequently assigned to an open position if the job opening has been posted on the organization's web site or elsewhere.) Employers are not impressed with applications that list "anything" as the position desired. It hints of desperation, a lack of confidence, or a lack of focus or direction.

- Since salary is such an influential factor in employment, use "negotiable" as the reply to the question of salary desired. Don't risk eliminating yourself before you have a chance to present your qualifications in the interview. Save discussion of salary until the employer has expressed a definite interest in you. (Besides, the employer could have more money in mind than you say you will require. Why lose such an advantage up front?)

If the position has been advertised at a set and non-negotiable salary, list that figure in the "Salary Desired" response area. Your circumstances and preferences will determine answers to the remaining position questions.

ABC Company

APPLICATION FOR EMPLOYMENT

This application is used in the selection process and both pages must be completed. Attach extra sheets if necessary (references to resumes are NOT acceptable).

APPLICANT INFORMATION

Last Name	First Name	M. I.	Social Security Number	Home Phone	Alternative Phone
Martinelli	Elizabeth	S.	606-00-0088	208-555-0106	208-555-0170

Permanent Address – No. & Street	City		State	Zip	Date
6518 Willow Way	Boise		ID	83706	01/15/--

Have you previously ...... ☐ applied to OR ☐ been employed by ABC Company? Where and when? *N/A* E-mail Address *emartinelli@communicon.net*

Do you have relatives working for the ABC Company? ☐Yes ☒No If yes, give names and departments where they work.

Figure 10-1: Personal Information Section

POSITION

Position Desired	Salary Desired (per month)
Sales Supervisor	Negotiable

Willing to relocate? ☒ Yes ☐ No Do you want ☒ Full-time ☐ Part-time Date Available for Work *Immediately*

Figure 10-2: Position Information Section

Education. Your education will be covered in a section of the application blank similar to Figure 10-3. Remember the following points when filling out this section:

- This sample lists one high school and one community college. If you have attended more than one high school, list the most recent one and indicate the year you received your diploma. List your GPA only if it is requested or if it is high. If you have attended more than one college, postsecondary school, or educational institution, list the most recent one first and work back to the first one attended. If necessary, attach a separate keyed list of additional schools you attended.

- If space is provided to list subjects of study, research, special skills (such as a foreign language), or other activities, list examples of these capabilities and activities that relate to your job objective.

Employment History. The employment history (or work experience) section of the sample application is shown in Figure 10-4. An explanation of the entries follows.

EDUCATION						
Highest Educational Level Completed:						
Name of School	Location	From	To	Degree or Diploma	Major	Minor
High School *Idaho Falls High School*	*Idaho Falls, ID*			*Diploma*		
Community College *Central Community College*	*Boise, ID*	*9/01*	*1/03*	*A.A.*	*Marketing*	
College or University						
Graduate School						
Special Training						
Languages Other Than English (if required in employment announcement):	Speak *Spanish*			Read *Spanish*		Write *Spanish*

Figure 10-3: Education Information Section

- If your application provides enough space, include key words and use action verbs to describe accomplishments in results-oriented terms—just as you would for your resume.

- Even if you have been fired before, do not list the reason for leaving as "fired." A better choice is "laid off" or "downsized." Because organizational downsizing is common, this terminology can get you into an interview.

References. Whenever possible, tie your references directly to your work experience. Most prospective employers value good references from former reputable employers because former employers know firsthand how you performed at work. Notice in Figure 10-5 how the first two references are tied to the employment history shown in Figure 10-4 on page 169.

Some applications specify that your references be people other than former employers or supervisors. In this case, you should not list former employers! This is an example of why it is so important to read every word of the application carefully.

EMPLOYMENT HISTORY & RELATED EXPERIENCE

List present or most recent experience first. Include armed services experience and volunteer work.

Employer Name	Employer Address	Dates (Mo./Yr.)
Kevington's Emporium (Part-time)	3315 Front Street Boise, ID 83705	From 12/00 To Present

Position Title	Supervisor	Phone
Assistant Sales Supervisor	Charlie Wu	208-555-0131 Ext. 125

Reason for Leaving	Salary: Start 7.50/hr End 10.58/hr	No. Hours Per Week:
Still employed		20

Duties:

Training, supervising, and scheduling staff of six

Promoted to Assistant Sales Supervisor after only six months

Employer Name	Employer Address	Dates (Mo./Yr.)
Crown Sportswear (Part-time)	1800 Orchard Street Boise, ID 83704	From 5/00 To 11/00

Position Title	Supervisor	Phone
Sales Clerk	Connie Pratt	208-555-0114 Ext. 418

Reason for Leaving	Salary: Start 7.00/hr End 7.00/hr	No. Hours Per Week:
Took new job		10-15

Duties:

Sales, customer service, design and set up of all merchandise displays

Performed managerial and closing duties for store three nights a week

Employer Name	Employer Address	Dates (Mo./Yr.)
Value Market Variety (Part-time)	460 Park Way Idaho Falls, ID 83402	From 12/98 To 3/00

Position Title	Supervisor	Phone
Sales Clerk	Tevia Levitt	208-555-0199 Ext. 420

Reason for Leaving	Salary: Start 6.00/hr End 7.25/hr	No. Hours Per Week:
Moved to college location		15

Duties:

Sales, customer service, and inventory stocking tasks

Selected "Customer Service Employee of the Month" twice in one year

Figure 10-4: Employment History Section

REFERENCES				
Name	Address	Telephone	Occupation	Years Known
Charlie Wu (Kevington's Emporium)	3315 Front Street Boise, ID 83705	208-555-0131 Ext. 125	Sales Manager	2 years
Name	Address	Telephone	Occupation	Years Known
Tevia Levitt	460 Park Way Idaho Falls, ID 83402	208-555-0199 Ext. 420	Supervisor	4 years
Name	Address	Telephone	Occupation	Years Known
Dr. Robert Cornwell	Business Department Central Community College 8500 College Way Boise, ID 83704	208-555-0143	Professor, Marketing and Sales	2 years

Figure 10-5: References Section

Request to Contact Your Current Employer. If your application asks for permission to contact your current employer, answer *yes* only if your current employer is aware of your job search and approves. Otherwise, protect your current job with a reply of *no*.

Background Information Check. Because employers are constantly monitored by regulatory agencies to ensure they are obeying the law, you may be asked on your application if you are legally available for work in the United States. You may also be asked if you have a criminal past that includes a felony or misdemeanor charge. Answer these questions truthfully.

Applicant Statement. As shown in Figure 10-6, be sure to date and sign your application. (Be careful to list the correct year. Incorrectly dating your application is a common error and can affect the time your application is retained in an active file.) And remember, some employers do not consider the application valid unless it is signed.

Prepare for Completing an Application On-Site

If you must complete the application on the employer's premises, have the following items with you for easy reference:

- Your completed sample application to be used as a guide

- Two or three black ink pens

- Your Social Security card, driver's license, proof of citizenship, certificates, union card, grade transcripts, and related items pertinent to your occupational field (to verify the accuracy of data you must record)

- Your resume (as a reference for details)

- A pocket dictionary and a calculator

ADDITIONAL INFORMATION

◆Are you currently employed? ☒ Yes ☐ No   ◆May we contact your employer? ☒ Yes ☐ No
◆May we contact your former employers? ☒ Yes ☐ No

Can you (if accepted for employment) provide proof of your legal right to remain and work in the U.S.? ☒ Yes ☐ No

A separate affidavit on felony and misdemeanor convictions is REQUIRED to be completed on the attached form.

I hereby certify that all statements on this application are true and complete to the best of my knowledge and belief. If employed, I understand that any untrue statements on the above record may be considered grounds for termination.

Date *01/15/--*   Signature *Elizabeth S. Martinelli*

Figure 10-6: Applicant Statement

Check Your Work. Once you have completed your application, always check it thoroughly for accuracy, neatness, completeness, and quality of answers. You will have completed a winning application if you can answer yes to the following questions:

- Did you follow all directions?
- Did you print in black ink or key information correctly? (Black ink copies best.) Or did you use a computerized application form and then print and check the final results carefully before submitting your application?
- Did you answer all questions?
- Is your application completely free from errors?
- Did you use complete and accurate addresses in the references section?
- Is the content of every answer correct and well phrased?
- Does the application look attractive and neat?
- Did you sign and date your application?

Submit Your Application at the Appropriate Time

The best time to submit employment applications depends on the status of job openings with your prospective employers, whether employers will give you applications, and employers' preferences. Once again, your research on the industry and prospective employers is essential.

Resources for obtaining this information include current employees of the firm, the human resources department of the firm, knowledgeable experts in the field, the area chamber of commerce, and your school career services staff.

Unless your research indicates that the employer does not want candidates to submit unsolicited applications, obtain an application and submit it along with your resume and cover letter. This demonstrates more initiative than applicants who don't bother to do this. However, some employers consider unsolicited submission of an application to be too pushy, so do your research.

Complete Career Action 10-1

171

Complete an Actual Application or a Sample Application

Directions: Using the guidelines presented in this chapter, print out and then complete the application for employment form on your Learner's CD. If at all possible, obtain and use an actual application from an employer in your job target industry—even one from your actual target employer. Using an application from your job target industry provides the best preparation and practice. Complete the application for practice, and use it as a model when you fill out actual applications for employment.

JUMP-STARTING YOUR COVER LETTER

Your cover letter introduces you to prospective employers. It must be well written, be designed to get the reader's attention and interest, and provide information that convinces the reader to interview you and consider you for employment. Review the section on good writing style and organization in Chapter 9. These techniques also apply to writing a good cover letter.

Most employers expect a cover letter because it demonstrates the type of professionalism and initiative they want in an employee. Sending or taking your resume to employers without a cover letter could cost you further employer consideration.

Tailor the content of your letter to fit each employer. In addition, vary the content somewhat, depending on which of the following three situations is applicable:

1. **Responding to an advertised opening for a specific job.** Figure 10-7 on page 173 is an example of a cover letter responding to an advertised opening.

2. **Contacting someone whom a member of your job search network has suggested (a networking cover letter).** Refer to Figure 10-8 on page 174.

3. **Writing to a potential employer who has not advertised a position opening.** See the example in Figure 10-9 on page 175.

Tailoring Your Letter

The cover letter should highlight your most important qualifications and stress how those qualifications can meet the employer's needs. Cover letters that are not tailored to meet the employer's needs are often eliminated. Customize every cover letter.

> *"The only place where success comes before work is in a dictionary."*
>
> Vidal Sassoon

Demonstrate Your Knowledge of the Organization/Industry. Make your cover letter personal yet professional. Use your company research to personalize your letter. Mention your interest in a new or popular product of the organization; expansion of the firm; recent organizational accomplishments; the company's reputation for reliability, quality, its product, or customer service; humanitarian efforts; a special achievement of the person you're writing to, or the organization in general.

Don't Overdo It. Don't use words that are too emotional for a business setting: "I love to design computer graphics to enhance specialized publications." Say instead, "I recently read in *Advertising Age* about the award your organization won for Outstanding Use of Computer Graphics in a Specialty Catalog."

148 Barrister Avenue
Tucson, AZ 85726
April 20, 20—

Mr. George O'Donnell
Office Manager
MegaMall Property Management Company
P.O. Box 555
Tucson, AZ 85726

Dear Mr. O'Donnell:

EXPERIENCED ADMINISTRATIVE ASSISTANT, JOB #4864

Please accept my application for the administrative assistant position advertised in last Sunday's edition of the *Arizona Bugle*. As a Scout Leader involved in a promotional project last fall, I appreciated MegaMall's offer to let us hold our event at no charge in the center of the mall. I would welcome the chance to work in such a civic-minded organization.

I am an energetic, detail-oriented person who has strong administrative and computer skills, retail and community service experience, and the ability to work well with people from all walks of life. In addition, I have held positions of responsibility in four community organizations over the last eight years and was chosen 2002 National Diabetes Foundation Volunteer of the Year.

As you can see from my resume, I thrive in a busy atmosphere that involves many different tasks, the opportunity to work with people, the satisfaction of meeting deadlines, and the chance to excel. I would appreciate an interview to discuss the possibility of my joining your staff. I will call you next week to request an appointment, or you may call me at your convenience at 520-555-0122.

Sincerely,

Kimi Okasaki

Kimi Okasaki

Enclosure

Figure 10-7: Cover Letter Responding to an Advertised Job Opening

2440 Windom Way, Apt. 34
Los Angeles, CA 90063
June 29, 20—

Ms. Stephanie Nolan
Manager, Auditing Staff
Nolan Henry O'Leary Public Accountants
1410 Granada Avenue, 7th Floor
San Francisco, CA 94115

Dear Ms. Nolan:

Meagan Gerena at Smythe and Associates indicated that you are interested in hiring an accounting graduate who has some experience in the field. My degree and special interest is in Accounting/ Information Systems. Please consider me for a place on your well-respected auditing team, which was recently named by the *San Francisco Business Reporter* as one of the Top 10 auditing firms in the greater San Francisco area.

During the last two years, I have worked for a CPA firm where I was able to develop a wide range of accounting and accounting-related skills. My responsibilities included:

- Performing full-charge bookkeeper duties, such as opening, posting, and closing the books; completing federal and state corporate tax returns; and creating templates using Excel.

- Assisting a consultant in upgrading software for a customized accounting system.

- Creating a procedures manual that identified common operating, maintenance, and troubleshooting situations that could occur between the two operating systems and providing directions and steps for reconciling those problems in a timely and cost-effective way.

During my senior year at the University of Los Angeles, I had the chance to lead an internship research team. We studied the operations of a local accounting firm, accompanied its auditors to several client sites, and assisted in the audit of a small retail store. These experiences cemented my interest in auditing as a career field.

I am confident in my ability to make a positive contribution to Nolan Henry O'Leary Public Accountants and am enclosing a copy of my resume for your review. I will call you next week to request an appointment, or you may reach me at 213-555-0156. Thank you for considering my request. I am looking forward to meeting you.

Respectfully,

Juan Tejada

Juan Tejada

Enclosure

cc: Meagan Gerena, Smythe and Associates

Figure 10-8: Networking Cover Letter

846 Cameron Way
Phoenix, AZ 85012
December 10, 20—

Mr. Gary Whaley
District Sales Manager
Computeriferals Company
Rallings City, NY 10099

Dear Mr. Whaley:

Computeriferals has earned my respect. I have used and repaired peripherals from most of the leading manufacturers in my studies as a Business Systems/Computer Repair major and in my job as a sales representative at ComputerChoice. I know you build quality products, and I want to sell quality products—Computeriferals.

Careful review of my qualifications and the requirements of a sales representative at Computeriferals suggests that I am well qualified for a sales position with your organization. Please consider the following highlights from my background:

- Initiated outside sales to small businesses and expanded customer base from 137 to 183 accounts in the past year—a 34 percent increase in number of customers served

- Increased yearly sales from $743,000 to $1,236,000—an increase of 66 percent

- Negotiated a $250,000 service contract with a client who has five office locations in this area

- Attained 100 percent customer retention through a service-first approach and frequent communication

Although I have enjoyed working in the local market, the wider scope of Computeriferals presents an appealing challenge. Even if you have no current openings, I would appreciate meeting with you to discuss your requirements for sales representatives. My resume is enclosed for your convenience. I will call next week to request an appointment, or you may reach me at 602-555-0160.

Respectfully,

Christopher Lipsmeyer

Christopher Lipsmeyer

Enclosure

Figure 10-9: Cover Letter Inquiring About an Unadvertised Position

Emphasize How You Can Meet Employer's Needs.
Identify in your cover letter the employer's needs outlined in the job opening announcements or advertisements. If your current job target deals only with accounting, a vague listing of accounting qualifications and computer specialization will not be as effective as a reference to strong accounting abilities (with the computer specialization referenced as a backup).

Also, if you are considering more than one position, such as an accounting technician or a computer specialist, highlight the appropriate skills, experience, and education for each job you target.

SUCCESS TIP

Tailor your cover letter to the employer, and make sure your cover letter is error free. Applicants who do a good job stay in the running!

In your cover letter, emphasize your specific abilities that meet the employer's needs for the particular job.

Addressing Your Letter

Some organizations don't accept unsolicited applications, resumes, or cover letters. Often applicants who address communications to the human resources department get a form letter stating that no applications are currently being accepted.

Find Out Who Hires. To boost your chances, address your letter to the person who has hiring authority for the position (particularly the one who would be your supervisor—the department head, manager, or person who would supervise your work). Never address your cover letter "To Whom It May Concern." This type of salutation may target your letter for the wastebasket.

How do you get the right person's name? If you don't yet know who to address your cover letter to, consider one of these methods:

1. Call your target employer and say you are doing career research and want to address a letter of inquiry to the person who specializes in your career area. Get the person's full name and title, and verify the spelling and mailing address. When you call, introduce yourself, get the name of the person you talk with, and thank that person by name for his or her help. Always say you are a student or are doing research. This person could possibly help you later, and using names establishes a courteous, friendly tone.

2. Go to the human resources office (if your target employer has one). Ask whether there is an organizational chart you could use as part of your career planning class or personal research. This information should provide you with the name of the department head you should address your cover letter to.

If this method seems inappropriate for your job search, ask members of your job search network to help you devise a workable approach. Use your creative ability, dare to be different, but always be courteous and businesslike.

Contacting the targeted department head personally can get you in the door sooner.

The Human Resources Department or the Specific Department Head? If you send your cover letter and resume only to the human resources department, the person who heads the department you are interested in might never see it. If you send your letter directly to the person you would work for, your chances of getting an interview will be greatly increased, but the human resources department could resent your circumventing them.

How do you handle this situation? If the employer is accepting applications, send one letter and resume to the human resources department and one to the department head. Indicate in your letters that you have sent similar communications to each party. At worst, both letters wind up in the human resources department. If the employer is not officially accepting applications, send your cover letter and resume to the department head only. If it is persuasive enough, you could still get an interview!

If you write a convincing cover letter, the employer will be eager to talk with you.

PERSONAL BEST
Writing Effective Cover Letters

- Create a positive first impression. The cover letter is the first thing that meets the reader's eye. Give it the same consideration and careful preparation as you do your resume.

- Use effective writing techniques and project a friendly, energetic, and professional image.

- Address your letter to the appropriate person, and use his or her correct full name and title (no abbreviations except *Mr., Dr.,* and so on).

- Relate your qualifications to the needs and interests of the prospective employer. Emphasize what you can do for the organization.

- Don't use overblown or empty words to describe your abilities. Use specific, measurable terms; for example, "My program increased reported customer satisfaction by 35 percent."

- Project confidence in your qualifications, and show interest and enthusiasm for the job.

- If the job will likely require you to relocate, state your willingness to move.

- Emphasize your skills as a team player. Don't try to convince the employer that you are a one-person miracle worker.

- Incorporate specialized terminology from your industry and job target where appropriate.

- Use a word processor and print your letter and resume on high-quality paper. Format your letter in an acceptable business style.

- Hand sign each cover letter.

- Be certain the final letter is perfect—no errors! Proofread and proofread again!

DEVELOPING WINNING COVER LETTER CONTENT

Help the employer by keeping your cover letter brief (four or five paragraphs—no longer than one page). Be sure your cover letter does not duplicate exactly the data in your resume. (What busy employer wants to read the same thing twice?) Also make sure that what you say in both your resume and cover letter does not contain contradictions.

Content of a Cover Letter

The following items should be included in the letter:

- If you had any previous communication with the person you're writing to, refer to it to help him or her remember you.

- If you have a contact who knows the person you are writing to, mention your contact's name in your letter.

- Explain how you learned of and why you are interested in the employer, and state the type of position you are seeking.

- Include at least one sentence that shows your knowledge of the company. This demonstrates initiative and interest.

- Emphasize your qualifications for the job (one or two results-oriented descriptions of accomplishments and capabilities that show how you can benefit the employer and handle the job).

- State that your resume is enclosed.

- Include a request for an interview (not a bid for a job) even if no openings are available now.

- Include a courteous closing sentence.

The Opening

Begin by introducing yourself and stating your purpose. Explain how you know of the employer and why you are interested in this particular organization; state the type of job you are seeking.

If you are responding to an announced job opening, refer to the position you are applying for and how or where you heard about it. If you learned about the opening through an advertisement or announcement, include the date of the notice and where you found it (newspaper, Internet job posting, professional journal, employment agency, or the company human resources department).

If you know someone who would be influential and recognized by the reader, get that person's permission and reference his or her name in your letter.

The following example is a networking cover letter sent by Kimi Okasaki, who is seeking an administrative support position. Kimi mentions the name of a person well known to the addressee.

"Carmine Garduno from the Health Services Bureau recommended I talk with you about the possibility that you may need an administrative support person with experience in educational and community activities. Your new five-year educational and community plan is soundly developed. I believe my five years of experience as a volunteer in the Valley Elementary School Parent-Teacher Organization (VES-PTO) and the Diabetes Foundation would be useful in helping you achieve success in the plan."

Your Sales Pitch

This section focuses on your qualifications for the job. Make this paragraph a results-oriented summary of your assets, specifically highlighting one or two accomplishments that demonstrate your suitability for the job. You must be able to verify these accomplishments with evidence. Do not duplicate information exactly from your resume. Whenever possible, use bullets to highlight the qualifications you most want to emphasize to capture the reader's attention.

"Through my volunteer work, I learned about the disease-prevention techniques your department teaches to day-care workers. The potential to combine helping families, defeating disease, and doing work I enjoy is irresistible. I recently completed an

Associate in Science degree, majoring in Information Management Technology, with an overall GPA of 3.5. As Secretary-Treasurer of the VES-PTO, I used Excel and Word to generate and merge letters and address labels for 500 student families."

The Closing

In the closing, ask for an interview (not a job). Research shows that an active close (in which you say you will call to request an interview) leads to more interviews. A passive close (in which you request the reader to call you), however, can lead to higher-quality interviews. A third approach, which is used below, combines the strengths of both styles.

"Enclosed for your review is my resume. I would appreciate meeting with you and discussing the possibility of our working together. I will call you on Thursday to request an interview, or you may reach me at 555-0122. I would welcome the opportunity to contribute to the community outreach efforts of the Department of Disease Prevention.

Sincerely,
Kimi Okasaki

Complete Career Actions 10-2 and 10-3

Your sales pitch should highlight the accomplishments that demonstrate your suitability for the job.

> ### SUCCESS TIP
>
> **In your cover letter, state the position you are applying for, highlight your related capabilities, and request an interview.**

Personal Review and Edit of Your Letter

Review and edit your cover letter draft by using the colored pen system recommended for the development of your resume. Be choosy (downright hypercritical) about the words you use. Every word counts!

Outside Critical Review

Ask a member of your network who has strong communications skills and who knows your background to critique your letter. Most people find it difficult to critique their own resumes and cover letters because they overlook important aspects (such as punctuation, omission of details, and so on) while concentrating on the wording. Your critic may think of additional items you should include that you have overlooked. Sources for outside reviewers and critics include:

- **A hiring expert you know** who can tell you how your cover letter stacks up against the ones he or she reviews and how you can improve yours.

- **A professional friend or acquaintance** who knows you and your work well enough to help clarify confusing statements or to spot where you have omitted or neglected to emphasize important information or qualifications.

- **A professional who does not know you well** to serve as a final test for your cover letter, reading to learn about you from the letter. Choose a good writer who will give honest criticism, not someone who will automatically say the letter is "fine." You want solid suggestions for improvement.

Complete Career Action 10-4

Use the Internet to Research Cover Letter Strategies

 Directions: Visit the sites listed below, the web site for this text, and/or other sites and search engines you favor to locate at least four strategies for writing a successful cover letter. Look for new ideas that may be useful to you. Write a summary of your findings, or print copies of the data. If you find new information or information that varies from that in your textbook, research further and discuss the topic(s) in the classroom, with your career services staff, and with interview specialists.

Monster.com
(Click on "Career Center.")
www.monster.com

CareerLab
(Look under "Cover Letter Library.")
www.careerlab.com

Your Career: How to Make It Happen web site
(Click on "Links"; then click on "Career planning and job search information links.")
www.levitt.swlearning.com

CareerJournal.com
(Enter "cover letter" in search window.)
www.careerjournal.com

JobStar
http://jobstar.org

Gary Will's WorkSearch
www.garywill.com/worksearch

Quinessential Careers
www.quintcareers.com
(Click on the "Featured Article of Week" link; then click on "Career Articles"; then click on "Entire Catalog of Articles.")

The Riley Guide
www.rileyguide.com

Create Cover Letter Outline and Draft

 Part A: Access Career Action 10-3 on your Learner's CD, or use the Cover Letter Outline form on page 187 to organize and outline your basic cover letter (keeping in mind it should be tailored to fit each employer's needs). Don't try to write a perfect letter at this point; just work at getting the essence of your message on paper. You will refine it later.

Review the sample cover letters provided in Figures 10-7, 10-8, and 10-9 on pages 173, 174, and 175, respectively.

Part B: Using your cover letter outline and related job target research information, compose a cover letter draft. Make it concise, tailored to the employer's needs, and courteous. Most important is to demonstrate how you can benefit the employer.

CAREER ACTION 10-4

Prepare Your Final Cover Letter

Directions: Now polish your cover letter draft, emphasizing your qualifications and making the content clear and concise. Use a thesaurus to find just the right shades of meaning. As you prepare your final cover letter, remember that the same four words used to describe a good resume apply to your cover letter:

IT MUST BE PERFECT!

After your cover letter is complete, review it with thorough attention to detail; even one error can eliminate you in the employer's paper screening.

When you think your letter is perfect, ask an outside critic to review it one more time slowly and carefully, looking for even the smallest error. This is critical to the success of your cover letter. Print the final letter on top-quality paper.

DISTRIBUTING YOUR COMPLETE JOB SEARCH PAPER PACKAGE

Once you have completed your resume and cover letter and know how to complete an employment application, you're ready to submit a solid job search paper package (application, resume, and cover letter).

How you distribute your job search documents is also important. Consider the following tips regarding distribution:

1. **Regular Mail.** If you mail your documents, put them into a large envelope so you don't have to fold them. If the employer faxes or scans your letter after receiving it, folds in the paper can cause errors in the process.

2. **E-Mail or Fax.** Some employers specify that they want you to e-mail or fax the documents; do what they say! Follow the e-mail instructions provided in Chapter 9.

PREPARING AN ELECTRONIC COVER LETTER

The emergence of the electronic job market has created the need for the electronic resume discussed in Chapter 9. In addition, many employers require electronic cover letters to be transmitted through e-mail or to be posted on their Internet home pages.

Listed below are some of the key strategies for preparing and writing an electronic cover letter:

1. **Stick with a plain style text.** Even if your e-mail allows you to enhance the appearance of the text, keep it simple and plain. (Refer to Chapter 9, page 132, for "Electronic Resume Formatting Guidelines.")

2. **Make sure lines are no more than 65 characters.** If your line length is longer than this, you risk the text fragmenting unevenly on multiple lines on the receiver's screen.

3. **Keep your cover letter concise, but clear.** Your e-mail cover letter should be only two to three paragraphs and under 150 words. This cover letter should reveal your interest and sell the target employer on one or two of your outstanding capabilities.

4. **Follow standard business letter guidelines.** Just because e-mail is less formal than a paper version does not mean you omit parts of the letter such as the salutation and closing.

5. **Make good use of your subject line.** The subject line should stimulate the reader to continue reading your letter. Consider a subject line with "Experienced CPA for Auditing Director" rather than "Re: Job No. 3872."

6. **Take advantage of keywords.** Focus on keywords and skill sets that will increase the chances of your letter being retrieved in a database search. Because of the possibility of a database search, it is more important to use noun phrases than action verbs in an electronic cover letter.

7. **Provide sufficient contact information to the prospective employer.** This information should include your name, address, and phone number.

8. **Do not attach files to an e-mail cover letter.** Some organizations actually block e-mail that contains an attachment.

9. **Follow company guidelines and submit only what they ask for.**

10. **Proofread.** Spell check and proofread again before you hit the send button.

Transmit your electronic cover letter in one of two ways: (1) copy and paste it into your e-mail program and send it to the employer as an e-mail message or (2) paste it into the cover letter block in the job application section of the employer's web site. Regardless of which way the letter is sent, if it is not well written, it will not arrive at its intended destination (the hiring desk).

Ask a member of your network who has strong communication skills to critique your cover letter carefully.

SUCCESS TIP

Format electronic cover letters to transmit correctly: Follow employer instructions and save as plain text.

MAXIMIZING YOUR ONLINE JOB SEARCH PROCESS

The following six steps explain how to conduct a savvy online job search.

Step 1: Define Your Specific Job Target

To access the job listings and/or post a resume on most job recruitment sites, applicants must first complete a registration or resume posting form. The applicant/job matching software used by most job listing sites requires applicant information to match to the job openings:

- **Keywords.** These are search terms describing the type of job you are seeking. Use terms that describe the skills, experience, and abilities you have that are required in jobs you want to pursue.

- **Desired employment industry.** You will typically be asked to specify the industry in which you are seeking employment.

- **Geographical preference.** You will need to specify one or more geographical areas in which you would like to work.

- **Desired salary.** Some sites require that you include the salary range you are seeking.

Step 2: Get the Edge With Employer/Industry Research

Completing employer and industry research is well worth your time for several reasons: Research demonstrates initiative on your part; employers prefer to hire people who know about their organizations; research provides common-ground information that helps you communicate easily and knowledgeably with interviewers; research helps you avoid choosing a job that is not right for you.

Step 3: Prepare Electronic Resume, Cover Letter, and Web Resume/Portfolio

You will definitely need a well-prepared electronic resume and cover letter. If appropriate for your career field, you may also want to develop a web resume and web portfolio. See Chapter 9 for details regarding development and transmission of these.

Step 4: Find Online Job Openings

Many good job-listing sites are available on the Internet. Resources for finding these include employers' direct web sites (the best source, if available—try entering the name of the employer followed by *.com* in your Internet browser); the *Your Career: How to Make It Happen* web site (see "Job

recruitment links" under the "Links" page); and The Riley Guide at www.rileyguide.com (see "Job Listings").

Step 5: Apply Online

Job listing and employer sites vary. Some require applicants to paste their resumes into an open resume block. Others require building a resume online. Still others require completion of an online application only—no resume is required in this case. Follow the web site instructions exactly. See Chapter 9 for more details regarding online application. Before you hit the transmit, send, or submit button, print copies of all forms you complete, proofread carefully, and make corrections. Reprint if corrections are needed; then file your final forms as a reference.

Step 6: Follow Up

Get the edge on your competition by following up as outlined below.

- **Call the employer directly.** Ask for the human resources department, and state that you are responding to the company's online job advertisement. (Give the source of the ad, the date, the job number, and so on.) If you have applied online, ask for the name, phone number, and regular and e-mail addresses of the hiring decision maker.

- Call and/or send an e-mail message to the decision maker. Let the decision maker know of your application and interest in the job.

Review the key steps for online job application illustrated in Figure 10-10.

TAPPING INTO YOUR NETWORK FOR JOB LEADS

Employers base their hiring decisions largely on trust. They are most likely to hire people they know or who are referred by people they know. For this reason, your job search network is the No. 1 source of solid job leads.

Step	Action	Process
1	**Define your job target** so you can complete job search forms on recruitment sites.	Identify keywords you could provide in keyword fields for job matches on recruitment sites. Identify preferred geographical locations, employment industry, and salary range (if required).
2	**Research employers.**	Review Chapter 8, "Research Prospective Employers." Research employers' web sites. See "Links" pages on the *Your Career: How to Make It Happen* web site for employer, salary, and relocation information.
3	**Prepare electronic resume and cover letter.** Prepare a web resume and e-portfolio, if appropriate, for your job target.	Prepare and transmit properly formatted electronic resume and cover letters tailored to each employer's needs, including targeted keywords (see Chapter 9). If appropriate, prepare web resume and online portfolio.
4	**Find online job openings.**	Check employers' web sites. Check job-listing sites. See "Links" (job links) on the *Your Career: How to Make It Happen* web site.
5	**Apply online.**	Follow job application instructions on sites carefully. Register or fill out access screens on job-listing sites with job target information (Step 1 above). Post electronic resume and cover letter as required by sites. Before submitting final online application, print a copy for your files.
6	**Follow up, if possible.**	Call employer; indicate you have applied online to a specific job ad. Contact the decision maker, if possible.

Figure 10-10: Key Steps for Online Job Application

Networking Process

Once you complete your job search package, contact your network to expand your employment options. Because network members are statistically the strongest job lead source, they can form the bridge to your perfect job. Follow the networking guidelines below for best results. They are listed in order of preference for maximum results.

1. **Make an appointment to meet in person.** Make appointments with the most viable of your networking members. Appointments get the best results. In each meeting, briefly review your job objective and ask for recommendations. Give each person a copy of your cover letter and resume, asking for feedback on the content and quality. Be organized; respect the person's time.

2. **Make a telephone call.** If you can't get an appointment, make a telephone call. Briefly review your job objective and ask for recommendations. Ask whether you can send a copy of your cover letter and resume to get his or her feedback.

3. **Send a networking letter.** If you can't get a meeting or reach the person by telephone, send a networking letter (see instructions below).

Networking Letter

A networking letter tells your network about your job search goals and requests specific help with the process. This letter contains a basic informational core, as well as personalized comments tailored to the recipient. The employment success rate from these letters is high.

Your networking letter should include the following features:

- A friendly, enthusiastic, and confident tone

- A professional format with no errors

- A complete but concise message that clearly identifies the job target and search goals

- A request for specific help

- A reference to the resume

Tailor your networking letter by considering the individual strengths of your network members. Ask a good writer for advice in improving your resume. Ask for help in identifying specific employers or finding direct job leads. You can also request meetings with some network members to brainstorm strategies

FOLLOWING UP WITH A TELEPHONE CALL

Applicants who follow up with a telephone call to employers after sending cover letters and resumes are dramatically more successful. Two important reasons for this are employers see follow-up as an indication of initiative and confidence, and busy employers may actually intend to call an applicant but get sidetracked. Applicants who call save the employer time and often speed a hiring decision.

Call about three or four days after the employer receives your letter, and say something like this: "This is Jennifer Ortiz calling from Raleigh. I sent you a letter and resume regarding the system support programming job and wanted to make sure you received it." This simple telephone call is often a deciding factor in getting an interview. Increase your odds by making this call.

SUCCESS TIP

After sending your job search package, follow up with a telephone call to increase your chances of securing an interview.

Increase your chances for success by following up your cover letter and resume with a phone call to your prospective employer.

✓ CHECKLIST:
Applications and Cover Letters

Check each of the actions you are taking to increase your career success:

☐ Making the applications perfect

☐ Tailoring cover letters to employers; making sure the cover letter is error-free

☐ Stating the position applyied for, listing related abilities, and requesting an interview

☐ Formatting electronic cover letters correctly

☐ Following up cover letters with telephone calls

critical thinking *Questions*

1. What are possible consequences of not filling out an employment application completely and according to the instructions?

2. Should you mention a salary figure in the application? Explain.

3. Think of a probable employer with whom you would like to interview. How would you go about finding out to whom you should address your cover letter? Write the name, title, and address of the person in your answer.

4. What are at least three features of an online cover letter?

CAREER ACTION 10-3

Create Cover Letter Outline and Draft

Part I: Cover Letter Outline

Your Mailing
Address:

_____

_____

_____

_____

Date:

_____

Name and Title
of Addressee:

_____

_____

_____

Salutation:

Dear: _____

Paragraph 1,
Opening:
(Include the name
of a referral if
you have one;
state your
position
objective.)

_____

_____

_____

_____

_____

_____

_____

_____

_____

_____

Continued on next page.

Paragraph 2,
Your Sales
Pitch:
(Tailor it to
the opening.
Where appropriate,
use bullets to
highlight strong
job-relevant
qualifications.)

_____
_____
_____
_____
_____
_____
_____
_____
_____
_____
_____

Paragraph 3,
Closing:
(State that
your resume is
enclosed and
request an
interview. Include
your telephone
number.)

_____
_____
_____
_____
_____
_____
_____
_____
_____
_____

Complimentary
Close:

Sincerely,

_____

(Key your name here.)

chapter **11**

INTERVIEW LIKE A PRO

In this chapter, you will:

- Prepare appropriate interview responses to demonstrate enthusiasm and interest in a position and an organization.

- Identify nonverbal behaviors to enhance your interview performance.

- Prepare a 60-Second Interview Commercial.

- Identify the core elements of successful interviewing and ways to succeed in your interview.

- Summarize the fine points for interview success that are applicable to your job search and career planning.

 Use the Internet to locate and summarize interview strategies.

"First, come prepared! Countless applicants arrive at our agency without a resume. Others are not able to provide accurate dates or addresses for their work history. The key to a successful interview is advance preparation. And, to make the very best impression, DRESS FOR SUCCESS!"

Sherri Neihaus
Adecco Employment Services
www.adecona.com

You have learned how to present yourself well on paper (the application, cover letter, and resume). Now for the main event—the job interview. The practical interview techniques presented in this chapter work. These techniques are based on widespread, ongoing research with professional interviewers. These hiring specialists represent diverse employment fields and organizations throughout the United States. Research also includes thorough review and testing of successful job-seeking program techniques.

KNOW THE CORE ELEMENTS OF SUCCESSFUL INTERVIEWING

You will be screened into an interview because you appear qualified on paper. The employer uses the interview to learn whether you have the personal qualities to fit into the organization and to further confirm your work performance qualifications.

The First 30 Seconds Count

When first meeting, people often form opinions about others within 30 seconds or less! This first 30 seconds can make or break an interview. Interviewers say they form strong opinions about an applicant in the time it takes the applicant to walk across the room, say "Hello," and sit down. Read on to learn how to make those 30 seconds work for you!

Interview and interpersonal communications experts have studied what applicants can do to make a favorable first impression and to best project professionalism and competence. They report that the attitudes, image, and appearance applicants project during interviews are as influential as their skills in getting ahead. Projecting strength in these areas gives job applicants a decided edge over their competition, as you can see in Figure 11-1.

The first 30 seconds count. Which woman is dressed more professionally?

Applicants Are Screened on Paper First

You are selected to interview on the basis of your resume, cover letter, and application. Employers request these beforehand so they can review your education, work experience, and qualifications and compare them with those of other applicants. Employers don't have time during the interview to evaluate this information in detail.

The Interview Focuses on You as a Person

One main purpose of the interview is for the employer to get to know the applicant as a person. Your image and appearance are the first things the interviewer will evaluate—and first impressions can influence the entire interview. Your *attitude* (the essence of your personality), however, is the biggest factor of your success in the interview. Job qualifications also count during the interview, and your responsibility is to summarize them well.

Your Attitude—The No. 1 Factor

Attitude is the No. 1 factor that influences an employer to hire. Following are ways you can exhibit a good attitude:

Impact on Interviews	
Areas:	Approximate Impact on Interview:
1. Attitude	40 percent
2. Image and Appearance	25 percent
3. Communication (verbal/nonverbal)	25 percent
4. Job Qualifications	10 percent

Figure 11-1: Impact on Interviews

1. **Concentrate on being likable.** As simplistic as it seems, research proves that one of the most essential goals in successful interviewing is to be liked by the interviewer. Interviewers want to hire pleasant people others will like working with on a daily basis. Pay attention to the following areas (detailed later in this chapter) to project that you are highly likable:

   ■ Be friendly, courteous, and enthusiastic.

   ■ Speak positively.

   ■ Use positive body language and smile.

   ■ Make certain your appearance is appropriate.

2. **Project an air of confidence and pride.** Act as though you want and deserve the job, not as though you are desperate.

3. **Demonstrate enthusiasm.** The applicant's level of enthusiasm often influences employers as much as any other interviewing factor. The applicant who demonstrates little enthusiasm for a job will never be selected for the position.

4. **Demonstrate knowledge of and interest in the employer.** "I really want this job" is not convincing enough. Explain why you want the position and how the position fits your career plans. You can cite opportunities that may be unique to a firm or emphasize your skills and education that are highly relevant to the position.

5. **Perform at your best every moment.** There is no such thing as "time out" during the interview. While in the waiting area, treat the assistant or receptionist courteously; learn and use his or her name. (The interviewer often requests this person's opinion of applicants.)

6. **Remember, the interview is a two-way street.** Project genuine interest in determining whether you and the employer can mutually benefit from your employment.

SUCCESS TIP

Project enthusiasm and a positive attitude in interviews. Often a less experienced applicant with greater enthusiasm for a job is hired over competitors who are more qualified.

Complete Career Action 11-1

Image and Appearance

Have you ever looked at a display of CDs or books and been drawn to one with an appealing cover? The same concept applies in your interview. Remember, by the time you walk into the room and sit down, the interviewer has decided whether you will be considered for the position. Your image and appearance, combined with the attitude you project, determine this first impression and may count as much as 25 percent as a positive or negative hiring factor.

CAREER ACTION 11-1

Project Enthusiasm, Positive Attitude, and Interest

Directions: Access Career Action 11-1 on your Learner's CD, or use a separate sheet of paper. Prepare a list of statements you can use in your interview that demonstrate sincere enthusiasm and interest in the job, company, and other relevant aspects of your target employer. Back up your statements by referring to your research.

Know How the Outer Package Helps the Sale.

Cosmetic firms are well aware of the impact of the package; some people spend six times as much for the package as for the product inside! Products packaged attractively far outsell those that are not.

Dress Conservatively. When applying for an office or professional position, most interviewers expect you to wear businesslike clothes. For men and women, a conservative suit of quality fabric is generally appropriate. For women, a conservative, tailored dress or coordinated skirt and blouse are also appropriate, especially when worn with a matching jacket. In most cases, women who wear slacks to an interview lower their chance of being selected.

Whenever possible, visit your target employer before the interview to observe the working atmosphere, conditions, and dress code. Use this information to determine how to dress for your interview. A word of caution: Even if the employer permits casual dress on the job, you should demonstrate initiative and enhance your professional image by dressing more formally for your important business meeting—the interview. This also projects respect for the employer, which increases your likability.

Appear Clean, Pressed, and Perfectly Groomed.

Make sure your clothes are clean, pressed, in good repair, comfortable, and well fitted. (Clothing or shoes that are too tight restrict comfortable, poised movement.) Visit top-notch clothing stores, and get help from experienced salespeople in selecting a coordinated interview outfit. You don't have to buy your outfit in an expensive store; you can usually duplicate it closely in a less expensive shop. Be immaculately groomed—head to toe. Be a model of cleanliness, and always use a deodorant. "Never let 'em see you sweat!"

Use Color to Your Advantage. Color is the most dynamic tool for dressing to enhance appearance. Learn what colors best complement your skin, eyes, and hair. A good test is to note when you get repeated compliments on a color you wear.

Traditionally blue and gray are reliable color choices for interview suits, jackets, slacks, and skirts. Strengthen your image by using your best colors in your accessories—scarves, ties, shirts, blouses, and so on.

Research Dress Expectations. A business suit is not appropriate for every interview. Base your clothing choice on employer and career field research. Would a sport coat and dress slacks be more appropriate for your employer target, or would less formal slacks and a neat shirt and tie be better? Would a skirt and blouse be more in line with the employer target? Never dress too casually. T-shirts, jeans, tennis shoes, and other casual or faddish items cost applicants the job.

SUCCESS TIP

Smile and project professionalism. Dress and groom yourself neatly and appropriately.

Lose the Nose Ring and Baseball Cap. If you try to make a bold statement against business-world conformity, you can probably kiss the job good-bye. People who wear baseball caps, nose rings, or too many earrings or finger rings to an interview might as well stay home.

Review the pictures of job applicants on page 193. Which outfit do you think is more likely to help the applicant get a job in a professional business or office setting? Why?

Look Alert! Being well-rested projects a healthy, alert image; get plenty of sleep the night before an interview. Taking good care of yourself with a healthy diet, exercise, and adequate rest is an important lifetime investment in a successful career.

Even though casual attire may be appropriate for some business offices, it is inappropriate when interviewing for a business or office position.

A conservative suit is appropriate when interviewing for a professional or business position.

Smile! Nothing leaves a better impression of likability than a pleasant smile at the point of meeting the interviewer and throughout the interview.

Verbal Communication

Start your verbal communication off right by using the interviewer's name in your greeting. This conveys respect, which aids your likability. (In some cases, more than one person will interview you at a time. See Chapter 13, "Be Prepared for Any Interview Style.") Learn and use the names of everyone who will be interviewing you.

State Your Name and the Position You're Seeking. When you enter the interviewer's office, begin with a friendly greeting and state the position you're interviewing for: "Hello, Ms. Levine, I'm Bella Reyna. I'm here to interview for the accounting position." If someone has already introduced you to the interviewer, simply say, "Good morning, Ms. Levine." Identifying the position is important because interviewers often interview for many different positions.

Project a Pleasant Tone of Voice. It isn't always what you say that creates a positive or negative reflection of your attitude, but how you say it. Using a pleasant tone of voice (friendly, courteous, and energetic) also enhances your likability.

Record Yourself for Practice. Ask a friend to conduct a practice interview with you to evaluate your tone of voice. Have your friend ask you some of the sample questions from Chapter 14. Tape your questions and answers and listen to them; then decide where you could improve. If your voice is high-pitched, work on lowering it; if you speak too softly, increase the volume; and so on. Above all, speak in a warm tone with energy.

Focus on How You Fit the Job. Near the beginning of your interview, as soon as it seems appropriate, ask a question similar to this: "Could you describe the scope of the job and tell me what capabilities are most important in filling the position?" The interviewer's response will help you focus on emphasizing your qualifications that best match the needs of the employer.

Use Positive Words and Phrases. One of the most important interview goals is to keep the content completely positive so the interviewer's final impression is "Yes, this is the person for the job!" Use a positive vocabulary and eliminate all negative terms.

Emphasize Your Strengths—Even When Discussing an Error. Emphasize your strengths and abilities that are relevant to the job. Although you want to avoid bringing up past shortcomings, do not try to dodge one that comes out during an interview. Face it head-on and explain what you learned from the experience. Turn a potential negative into a positive by demonstrating that you learn from your mistakes.

> *"Remember that a person's name is, to that person, the sweetest sound in any language."*
>
> Dale Carnegie

If the interviewer asks you about the circumstances, explain briefly; don't make excuses or blame others. Remember, the interviewer is human too and has probably made his or her share of mistakes. You create a better impression by being honest, candid, and sincere.

Do not lie during an interview, and be prepared to state why you left previous employment if you're asked. Do no speak unfavorably about your previous supervisor or firm. Interviewers often believe you would do the same after leaving their companies. Maintain your business and professional integrity throughout the interview.

Speak Correctly. Grammatical errors can cost applicants the job. Use correct grammar, word choice, and a businesslike vocabulary, not an informal, chatty one. Avoid slang. When under stress, people often use pet phrases (such as *you know*) too often. This is highly annoying and projects immaturity and insecurity. Ask a friend or family member to help you identify any speech weaknesses you have. Begin eliminating these speech habits now.

Avoid Credibility Robbers. Avoid using words and phrases that rob credibility and make you sound indecisive or lacking in credibility. Eliminate the following credibility robbers from your vocabulary:

- *Just or only.* Used as follows, "I *just* worked as a waiter" or "I *only* worked there on a part-time basis" implies that you are not proud of your work or that you don't consider the work meaningful. Any work is meaningful; it demonstrates initiative. Leave out the credibility robbers.

- *I guess.* This sounds uncertain— definitely not the image you want to project!

- *Little.* Don't belittle your accomplishments, as in "This is a *little* report/project I wrote/developed."

- *Probably.* This suggests unnecessary doubt: "The technique I developed would *probably* be useful in your department." This statement sounds more convincing: "I believe the technique I developed would be useful in your department."

This is a small sample of words and phrases that can diminish your image, but it is designed to illustrate the concept. Ask members of your support system to help you identify other verbal credibility robbers and to remind you when you use them.

Meet Business Etiquette Expectations. Business etiquette refers to expected professional behavior in business, and it is based on courtesy and cultural norms. Etiquette blunders include leaving your cell phone ringer on during a business meeting and licking gravy off your fingers during a business lunch. Appropriate business etiquette is also important in conducting global business successfully; an unintentional etiquette breach can quickly squash a delicate international transaction. For example, in Asia, presenting your business card using only one hand is considered rude.

Business etiquette is a key factor in hiring. Your behavior in an interview gives your potential employer clues to how you'll treat clients and customers. For example, during an interview lunch, one applicant lost the job when he wiped his nose with his napkin. Any error in etiquette can cost you the job during an interview situation. Etiquette expectations are getting more attention in the interview process. To learn more about this topic, conduct an Internet search for current tips on business etiquette.

Heed These Additional Tips. The following are additional tips for effective communication:

- **Keep the interview businesslike.** Do not discuss personal, domestic, or financial problems. The purpose of the interview is to explore how well your qualifications and interests match the needs of the employer. This is where you need to focus your remarks.

- **Try to demonstrate a sense of humor.** Most employers look for job applicants with a sense of humor. Humor is an important factor in working well with other people and is a sign of intelligence. Use humor only when appropriate, however, and don't tell jokes; they're not suitable for an interview. Making yourself the subject of the humor is usually safe.

- **Don't ramble.** Be concise, yet not curt, with your replies. Rambling is frequently a nervous response. Answer questions with required information, adding anything you think is relevant or especially important; then stop talking or ask a question.

- **Focus on your goal.** Keep coming back to the main purpose in the interview: determining how you and the employer can mutually benefit. If the conversation strays too far from this subject, bring it back in that direction. Get feedback from the interviewer to clarify how you're coming across. Stop and ask: "Do you think my skills in that area would be helpful to you?" If the answer is yes, you know you're on the right track. If the answer is no or unclear, clarify how you are qualified for the job.

SUCCESS TIP

Keep your verbal communication positive, focused on how you fit the job, and courteous.

Body Language

Through life experiences, people become experts at sending and interpreting nonverbal messages. Nonverbal communication, or *body language*, is powerful. A severe frown can melt the warmest smile; a yawn during a speech speaks for itself. What emotions or qualities do you associate with these behaviors: (a) hands on hips and glaring face, (b) extreme fidgeting, (c) lack of eye contact, (d) slouched posture, (e) uplifted posture, (f) pleasant smile, (g) limp handshake?

See How Body Language Packs a Punch! Body language has the greatest impact of the three sources of communication; it carries more impact than the words you say. To succeed in interviews, keep your body language positive.

During an interview, your body language is a major factor. If you speak persuasively during your interview but your body language conveys arrogance, lack of enthusiasm, excessive nervousness, or other negative messages, the interviewer typically will be more influenced by your negative body language than by what you say.

In face-to-face communication, the three elements of communication that affect the listener or receiver are verbal communication, voice qualities, and nonverbal communication. The impact of each of these sources is illustrated in Figure 11-2. Because body language impacts communication so highly, focus on sending positive nonverbal messages to maximize your interview effectiveness.

Even though words have the least impact in communication, the content must be appropriate for the situation. (This is where your research pays off.)

You must also speak correctly (to project professionalism and competence). A glaring grammatical error could vaporize your chances for a job.

Use Positive Body Language to Your Advantage.

Follow the easy body language pointers below. They will speak well for you during your job search and will help you achieve important goals throughout your career. Also pay attention to the body language of others.

1. **Relax.** If you're tense, your body language will project that tension.

   a. Most importantly, be well rested for the interview so you will be alert.

   b. Complete your research on the industry, organization, and interviewer ahead of time. Stop preparing the night before the interview; then relax and let your preparation pay off the next day.

   c. On the day of the interview, exercise; do some stretching, running, and/or yoga. Exercise is one of nature's best techniques for relaxing your body and your mind. Be sure to allow adequate time in your day to do some form of exercise prior to your interview. You will feel greater energy and more relaxed—both excellent reasons to do so.

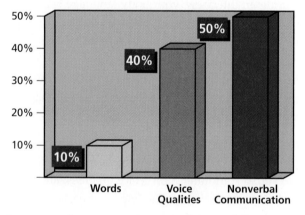

Figure 11-2: Three Sources of Communication and the Impact of Each

   d. During the interview, occasionally change your position in your seat; this relaxes muscular body tension and breaks the rigid feeling that nervousness can cause.

   e. Don't hurry movements and breathe deeply to aid relaxation. This will help you project confidence and will also reduce anxiety.

   f. Smile—it's an effective tension breaker (for you and the interviewer)!

   g. Visualize your success in detail. Project enthusiasm and likability; concentrate on your capabilities.

2. Give a firm **handshake.** Because touch is the keenest physical sense, your handshake will greatly bolster or detract from your credibility. The best handshake is firm and is accompanied by confident eye contact and a pleasant smile.

3. **Make eye contact.** Making good eye contact is essential to achieving effective communication. It conveys that you really care about what the person has to say. It also conveys confidence, intelligence, competence, and honesty. This doesn't mean you should glue your eyes to the interviewer; it does mean you should look at the interviewer, especially when he or she is talking. Break the eye contact at natural points in the discussion. Avoid letting your eyes dart back and forth around the room. If you are extremely uncomfortable looking directly into the eyes of the interviewer, look at the forehead. This gives the impression of looking into his or her eyes. In a group interview, periodically make eye contact with each person.

4. **Maintain good posture.** Good posture conveys that you're composed, respectable, alert, and strong. Sit, stand, and walk with your head up and your back straight. Slouching conveys that you're bored, disinterested, lazy, or unintelligent. Crossing your arms and legs can be interpreted as being closed or stubborn.

Use assertive eye contact and a pleasant facial expression.

5. **Maintain a pleasant facial expression.** Aim for a pleasant, uplifted facial expression. Avoid frowning, licking your lips, clenching your jaw, or any other nervous or downturned expression.

6. **Don't fidget.** Fidgeting is distracting and makes you look nervous, self-conscious, and unsure of your ability to get the job.

7. **Mirror communication behaviors of the interviewer.** Some people have intense, highly energetic body language and voice qualities; others are more relaxed in both. People are most comfortable communicating with others who have styles similar to their own. Subtly mirror, or match, your interviewer's style, speed, and tone of voice, but don't overdo it. Never mirror negative behavior. Much has been written about this technique of mirroring communication behaviors (called neurolinguistic programming)—more than can be

included here. Consider reading more about this skill and developing the technique.

Communicate Trustworthiness. During your interview, conveying trustworthiness, which also conveys believability, is essential. Interviewers will not hire people they think are untrustworthy.

Conveying trust is almost entirely a nonverbal function. Trust is conveyed through positive nonverbal messages that convince the listener's emotional brain center. Trust is a dynamic emotional response that is learned in infancy and childhood and that remains permanently embedded in the brain. We learned to trust people who projected caring, competence, warmth, and self-confidence through their body language. As adults, we still evaluate the trustworthiness of others this same way.

How can you convey these trustworthy, believable qualities: *warmth, caring, competence,* and *self-assurance?* You can do this through positive nonverbal communication:

- A firm, warm handshake
- A pleasant facial expression and direct eye contact
- Erect posture (sitting and standing)
- An energetic, pleasant voice tone
- A tall, deliberate walk

Develop Assertive Body Language. Concentrate on sending assertive messages and eliminating passive or aggressive nonverbal habits. Three styles are defined below.

1. **Assertive Body Language.** This body language is relaxed, open, and confident. It agrees with and supports your words and conveys competence, self-assurance, caring, and credibility.

2. **Passive Body Language.** This body language looks nonenergetic and diminishes credibility by conveying insecurity, weakness, anxiety, and a lack of self-assurance and competence.

3. **Aggressive Body Language.** This body language appears brash and overbearing and sends offensive messages that convey hostility, pushiness, intimidation, and a domineering attitude.

Observe Additional Body Language Tips. Also pay attention to the following nonverbal do's and don'ts:

DO

- Do sit with your body slightly to the side, rather than directly facing the interviewer. This tends to promote an attitude of openness and a relaxed atmosphere.

- Do keep your hands apart to avoid fidgeting. Rest them on the arms of the chair and keep them still. Keep your hands relaxed, not in tight fists.

DON'T

- Don't bring you hand to your face; it can be interpreted as insecurity.

- Don't nod your head too much or tilt it to one side. Both actions detract from your message.

- Don't grimace or frown and don't blink too frequently.

To practice developing positive body language, arrange your own videotaped practice interview. Review the tape, watching carefully for body language that needs correction.

Complete Career Action 11-2

Watch Your Interviewer's Body Language. Watch to see what the interviewer's body language is saying. The interviewer may lean forward, signaling you to expand on what you are saying. If the interviewer shuffles papers, looks around the room, or gives other nonverbal clues that you should finish speaking, heed the signal.

Keep listening and watching to determine whether what you are saying is clearly understood. Retreat from a subject if you observe that it's not being well received.

SUCCESS TIP

To project trust and credibility quickly, use positive body language in the first 30 seconds and throughout the interview. Focus on pleasant facial expression, good posture and eye contact, and a strong handshake.

CAREER ACTION 11-2

Body Language Self-Inventory

 Directions: Access Career Action 11-2 on your Learner's CD, or turn to page 210 and complete the Body Language Self-Inventory. This assignment will help you identify passive and aggressive body language habits you can begin eliminating to increase your communications effectiveness.

PERSONAL BEST

Listening Skills

While you may think of the interviewing process primarily in terms of talking, listening is just as important. You need to listen to the interviewer carefully for important details regarding the job requirements, the organization, and the department so you can respond appropriately. Follow these tips to become a more effective and active listener:

- Address your interviewer using his or her proper name.

- Communicate with undivided attention; resist distractions.

- Nod as appropriate.

- Repeat or summarize main ideas.

- Ask questions as appropriate to clarify meanings.

- Listen "between the lines" for the underlying messages.

- Don't argue or interrupt.

- Maintain eye contact (not too intense).

- Maintain an "open" position (don't cross arms or legs; keep hands unclenched).

- Maintain same eye level (sit or stand as appropriate).

LISTENING: THE SILENT POWER PLAY

Concentrate on listening to every word the interviewer says. Never interrupt the interviewer; this is considered rude. If the interviewer asks a question you don't understand, politely ask him or her to repeat it. If you don't understand the question fully, you won't be able to respond adequately.

Silence Is Sometimes Used as a Power Play. The interviewer may ask a question, you then provide the proper response, but the interviewer doesn't respond—a technique to test your confidence and ability to handle stress or uncertainty.

If you experience this silence power play, do not retract your statement—just wait calmly. You have no obligation to continue talking if you answered adequately. By doing this, you will pass the "test" and project a mature, confident image. Break a long silence by asking whether the interviewer needs more information or by asking a related question. Be prepared to handle silence.

You Can Also Use Silence. If you are asked a difficult question, giving an answer too quickly and without enough thought could be detrimental. You're entitled to think carefully about the question and prepare your response. The employer wouldn't want you to solve problems on the job without adequate thought and planning. However, avoid long pauses in a telephone or video-based interview; such pauses can project slow thinking abilities.

Emphasizing Your Qualifications

In your interview, you need to convince the employer that you are the best-qualified person for the job. If you don't, you won't be hired. To convince the employer, focus on how your skills and experience can benefit the employer. The way you handle discussion of your qualifications will be a determining factor in whether you get the job.

Getting hired can be compared to making a sale. In this case, the products are you and your capabilities. You complete the "sale" by effectively emphasizing how your capabilities can benefit the employer.

Develop and Use a 60-Second Commercial.

To help make the sale, develop a 60-Second Commercial. This commercial is a power-packed summary of the benefits you can offer. As a starting point, think of times you provided benefits to an employer or a volunteer organization. Employers are persuaded to "buy" (hire) the person who can offer benefits in one or more of these areas:

- Increasing sales/profits/productivity

- Decreasing costs

- Saving time

- Solving problems

- Increasing convenience

- Enhancing image

- Improving relationships

- Increasing accuracy or efficiency

Give Examples of Measurable Accomplishments and Transferable Competencies. The key is to provide evidence of your capabilities, or proof by example. For instance, if you are skilled at improving work efficiency, give specific examples of demonstrated ability. Use numbers to boost credibility. For example,

> NO: "I work efficiently."

> YES: "I developed an order processing system that reduced processing time by 20 percent."

Since employers are looking for flexible employees, also emphasize your transferable skills, such as your ability to handle diverse responsibilities, manage yourself (attendance, punctuality, and problem solving), and work well with others.

Be sure your 60-Second Commercial represents you authentically. If it doesn't, it can lead to a mismatch between you and the company. A lack of honesty can eliminate you from the competition; don't sell what you can't deliver.

Keep Your Commercial Concise. Assume that your target employer requires you to summarize your job qualifications in a 60-second videotape. Just as in a television commercial, your interview commercial must be short, relevant, and convincing.

During your interview, use your 60-Second Commercial to focus on your qualifications for the job.

Tailor Your Commercial to Each Employer. Career Action 11-3, on page 202, guides you through the development of a persuasive summary of your qualifications tailored for each employer.

SUCCESS TIP

Make the sale: Deliver a polished "interview commercial" emphasizing the heart of your qualifications. Include measurable accomplishments whenever possible.

Review the 60-Second Commercials in Figure 11-3. See how they focus on employer benefits, emphasizing the results-oriented accomplishments and transferable competencies. Notice how they are phrased in the proof-by-example format and are concise phrases, rather than complete sentences. (In an actual interview, use complete sentences.)

Complete Career Action 11-3

60-SECOND COMMERCIAL SAMPLE #1

Job Target: Sales representative with Axion Inc., a consumer product company

Experience Credentials: Two years in retail sales at Computer Logistics, Inc.

Education Credentials: B.A. in sales and marketing

Proof of Benefits Provided

- Increased school newspaper revenues 22 percent as advertising assistant

- Voted "Most Helpful Clerk" by customers in Service Excellence contest at Ralston Pharmacy

- Received performance ratings of "excellent" in accurate, quick sales for two years at Computer Logistics

Related Job Skills/Preferences

- Highly skilled in record keeping, use of personal computers, business math

- Enjoy travel, open to relocation

Transferable Competencies

- Maintain a professional appearance and have good communication skills

- Strong interpersonal relations skills

60-SECOND COMMERCIAL SAMPLE #2

Job Target: Graphics/text specialist position with Action Publishers

Experience Credentials: Worked 18 months as graphics/text processing assistant, Westville State College Print Center

Education Credentials: Associate of Applied Business Degree, Westville State College

Proof of Benefits Provided

- Developed priority scheduling method, resulting in 99 percent on-time delivery

- Developed three graphic-intensive brochures that were selected by school for national student recruitment campaign

Related Job Skills/Preferences

- Key 70 wpm

- Skilled in English usage

- Proficient in Word, Excel, graphics design, and desktop publishing software

- Operate personal computers, printers, networks, and other office equipment

- Enjoy all aspects of document/graphic development

Transferable Competencies

Punctual, self-starter, resourceful in information management, skilled in computer technology, excellent language skills

Figure 11-3: 60-Second Commercial Samples

60-Second Commercial

 Directions: Access Career Action 11-3 on your Learner's CD, or follow the steps outlined below. Prepare your own 60-Second Commercial.

1. **Prepare a rough draft.** On separate paper, prepare a rough draft of your basic commercial.

2. **Use short phrases, not full sentences.** The goal is to say the most about your qualifications in the fewest possible words.

3. **Name your targeted job position and the employer.**

4. **Briefly summarize education and training.** Review your resume and Career Action 2-1: Education, Training, and Organizational Activities Inventory as a reference.

5. **Focus on "Proof of Benefits Provided."** Describe relevant examples of your work performance and accomplishments and successful use of your job-specific skills. Whenever possible, use numbers or percentages to measure the success. Also emphasize benefits you can provide for the employer.

6. **List your job skills and transferable competencies most relevant to the job target.** Review Career Actions 3-1 and 3-2 on pages 36 and 37 for the lists of top job-specific and transferable skills.

7. **Tailor each commercial.** Use your commercial draft as a base, and tailor it for each target employer. Practice delivering your commercial aloud, but don't memorize it word for word, sounding as though you are reading a script and lacking energy. Take a copy of your commercial with you to the interview. If you have a momentary brain drain, quickly scan it, but don't read from it directly.

Polish and Focus the Content. Your aim is to prepare a brief, polished summary of your qualifications. The heart of your 60-second sales message should emphasize how you can benefit the employer. It is your interview billboard saying "Here's what I can do for you!" This helps the interviewer focus on the strengths you have to offer.

Deliver Your 60-Second Commercial. To target an opening for your commercial, ask the interviewer to review the scope of the job responsibilities and the reason for the opening. Pay attention to the answers. If necessary, probe further to clarify what the employer really needs. Then discuss the benefits you can offer to meet those needs. Pick from your master 60-Second Commercial those items that best fit the needs expressed by the interviewer—that's good selling!

Be ready for any situation; practice delivering the full-length version of your commercial as well as a shorter one (a 60-second and a 30-second version). Remember, the more often buyers see or hear a sales message, the more likely they buy. Whenever possible, weave your commercial into the interview—perhaps the longer version first, followed later by the shorter one. However, don't overdo it; twice is probably enough.

If the person interviewing you isn't an experienced interviewer (which can happen), you must take the initiative to deliver your commercial. An untrained interviewer may never ask you directly about your qualifications. Be sure you present them in your interview.

Complete Career Action 11-4

CAREER ACTION 11-4

Summary of Core Areas of Successful Interviewing

Directions: Write a summary discussing how you can apply in your own job search the interview strategies presented thus far in Chapter 11. Explain specifically how you can apply the techniques presented relating to each of the following:

1. Attitude
2. Image and Appearance
3. Verbal Communication

4. Nonverbal Communication
5. Listening
6. Job Qualifications

SUCCESS TIP

Help interviewers remember your strengths: Always deliver your interview commercial—even if you only get 30 seconds to do it!

USE YOUR PORTFOLIO ITEMS AND INTERVIEW MARKETING KIT

Interviewers agree that applicants who prepare well for interviews gain a decided advantage over those who don't; those who prepare always perform better. By preparing well, you will project professionalism and organizational skills and increase your own sense of readiness.

Select Portfolio Items

Before each interview, select the items most appropriate for your current job target from your Career

"When your work speaks for itself, don't interrupt."

Mark Twain

Portfolio (see Chapter 3, "Your Career Portfolio"; also see "Career Portfolio" and "Interview Marketing Kit" in Appendix B: Career Management and Marketing Tools). Place the portfolio items you select in the Interview Marketing Kit described below.

Prepare and Use an Interview Marketing Kit

To round out your interview preparation, assemble and take with you an Interview Marketing Kit. Use a professional-looking binder or small attaché case to carry selected portfolio and other items. A regular briefcase is not recommended because interviewers might view it as overkill. The items to include in your kit are listed in Figure 11-4.

Well in advance of your interview, prepare your 60-Second Commercial and the list of questions you want to ask. For guidelines in developing your questions, refer to "Plan Now: Your Questions Count!" in Chapter 14.

Arrange the portfolio items in your Interview Marketing Kit to best show how your abilities relate to the employer's needs.

INTERVIEW MARKETING KIT CONTENTS

1. **Items from Career Portfolio for this interview:**

   - Job-related samples of your work, if applicable (from your work and/or educational or training experience)

   - Required certificates, licenses, transcripts, or other related documents

   - Spare copies of your resume

   - Letters of recommendation

   - List of references appropriate for the job

2. **A copy of your 60-Second Commercial** summarizing your qualifications for the job (skills, education, and experience)

3. **A notebook with a list of pertinent questions** you can ask during the interview (see Chapter 14)

4. **Professional preparation items**

   - Pens and pencils

   - An appointment calendar

Figure 11-4: Interview Marketing Kit Contents

Practice Using Your Marketing Materials

To capture the interviewer's attention, refer first to an item representing one of your most outstanding accomplishments. Save another exceptional item to use toward the end of your interview to leave a favorable last impression.

Practice using your portfolio items so the actual delivery will be smooth. Have a friend give you a mock interview, and practice referring to your portfolio items at key points during the interview.

Suppose the interviewer asks, "How important do you think it is to keep up with changing technology?" At this point, you could say, "I think it is very important, and I have taken several classes to update my software skills." Then provide an appropriate example of remaining up to date with technology in your field. By rehearsing, you will be able to work the portfolio into the interview naturally.

SUCCESS TIP

Be prepared and organized; take with you an Interview Marketing Kit containing items from your career portfolio and other items you may need in the interview.

Use Portfolio Items Wisely

Relying only on the portfolio items during interviews to convince the interviewer of your qualifications is a big mistake. It's like a speaker relying on only one set of slides. The focus of the interview is still on you. Your personal appearance and your nonverbal and verbal communication skills are essential. The portfolio items are a visual aid to add further dimension to selling your qualifications.

Where appropriate, use your portfolio materials to enhance your demonstration of qualifications.

Do no misrepresent yourself in the portfolio items; the work must be your own. Be prepared to reproduce the work if requested to do so during pre-employment testing. Select your portfolio items to match specific employers and jobs. Do not use every item in your primary portfolio for every interview.

An important part of your research is learning whether your targeted employers would likely be interested in reviewing a career portfolio during interviews. Some employers don't want or have time to review portfolios during interviews.

Refer to Your Portfolio Items and Take Notes

Before you refer to any portfolio items in your Interview Marketing Kit and before you make notes, ask whether the interviewer has any objections. Pay attention to the answer, and follow the interviewer's wishes.

An exception is referring to your appointment calendar. If you need to schedule a follow-up meeting or an activity, having your appointment book handy

projects organization. You want to confirm future appointments immediately. Doing them at a later time could result in a lost opportunity; the interviewer is likely to make a future commitment while you're still in the interview.

Prepare an Interview Survival Pack

With a little planning, you can avoid an interview sabotaging experience. Prepare a separate survival pack containing personal hygiene items (toothbrush and toothpaste, comb, even deodorant); a spare tie or nylons; and anything else you might need to look, smell, and be your best under any circumstances. Put your gear in a zippered pouch that fits neatly into your Interview Marketing Kit, or if you travel by car, store it there.

Limit Interviews to Two a Day

After two interviews in a day, performance levels typically drop. Don't jeopardize your chances; take a breather and gear up for the next day.

AVOID INTERVIEW DISQUALIFIERS

The following is a list of important reminders. Avoid committing any of these blunders. Any one of these could cost you the job:

1. Don't sit down until the interviewer invites you to; waiting is courteous.

2. Don't bring anyone else to the interview; it makes you look immature and insecure.

3. Don't smoke.

4. Don't put anything on or read anything on the interviewer's desk; it's considered an invasion of personal space.

5. Don't chew gum or have anything else in your mouth; this projects immaturity.

6. If you are invited to a business meal, don't order alcohol. When ordering, choose food that's easy to eat while carrying on a conversation.

7. Don't offer a limp handshake; it projects weakness. Use a firm handshake.

WRAP UP THE INTERVIEW IN YOUR FAVOR

To wrap up the interview in your favor, clarify what to expect next in the interview process and restate your qualifications.

Clarify What to Expect Next

You must know what to expect next in the interview process. Before you leave the interview, clarify:

1. What, if anything, you should do in the way of follow-up to the interview.

2. How long you should expect to wait before the hiring decision is made. (If you're considering another job, this is especially important.)

3. How the interviewer prefers you to follow up (by telephone, by letter, or in person).

The following sample dialogue shows how to get this information:

You:	When should I expect to hear whether I am selected for the position?
Interviewer:	We'll notify all applicants of our decision within two weeks.
You:	Do you mind if I check back with you?
Interviewer:	I prefer that you don't until we notify you.
or	
Interviewer:	No, I don't mind.
You:	How would you prefer I do that—by telephone, by mail or e-mail, in person?
Interviewer:	I prefer that you telephone my assistant.

> *"We judge ourselves by what we feel capable of doing, while others judge us by what we have already done."*
>
> Henry Wadsworth Longfellow

You are clarifying *how* you will be notified of the hiring decision, *when* you will be notified, *whether* the interviewer objects to your checking back, and *how* the interviewer prefers that you check back. In every instance, you are helping yourself in the job campaign.

Use the Clincher

As you near the close of your interview, make a point of leaving your interviewer with a clear picture of how you fit the job. Bring the interview full circle by asking a question in a courteous tone, similar to this example:

"Would you please summarize the most important qualifications you're looking for in filling this position?"

Once the interviewer has answered, you can restate your skills, experience, and other assets that meet these needs. (Run your 60- or 30-Second Commercial one more time.) This important clincher gives you one last chance to make the sale—to market the products (you and your qualifications for the job). People remember best what they hear first and last in any communication.

CLOSE THE INTERVIEW SKILLFULLY

Some applicants lose the race for the job by not clearing the final hurdle—closing the interview skillfully. Don't let down for a moment with regard to your posture, attitude, and verbal and nonverbal communication skills. Use the following techniques to close your interview skillfully:

- Watch for signs from the interviewer that it's time to wrap up. Signs include asking whether you have any further questions, tidying up papers on the desk, pushing the chair back, or simply sitting back in the chair. Heed the cue. Don't make the interviewer impatient by droning on at this point.

- If the interviewer is not skilled at interviewing, help wrap up the interview smoothly by asking: "Is there anything else you need to discuss with me? I know you are busy, and I appreciate the time you have given me for this interview."

- Request a commitment from the interviewer to notify you when an applicant has been selected. Imply that this is not the only job you are considering: "By what date will you make your decision on this position? I'd appreciate knowing within the next two weeks so I can finalize my plans."

- Before you leave, clarify any follow-up activities the interviewer expects from you. If a second interview is arranged, write down the date, time, place, and name of the person who will be interviewing you. If you are to provide additional information, credentials, or references, before you leave, make a note and verify what you are supposed to do.

- If you're seriously interested in the job, say so! Just as in effective sales, the person who asks is most likely to get. Interviewers are impressed with expressions of interest; candidates who directly express their interest strengthen their position. Offer a simple statement; for example, "I'd be pleased to be a part of this organization" or "After talking with you, I'm convinced this is the job I want, and I believe my qualifications would be an asset to the XYZ Corporation. Please consider me seriously for this position."

SUCCESS TIP

Close the interview skillfully. Pay attention to the interviewer's signals for closure. If possible, run your commercial one more time to focus on your capabilities. Find out how you should follow up and when a hiring decision will be made.

- As you leave, remember to use the interviewer's name: "Thank you for providing me with this interview, Mr. Carpenter."

- Be conscious of your posture as you stand up, keeping your shoulders back and your head up. A warm smile with a firm handshake confirms your friendly and positive attitude. Once you leave the interviewer's office, you are still interviewing! Thank the receptionist or assistant by name, and add a brief parting greeting.

Review Figure 11-5 to reinforce the areas that employers consider most important during the interview.

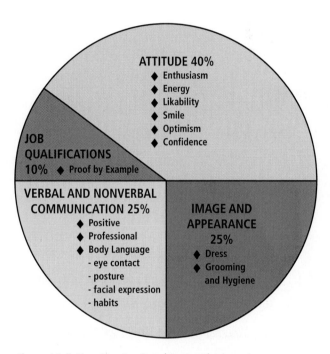

Figure 11-5: How You Are Rated During the Interview

Complete Career Action 11-5

Complete Career Action 11-6

Summary of Fine Points for Interview Success

 Directions: Write a summary of how you plan to apply the information presented for each of the following aspects of interviewing.

1. **Your Interview Marketing Kit.** What will yours consist of?

2. **Your Interview Survival Pack.** What should be in yours?

3. **Interview Disqualifiers.** Which apply to you?

4. **How to Wrap Up the Interview in Your Favor.** Summarize how you plan to wrap up your interview favorably. Explain how you will find out what method of follow-up contact the interviewer prefers.

5. **Close the Interview Skillfully.** Summarize how you plan to end your interview.

Use the Internet to Research Interview Strategies

Directions: Visit the web sites listed below, visit other sites you favor, or use search engines to locate and summarize at least four strategies for effective interviewing. Look for new ideas that will be useful to you. Write a summary of your findings. If you find new information, research further and discuss the topic(s) in the classroom, with your career services staff, and with interview specialists.

Search strings and topics to check: *Interview tips, techniques,* or *strategies and interview portfolios*

The Black Collegian Online (see "Monthly Issues")	www.black-collegian.com
CareerJournal (*The Wall Street Journal*)	www.careerjournal.com
Quintessential Careers	www.quintcareers.com
FlipDog.com	www.flipdog.com
Job.Interview.net	www.job-interview.net
JobWeb.com (National Association of Colleges and Employers)	www.jobweb.com
Monster.com	www.monster.com

✓ CHECKLIST:

Interviewing Like a Pro

Check each of the actions you are currently taking to increase your career success:

☐ Projecting enthusiasm and a positive attitude in interviews, which are big factors in hiring

☐ Projecting professionalism; smiling, dressing neatly and appropriately and being clean and neat

☐ Using positive verbal communication; using positive terms; and avoiding grammatical errors, slang, and credibility-robbing terms

☐ Using positive body language in the first 30 seconds and throughout the interview to project trust and credibility quickly

☐ Making the sale by delivering a polished interview commercial that emphasizes qualifications and includes measurable accomplishments whenever possible

☐ Being prepared and organized; taking to the interview an Interview Marketing Kit containing appropriate portfolio items

☐ Closing the interview skillfully; paying close attention to the interviewer's signals for closure; running the commercial one more time to focus on capabilities; and finding out how to follow up and when a hiring decision will be made

critical thinking *Questions*

1. What aspects of the applicant do interviewers focus on most?

2. How can the job applicant demonstrate a positive attitude during the interview?

3. What negative nonverbal habits are the most important for you to eliminate to improve your interview abilities?

4. What is the most important information the applicant must convey to the interviewer?

5. What are the two most important items of information you should include in your 60-Second Commercial?

Body Language Self-Inventory

Part 1

Directions: Review the following nonverbal descriptions, and place a check mark next to each item that describes your body language habits. Review your answers and circle any that are aggressive or passive; make a list of them. Then in Part 2, prepare a list of the habits you think are most important to change. Finally, take action to correct these habits, and get others to remind you when you exhibit them.

POSTURE

Behavior	Style	Behavior	Style
☐ comfortably upright	Assertive	☐ overbearing, intimidating	Aggressive
☐ relaxed, balanced	Assertive	☐ wooden, tight	Passive
☐ open, not constricted	Assertive	☐ slumped shoulders	Passive
☐ overly stiff	Aggressive	☐ slumped back/spine	Passive
☐ arms/legs crossed	Aggressive		

HANDSHAKE

Behavior	Style	Behavior	Style
☐ appropriately firm	Assertive	☐ held too long	Aggressive
☐ connect between thumb/first finger	Assertive	☐ limp	Passive
☐ shake from elbow through hand	Assertive	☐ from wrist through hand	Passive
☐ held appropriate length of time	Assertive	☐ held too briefly	Passive
☐ a "bone-crushing" grip	Aggressive	☐ grasping fingers only	Passive

FACIAL EXPRESSION

Behavior	Style	Behavior	Style
☐ open, relaxed, pleasant	Assertive	☐ clenched jaw	Aggressive
☐ frowning	Aggressive	☐ wrinkling forehead	Passive
☐ moody, sulking	Aggressive	☐ biting or licking lips	Passive
☐ tight upper lip, pursed mouth	Aggressive	☐ continual smiling	Passive

Continued on next page.

CAREER ACTION 11-2 (CONTINUED)

EYE CONTACT

Behavior	Style	Behavior	Style
☐ comfortably direct	Assertive	☐ constantly looking down	Passive
☐ staring off, bored expression	Aggressive	☐ blinking rapidly	Passive
☐ sneer or looking down nose	Aggressive	☐ frequent shift of focus	Passive
☐ direct stare	Aggressive	☐ no eye contact or avoidance	Passive

VOICE QUALITIES

Behavior	Style	Behavior	Style
☐ distinct and clear	Assertive	☐ too loud	Aggressive
☐ controlled, but relaxed	Assertive	☐ arrogant or sarcastic	Aggressive
☐ warm, pleasant tone	Assertive	☐ dull monotone	Passive
☐ energized/suitable emphasis	Assertive	☐ whiny tone	Passive
☐ too rapid	Aggressive	☐ too soft or too slow	Passive
☐ too demanding or urgent	Aggressive	☐ too nasal	Passive

GESTURES

Behavior	Style	Behavior	Style
☐ natural, not erratic	Assertive	☐ hands on hips	Aggressive
☐ occasional gestures to emphasize	Assertive	☐ wooden gestures	Passive
☐ occasional positive head nodding	Assertive	☐ tilting head to one side	Passive
☐ open hand (conveys trust)	Assertive	☐ bringing hand to face	Passive
☐ leaning toward speaker	Assertive	☐ too much head nodding	Passive
☐ pointing finger	Aggressive	☐ fidgeting	Passive
☐ clenched fists	Aggressive		

Continued on next page.

DISTRACTING NONVERBAL HABITS

	Behavior	Style		Behavior	Style
☐	drumming fingers	Passive	☐	fiddling with any object	Passive
☐	use of fillers (*um, uh, you know*)	Passive	☐	rubbing beard or mustache	Passive
☐	jiggling leg/arm	Passive	☐	biting nails	Passive
☐	fiddling with hair/glasses	Passive	☐	scratching	Passive

OTHER HABITS (List other similar habits you have.) _____

	Behavior	Style		Behavior	Style
☐	_____	_____	☐	_____	_____
☐	_____	_____	☐	_____	_____
☐	_____	_____	☐	_____	_____

Part 2

Directions: Review your self-assessment; then list the negative nonverbal habits you plan to change. List them in order of importance (most important change first).

MY GOALS FOR IMPROVING NONVERBAL COMMUNICATION

1. _____

2. _____

3. _____

4. _____

5. _____

chapter 12 MASTER THE ART OF
GETTING INTERVIEWS

In this chapter, you will:

- Develop written scripts for interview requests to be made through a personal visit or by telephone.

- Practice delivering your request for an interview.

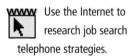 Use the Internet to research job search telephone strategies.

"Present yourself with confidence when communicating with a potential employer. Your own confidence will help convince them that you are the best person for the job. A genuine sense of enthusiasm conveys the high energy and interest level that employers want. Enthusiasm also helps sustain you during the job-search process, encouraging you to follow up, maintain contact and keep a positive outlook—all things that, ultimately, will distinguish you from the crowd."

Charlene Crusoe-Ingram
Vice President of Organization and People Development
Coca-Cola USA

To land your target job, you first need to get an interview. Sound strategies for succeeding in this essential job search step are outlined in Chapter 12. Techniques for arranging interviews directly and indirectly are presented.

DIRECT REQUESTS FOR INTERVIEWS

You can use four direct methods of contacting employers for an interview:

- Personal visit

- Telephone

- Standard letter

- Internet communication

Once you identify a promising employer prospect, your goal is to get an interview. Statistically the most productive methods are face-to-face or telephone contact. Don't write a letter when you can call, and don't call when you can make a personal visit. If you can't visit or call, a standard letter or Internet communication is appropriate. Review your 60-Second Commercial, resume, and cover letter that you prepared earlier. Tailor your request for an interview by emphasizing your strengths and experience that are most relevant to the needs of each prospective employer.

Developing Verbal Effectiveness in Interview Requests

To increase your success rate in landing interviews, focus on being courteous, likable, professional, persuasive, and resourceful. Follow the guidelines below to project likability and professionalism in face-to-face and telephone interview bids:

- Use a friendly tone and moderate pitch and speed.

- Use correct grammar.

- Speak distinctly and confidently.

- Eliminate slang and annoying filler expressions (*um, uh,* or *you know*).

- Be courteous.

- Communicate your message clearly and concisely.

- Emphasize your qualifications before requesting an interview.

Personal contact—in person or by phone—is the best way to make contact for an interview.

Respect the person's time. Most businesspeople will have only a few minutes for your visit or call. If you sense this is not a good time, say something like, "I'd be glad to call/visit you at a more convenient time, if necessary." Remain composed and professional. Do no act inconvenienced or become irritable.

SUCCESS TIP

When you ask for an interview, provide a reason for the receiver to answer yes by emphasizing your qualifications before requesting the interview!

Focusing Your Interview Request

The focus of an effective interview request should be on how your abilities can benefit (even be essential to) the employer. Identify for yourself what advantages your specific qualifications provide and then translate that information into a benefit for the prospective employer. Your employer research is vital and should include finding out who is in charge of the department that could benefit most from your abilities. This is the target person for your interview request.

Review the 60-Second Commercial you developed in Chapter 11 (Career Action 11-3, on page 202). Use a brief modification of it as the base for your request for an interview.

Making a Request Through a Personal Visit

A direct request for an interview through a personal visit is statistically the most successful method of getting an interview. It is difficult for people to ignore you when you're standing in front of them. Here are guidelines for making a successful request for an interview in person:

1. **Dress for the part.** Dress and groom yourself as if you were going to an actual interview.

2. **Research the firm thoroughly beforehand.**

3. **Be prepared.** Take your Interview Marketing Kit (Chapter 11) with you, including your 60-Second Commercial and your resume.

4. **Pay special attention to the gatekeeper** (the person between you and the employer): the administrative support person, supervisor, or human resources specialist. Actively and courteously seek that person's help (see "Breaking Gatekeeper Barriers" later in this chapter).

5. **Present the most concise, action-packed version of your 60-Second Commercial,** and then request an interview.

6. **Thank your contact by name** for his or her time and consideration.

If you don't get an interview, ask for referrals to another department or company that might need your abilities.

Study the example on page 216 of a request made for an interview during a personal visit to an employer. The applicant highlights qualifications, demonstrates knowledge of the employer and the industry, and expresses interest in the job—just the right approach!

SUCCESS TIP

When you make a request for an interview in person, prepare as if you were going to an actual interview. First impressions influence the outcome.

Complete Career Action 12-1

The following paragraphs represent a sample script that someone applying for an administrative support

CAREER ACTION 12-1

Develop Your Personal Request for an Interview

Directions: Read the sample script directly following this Career Action on page 216. Then write or key a script that would be appropriate for you to use when requesting an interview from your prospective job target(s).

position in a medical center might use to make an in-person request for an interview. Please note that there are four parts or sections to this request.

SAMPLE IN-PERSON REQUEST FOR AN INTERVIEW

- **The Opening—**"Hello Mr. Selland; my name is Jaleesa Williams. My instructor, Gerald Johnston, recommends your Information Services Department at Saint Mary's Hospital for its well-organized systems design. I recently completed my education at Mesa College, earning two A.S. degrees—one in Information Management Technology and the second in Medical Administrative Assistant."

- **The 60-Second Commercial Excerpt—**"I worked 18 months as a clerical assistant in the Business Office at Lewis State College while attending school. I'm proficient in Word, Excel, Access, PowerPoint, and Outlook software and have received MOUS certification in each of these software packages. I operate personal computers, networks, and general office equipment. I also type at 70 words per minute and am skilled in English usage."

- **The Request—**"I've developed some time-saving methods for creating templates and macros that are appropriate for your department. Would you have time for me to review them with you today, or would one day next week be more convenient?"

- **The Close—**"Next Tuesday at 10 a.m.? I appreciate your willingness to meet with me so soon, Mr. Selland. I look forward to meeting with you then. Thank you and good-bye."

SUCCESS TIP

Prepare your script and practice asking for an interview before you make a real request.

Requesting an Interview by Telephone

The telephone can be a powerful ally. It demands immediate attention from the person who answers it and reduces the time you need for initial inquiries because delivery is instantaneous. It also can be as informal as you wish and allows for two-way communication. Use the telephone to survey employers and to determine whether they're viable targets for employment. Follow up with personal visits to the most likely prospects.

Using the Telephone Persuasively

Good telephone communication skills will affect the success of your entire working career. You can develop these skills just as you develop any other skill. To prepare and make persuasive job search telephone calls, follow the methods outlined on pages 217-218 in the Personal Best feature and under "Organizing and Placing Telephone Calls" and review the script of a telephone request for an interview on page 218, preceding Career Action 12-2.

Good telephone communication skills are important to your career success. Develop your telephone skills so you can project confidence and enthusiasm in your voice for a positive impression.

PERSONAL BEST

Telephone Skills

Your voice is your personality over the telephone. It makes an immediate impression that can portray you as friendly or distant, confident or timid, relaxed or nervous. These tips from the Dallas, Texas, Online Women's Business Center can help you improve your telephone presence.

- Smile when you speak on the telephone. The muscles used to smile actually relax the vocal cords and create a pleasant voice tone. Try it!

- Don't talk on the phone with food or gum in your mouth; don't drink while talking on the phone. The sounds of drinking and eating are amplified over phone lines.

- When you place a call that you know might be lengthy, ask if it's a good time to talk before you dive into your spiel.

- Know what you want to say before making an important call. Practice the words aloud until they feel comfortable.

- Don't read from a script during a call. Either memorize your script as an actor would or use notes to guide you from one idea to another.

- Don't read your e-mail or catch up on other activities while on the phone. The person you're talking with will know you're distracted.

- Listen and respond to the person on the other end of the line. When you focus on him or her rather than on what you're going to say next, the phone call becomes more conversational.

- Evaluate your voice. Make a tape recording of yourself speaking on the telephone. Is your voice too shrill or strained? Do you speak in a monotone? Are you too soft or too loud? Do you speak too quickly? Too slowly? Do you speak clearly?

Organizing and Placing Telephone Calls

To prepare for and place effective phone calls for your job search, follow the steps outlined below.

1. **Determine the purpose of your call.** Is it to get the name of the hiring individual? Is it to request information? Is it to request an interview?

2. **Learn all you can about the organization before calling.** Get the name of the person you need to contact before you call to request an interview. You may need to make a preliminary call to get this information.

3. **Write out your script completely.** Summarize the key points you need to cover in your call prior to placing the call. Pattern your script after the samples in this chapter, and refer to your 60-Second Commercial. List all the information you need to obtain from your contact. The script or outline is essential. It helps you organize your message, making you sound intelligent and well prepared. It also provides a good reference in case you forget items.

4. **What do you say when someone answers the telephone?**

   a. Identify yourself: "Hello, this is Brenda Bernstein." (Support personnel who screen calls are immediately suspicious of callers who don't give their names or don't state why they are calling. Therefore, be straightforward to eliminate any suspicions instantly.)

   b. Identify your purpose for calling: Deliver your request for an interview, or use a practiced indirect strategy for getting through to the employer.

   c. Get the name of the person who answers: Ask, "Could I please have your name in case I need to talk with you again?" (Write it down. Using this person's name can make him or her far more receptive to helping you.)

   d. Clarify the details: Clarify any follow-up activities you are to complete (pick up an application, supply additional information or references, keep an appointment, and so on). Verify the time and place of any meetings; get the correct spelling and pronunciation of the names of people you will meet.

e. Thank the person by name.

If you need practice before actually calling for an interview, refer to the samples of indirect strategies for getting an interview on page 220. You can ask all the sample questions by telephone or request a meeting to discuss them. Study the telephone script of an interview request, which follows. Qualifications, knowledge of the employer and the industry, and interest in the employer are incorporated.

Like the sample script for an in-person request for an interview, the request for an interview by telephone also consists of four parts. This sample script reflects what might be said in a telephone conversation when trying to secure an interview for a sales representative position.

SAMPLE TELEPHONE REQUEST FOR AN INTERVIEW

- **The Opening**—"Hello, Ms. Hope. This is Stephen Rogowski. I'm just completing research comparing the product quality and service records of computer network manufacturers. I'm impressed with the results XYZ Company has achieved, and I'm interested in learning about your sales representative position."

- **The 60-Second Commercial Excerpt**—"I'm completing my degree in sales and marketing at Lewis State College and have two years of successful retail sales experience. I also was the advertising assistant for our school paper and increased sales by 18 percent this year."

- **The Request**—"Would it be possible to arrange a meeting with you to discuss your sales goals and how I might contribute to them?"

- **The Close**—"Thank you, Ms. Hope. I look forward to meeting with you next Tuesday, the 18th, at 2:30. Good-bye."

Complete Career Action 12-2

CAREER ACTION 12-2

Develop and Practice Requests for an Interview

Part A: Write or key a script that would be appropriate to use in making a telephone request for an interview with your prospective job target(s).

Part B: Turn to your support system for assistance. Do some role-playing and practice following the guidelines below. Deliver your telephone request for an interview to your support system helper.

1. Tape your delivery, play it back, critique it, and improve on it where necessary.

2. Request your helper to ask you questions that require more detail about your qualifications.

3. Practice responding when your helper makes excuses for not scheduling an interview.

4. Practice presenting your qualifications persuasively.

5. Practice turning objections into acceptance.

6. Persevere.

Requesting an Interview by Letter

If you are relying on your cover letter and resume to attract interviews and you have prepared these documents well, you are ready to make your interview request.

First, find out which method is appropriate for your target employer: sending your request by regular mail, by fax, or by e-mail. As a general rule, e-mail is appropriate for a first communication only under these circumstances:

- In communications with peers.
- When it has been requested.
- With high-tech or Internet-oriented companies.

Second, review the instructions in Chapter 10 for preparing and distributing your cover letter. You may also want to use e-mail and a letter to cover both bases. By using both media, you give extra emphasis to your message and increase the likelihood it will be read.

If you don't receive responses from your cover letter and resume within a week to ten days, reinforce the request through a telephone call or personal visit.

Responding to a Job Posted on the Internet

If you find a job posted on the Internet through a general job-posting site or a specific employer's web site, follow the instructions provided exactly. Often employers want you to e-mail or fax your resume and a cover letter to them. They may use a special code to identify a specific job opening; be sure to include it in your cover letter. They may also have an online resume form you fill out or a block into which you paste your resume or letter. All of these options become your technical "request for an interview."

INDIRECT STRATEGIES FOR LANDING INTERVIEWS

To reach an employer, to bypass a gatekeeper, or to find the hidden job market, you may need to use an indirect strategy that will lead to a request for an interview. Indirect requests for interviews are especially important during times of high job competition.

Getting Through to the Employer

When job competition is high, many employers are flooded with applicants. They may issue a temporary no-hire policy, which makes personal contact difficult because employees are instructed to notify applicants that no interviews are being scheduled.

This is the time you need to use initiative and persistence. Develop a persuasive reason to contact the person with hiring authority in your target organization.

> *"The people who get on in the world are the people who get up and look for circumstances they want, and if they can't find them, make them."*
>
> George Bernard Shaw

An indirect strategy can create opportunities to meet people in your job target organization who can arrange an interview for you. Although you should not make a direct request for a job during a meeting arranged indirectly, you can discuss your experience and abilities. You may actually convince your contact you would be an asset to the organization—exactly your intention! Also ask whether the employer might need your skills in the future or if your contact could suggest another organization or department that might need someone with your qualifications.

Meet to Discuss Resources Related to Your Field

The indirect strategy samples that follow provide a natural lead to discussing your qualifications. One effective indirect strategy is to arrange a brief meeting with a prospective employer to discuss professional associations and publications in your field. Once you meet, ask the following questions:

- What professional association would keep me informed of industry developments, technological advances in the field, and emerging trends?

- Which professional publications or Internet resources deal specifically with our field?

- Who else could I speak with for further advice on this topic?

Ask for Assistance with Your Career Preparation

If you have limited work experience related to your job target, call to ask for assistance with your career planning and educational preparation. The conversation you have with a prospective employer may be similar to one of the two samples below:

"Hello, Mr. Cuevo. This is Celia Lee. I'm completing an assignment for my career planning course and would appreciate your assistance with some of the research. I'm seeking opinions from people who are recognized and experienced in the field of (your field), which is why I'm calling you. My skills lie in the area(s) of _____. Could you help me identify positions within (your career field) for which these skills would be most useful? I'd also appreciate your recommendations regarding additional course work and preparation I might need."

"My major is _____, and my career objective is _____. I would appreciate your helping me identify elective course work or a minor (another minor) that would strengthen my educational preparation and support my career goal."

If you are seeking help to develop your resume into one prospective employers will not pass over, you can place a telephone call to someone and ask for his or her help in the following manner:

"Hello, Ms. Pappas. This is Nhon Tran. You've been highly recommended to me by Dr. Ivarsen of the Computer Information Systems Department of Nevada College. I'm developing a professional resume and would very much appreciate your critiquing it."

Follow Up

Then four to six months later you should follow up on your telephone call requesting information on additional preparation to make you more employable and/or your telephone call requesting help to develop your resume. The conversation may be similar to the following:

"Hello, Mr. Cuevo. This is Celia Lee. You gave me some excellent advice six months ago. Would you consider evaluating my preparation now?"

Ask to arrange a meeting, and then approach it as you would an interview—totally prepared! Remember, this person advised you earlier. If you followed the advice, he or she could consider hiring you for demonstrating initiative and intelligence. (After all, it was his or her idea, so it must be a good one!)

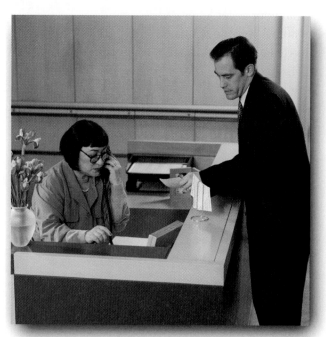

The gatekeeper can be a barrier or a resource in your pursuit of an interview.

Breaking Gatekeeper Barriers

The gatekeeper (the administrative support person, receptionist, or human resources staff) who must screen all job applicants can help, hinder, or destroy your chances for a job with the organization. This person's influence on your job campaign could be considerable, so you need to use good diplomacy skills. The following recommendations will help you establish a good relationship:

- Express respect for the organization, perhaps referring to its reputation for professionalism, reliability, or leadership. A gatekeeper who is happily employed with the organization will likely agree with your comments and may help you.

- Make as much effort to get the gatekeeper on your side as you do to get the employer to hire you. Be personable, courteous, and enthusiastic.

- As in the interview itself, notice the gatekeeper's surroundings. An interested comment from you about a family portrait, a wall decoration, or a desk item can relax the atmosphere. If the gatekeeper seems receptive, you can discuss your job search; you may get useful assistance!

- Ask for the gatekeeper's help in arranging an interview with the employer, indicating your awareness of busy schedules; ask the gatekeeper to suggest the best time to contact the employer. Ask if you could speak with someone else who could tell you more about your areas of interest.

- At the end of your conversation, call the gatekeeper by name and thank the person for his or her assistance. Remember the importance of developing a good rapport with all gatekeepers. Your efforts to do so could help you considerably in your job search campaign.

SUCCESS TIP

Treat gatekeepers (administrative support personnel and receptionists) courteously and professionally. They are often the keys to connecting with the hiring authority.

> *"If you only knock long enough and loud enough at the gate, you are sure to wake up somebody!"*
>
> Henry Wadsworth Longfellow

Uncovering the Hidden Job Market

Seek to uncover the hidden job market mentioned in Chapter 6. These jobs are not advertised. In fact, employers may be unaware they have positions you could fill. It's up to you to make an employer aware of your potential and possibly create a job in the process.

Research and Prepare. To uncover the hidden job market, you need to research carefully and learn as much as possible about the employer's products or services, structure, and so on. Then you need to:

- Analyze how your qualifications can be useful, even essential, to the employer.

- Prepare a dynamic 60-Second Commercial emphasizing how you could benefit the employer and get someone skilled in writing to help you polish it.

The key is to identify how you could provide a useful service or how you could save or make money for the organization.

Find out who is in charge of the department that could use your assets—your hidden job market target. Practice and polish your hidden job market sales pitch. A member of your support system could help by playing the role of your contact and critiquing your presentation.

SUCCESS TIP

Tap into the hidden job market. Resourceful applicants create jobs by researching employer's needs well and by showing how their abilities meet those needs.

Encourage the Need for Your Capabilities. Armed with thorough employer research and a 60-Second Commercial that illustrates how you can benefit the firm, you could uncover a job the employer hasn't even considered.

Think big! The hidden job market is limited only by your imagination. You have everything to gain by tapping into this market in your bid for an interview.

Going Through the Human Resources Department

If your target employer has a strict policy requiring all applicants to be processed through the human resources department, you may have to follow the procedures. Usually, your first step will be to submit an application, a resume, and a cover letter.

If the organization is interviewing, the first interview will likely be a screening interview given in person by a member of the human resources staff. Note, however, that some screening interviews are conducted by telephone to save time and money. One purpose is to verify the information in your cover letter, application, and resume. You will also be judged on your self-confidence, composure, intelligence, and personality. Projecting energy, enthusiasm, and confidence are essential during screening interviews.

If you perform well during a screening interview and if your qualifications appear to be adequate, you may be scheduled for a departmental interview. If the employer doesn't have openings in your area,

find out how to keep your file active and how you can remain informed of the hiring status for the position.

Using Employment Agencies/Contractors

If you are planning to use employment or staffing agencies or employment contractors in your job search, interviews for jobs will be arranged by them. Read each agency's agreement thoroughly to be certain you are satisfied with the method of interviewing. Clarify the procedure carefully before agreeing to it. Review the information presented on employment and staffing agencies and employment contractors in Chapter 6.

Developing a Plan When Your Targeted Job Is Not Open

If your preferred employer is not scheduling interviews because the company has no openings, reevaluate your goal.

If your ultimate goal still is to work for this organization and you think a position is worth waiting for, develop an effective waiting plan. The following guidelines may help:

1. **Take another job during the waiting period.** This work experience can increase your value. During your interim job, you can polish your current skills, develop new ones, and establish a reputation as a valuable employee.

2. **Follow up.** Call your target employer after you have been in your interim job some time and when you think employment opportunities have improved. Ask whether the employer would consider reevaluating your qualifications in light of your new experience, or ask for additional suggestions to improve your employability.

3. **Check back periodically.** Call the human resources department of your target employer to remain informed of the hiring status and to reaffirm your interest. This helps keep you first in line for openings.

If you consider more than one organization to be a prime employer, don't let one discouragement slow you down. Review the techniques presented in this chapter, and rally your efforts toward your next target. Preparation, practice, action, and perseverance pay off!

SUCCESS TIP

Make those calls; send letters; check the Internet. Successful achievement never starts with *if*, *but*, or *later*.

Complete Career Action 12-3

If you have a screening interview with a human resources staff member, project poise and enthusiasm.

CAREER ACTION 12-3

Use the Internet to Find Strategies for Getting Job Interviews

 Directions: Conduct an Internet search to find additional tips for getting job interviews. You may want to look for special tips on using the telephone effectively in the job search. Look for new ideas specifically useful to you. Write a summary of your findings.

Use the following Internet resources or others of your choice to conduct this search.

Quintessential Careers	www.quintcareers.com
Monster.com	www.monster.com
CareerLab	www.careerlab.com
job-interview.net	www.job-interview.net
CareerJournal.com	www.careerjournal.com

✔ CHECKLIST:

Mastering the Art of Getting Interviews

Check each of the actions you are currently taking to increase your career success:

☐ When asking for an interview, providing a reason for the receiver to answer yes by emphasizing qualifications before requesting the interview

☐ When making a request for an interview in person, preparing as if it were an actual interview because first impressions can influence the outcome

☐ Preparing a script and practicing asking for an interview before making a real request

☐ Treating gatekeepers (administrative support personnel and receptionists) courteously and professionally because they are often the key to connecting with the hiring authority

☐ Tapping into the hidden job market because resourceful applicants create jobs by researching employers' needs and by showing exactly how their abilities meet those needs

critical thinking *Questions*

1. What method of making a request for an interview do you think will be most effective in your job search? Why?

2. What are some advantages to making requests for interviews by telephone, rather than by letter?

3. Get creative. Think of an employer you could realistically target for a hidden job market position. What are the needs of this employer based on your research? What special skills and knowledge do you have that represent a hidden job you could perform to meet the employer's needs?

chapter 13 BE PREPARED FOR ANY INTERVIEW STYLE

In this chapter, you will:

- Conduct direct employer research to learn about styles of interviews used in your field.

- **WWW** Use the Internet to search for additional information on interview styles.

- Prepare a summary of the information from this chapter and from your research that is most pertinent to your job search.

"We give a one-on-one interview the first time we interview an applicant. If we bring them back for a second interview, we have two people interview them. Usually, we can get more in-depth in the second interview because the applicant is less nervous. If we are seriously considering hiring the person, we will send them to a staff member that is equal to their level to ask any questions and ensure a good match."

Ron Taylor, CPA
Partner
Robinson, Maynard & Associates

Although employers use several styles of interviews, interviewing basically consists of two approaches: the structured and the unstructured. Sometimes styles are combined within one interview. At other times, the interview usually falls into one of the two approaches. Once you have a job interview scheduled, you greatly improve your chance of success if you find out what style of interview will be used. Usually, the human resources department or receptionist will explain the general interview style and process to you.

THE INTERVIEW CONNECTION

In all interviews, try to give the interviewer a picture of your personal attributes as well as your experience, skills, and other job qualifications. Make your verbal and nonverbal messages positive, incorporating posture, facial expressions, and voice qualities that convey competence, friendliness, energy, and enthusiasm. This helps the interviewer feel comfortable and creates an open tone, which improves the chance for a successful interview. This helps both you and the interviewer relax and improves the natural flow of conversation. When under less tension, you can better communicate the information necessary for a good interview.

THE STRUCTURED INTERVIEW

The structured interview is often used by professional interviewers who work in the human resources department or who are part of a corporate team, panel, or other trained interviewing group. The interviewer often uses a planned pattern of questioning, sometimes recording your responses and making notes on a checklist or interview rating form. Many use the same list of questions for each job applicant to ensure fairness in interviewing. The approach is formal and focuses on obtaining factual information. Because it is highly structured, sometimes this approach doesn't give the interviewer adequate information about the applicant's personality and attitudes.

> *"The spirit, the will to win, and the will to excel are the things that endure."*
>
> Vince Lombardi

SUCCESS TIP

Be friendly, courteous, and positive to establish a good rapport with interviewers and to help relax the tone of overly structured interviews.

The Human Resources Department (Screening) Interview

Large organizations often require applicants to be interviewed first through the human resources department. The *screening interview* is used to identify qualified applicants for the next level of interview and to screen out those who don't have the basic qualifications. Your objectives in this interview are to make your qualifications clear and to try to find out who makes the final hiring decision.

If the interviewer doesn't give you this information during the interview, politely ask who will make the final hiring decision. If you are qualified for the job, this will accomplish two things: The interviewer will feel more obligated to arrange an interview for you with the hiring authority, and you can attempt to arrange the interview if the human resources department does not.

Although it's best to work through regular organizational channels, if your attempts are unsuccessful, try to arrange the interview yourself. Some employers are impressed with an applicant who doesn't give up; other employers may be annoyed the applicant didn't follow protocol. If the human resources department will not help you, setting up your own interview is worth a try—and you just might get the job! Take this approach with care; be assertive, not aggressive.

The interviewer may use a rating sheet to evaluate each applicant. Review Figure 13-1, a typical interview rating form, and notice the categories of evaluation.

The goal of your screening interview is to be scheduled for the next required interview. If the screening interviewer does not tell you, ask what to expect next, who is responsible for making the final hiring decision, and when this decision will be made.

INTERVIEW EVALUATION

Applicant: _____ **Date:** _____

Position: _____

	POOR	FAIR	GOOD	VERY GOOD	EXCELLENT
Resume, Application, Cover Letter					
Attitude, Interest, Enthusiasm					
Communication Skills					
Knowledge of Job/Company					
Education/Training					
Related Experience					
Team Interactive Skills					
Leadership Ability					
Coping Ability (stress, conflict, time demands, and so on)					
Motivation/Goals					
Judgment, Decision Making, Maturity					
Organizational/Planning Skills					
Demonstrated Performance/ Achievements					
Appearance (appropriate dress, grooming)					

Comments: _____

Conclusion: Considering the observations made above and the applicant's qualifications, do you think this person should be considered for the position?

Yes__ No__ Reservations: _____

Interviewer's Signature: _____

Figure 13-1: Typical Interview Rating Form

As a rule, you should expect to have no fewer than two interviews with an employer before a hiring decision is made. Some organizations give three or four interviews before selecting an applicant. A hiring decision is rarely made during the first interview. If you are scheduled for a follow-up interview, you're definitely in the running, so review and polish your interviewing skills. Keep your chin up and your smile broad, and go for the win!

SUCCESS TIP

In screening interviews held on campus or given by an employer's human resources department, find out what the next step in the hiring process will be, who makes the final hiring decision, and when it will be made.

In a behavioral interview, the interviewer might ask you to role-play a situation, such as counseling an unhappy employee.

The Behavioral Interview

In the *behavioral interview*, the interviewer asks questions aimed at getting the applicant to provide specific examples of how he or she has successfully used the required job skills of the job target. This allows the interviewer to evaluate a candidate's experience and behavior as an indicator of the applicant's potential for success. In fact, behavioral interviewing is said to be 55 percent predictive of future on-the-job behavior. If you have completed the activities in Chapter 12, you are ready to handle this style of interview. Your 60-Second Commercial contains the proof-by-example descriptions of your capabilities most relevant to the job target. This is exactly what interviewers are looking for in a behavioral interview.

In the behavioral interview, employers are looking for evidence of skills in the following three areas:

- **Content skills**—work-specific skills, such as computer programming, CAD, and medical transcription.

- **Functional or transferable skills**—skills used with people, things, or information. These are applicable from one job to another, such as good communication or math skills.

- **Adaptive or self-management skills**—personal characteristics, such as being dependable, a team player, a self-directed worker, a problem solver, or a decision maker.

The following are examples of typical behavioral interview questions:

- Give me an example of how you have managed conflict well.

- Give me an example of a time when you had to go above and beyond the call of duty in order to get a job done.

- Describe your leadership experience. Give examples that show your leadership style.

- Describe exactly how you have used this software, equipment, or tool in the past.

S U C C E S S   T I P

In behavioral interviews, provide the proof-by-example descriptions of your capabilities; include relevant parts of your 60-Second Commercial.

Review the techniques in Chapter 11 that deal with attitude and relaxation.

Before the interview, get and memorize the names of every member of the panel. Then during the interview, draw a diagram of the interviewers as they are seated and label the seats with their names (see Figure 13-2). At the close of the interview, thank each one by name and shake hands with each as you leave.

The Campus Interview

Some organizations give *campus interviews* for graduating students in such fields as engineering, electronics, business management, legal, accounting, computer information systems, and marketing. These are prearranged screening interviews, and the techniques vary depending on the organization. They are usually structured interviews, but several styles are used, including the stress interview, the "tell me about yourself" interview, and the panel interview. Each style is explained in detail later in this chapter.

Campus interviews are generally scheduled through the school's career services office. The schedule is closely observed, and the interviewer is forced to evaluate each candidate quickly. (The average interview time is 20 to 30 minutes.) In this type of interview, keep your remarks as concise and to the point as possible. Most interviewers are professionally trained and know how to guide applicants through the fact-finding process. Let the interviewer take the lead, and respond as concisely as possible without omitting pertinent information about your qualifications.

The Board or Panel Interview

In a *board or panel interview*, you talk with more than one person. Focus on the person questioning you at the time, but don't ignore the others. Being relaxed and projecting a self-assured attitude are important.

"Things turn out best for people who make the best of the way things turn out."

John Wooden

The Team Interview

The team interview may be given by a group of three to five employees. Usually, these people have been trained in interviewing techniques. They meet prior to the interview to determine the subject areas each team member will cover with the applicant. A few common questions may be asked by all the team members to give the applicant more than one chance for adequate expression.

In this style, the applicant meets individually with each member of the team; the team and the applicant do not meet together at one time. After the interviewing is completed, the team members meet to discuss the applicant's performance. Using common criteria, members of the team assess the information from the individual sessions and their reactions before identifying the best candidate.

The team interview gives applicants a chance to meet with several people who may be their peers or supervisors on the job. This method of interview ensures a personality fit and increases the chances of establishing rapport with one or more members of the team.

Another team interview tactic is for several interviewers to meet with an applicant at the same time. This method is used when a future hire will be working directly with several managers. Having a candidate meet with several people at once saves time. For out-of-town candidates, meeting several interviewers in a single setting eliminates the need to travel to the prospective employer multiple times, saving money and time.

Before a team interview, learn the names of the members and, if possible, learn something about their areas of expertise. Use this information to help enhance your performance. Also give consistent answers to the individual members' questions.

Figure 13-2: Seating Diagram for a Panel Interview

The Stress Interview

The *stress interview* is usually structured and is designed to test your behavior, logic, and emotional control under pressure. This form of interview is not used routinely. Stress makes it more difficult to assess job qualifications and personal attributes because applicants often become guarded in response to the stress. Stress questions are often reserved for jobs that involve regular pressure. Some stress questions, however, are routinely asked in other types of interviews—even informal ones. Every job has a crisis situation occasionally.

A skillful interviewer may use some stress techniques in combination with an unstructured interview approach to get a well-rounded picture of

your personality. Some techniques used in stress interviewing include (a) remaining silent following your remark, (b) questioning you rapidly, (c) placing you on the defensive with irritating questions or remarks, and (d) criticizing your responses or remarks.

An interviewer may use a stress technique unintentionally. If you encounter one, do not react. Take a deep breath, demonstrate control, and be courteous. This type of behavior earns perfect marks in the stress test! (Refer to Chapter 14 for specific examples of stress questions and suggested responses.)

The "Tell Me about Yourself" Interview

In the *"tell me about yourself" interview*, the interviewer takes a few minutes to build rapport and then says, "Tell me about yourself." Be prepared to handle this style effectively. Once the interviewer asks this question, he or she makes only enough comments to encourage the applicant to keep answering. The purpose is to see whether applicants focus on their qualifications for the job and how the employer would benefit by hiring them. Do not ramble on about your life history—a sure way to disqualify yourself on the spot. Ask questions such as "What exactly do you want to know about—my work experience, educational experience, skills, or extracurricular and community activities?"

Your objective in this case is to highlight your capabilities (personal attributes, accomplishments, skills, pertinent training, work experience, and so on). After you think you have covered these topics, ask, "Would you like me to clarify or expand any area for you?" This helps you focus on the information the interviewer wants.

SUCCESS TIP

If the interviewer says "Tell me about yourself," focus completely on your qualifications for the job. Don't talk about your life history.

During a job interview, ask questions to be sure you are providing the information the interviewer wants.

SUCCESS TIP

To ace multilevel interviews in which you are interviewed by several people, keep your answers consistent and maintain energy and enthusiasm.

The Telephone Interview

The *telephone interview* is a cost-effective screening device. If you expect to be interviewed by telephone, prepare by getting a member of your network to role-play the interviewer. Practice delivering your 60-Second Commercial and giving responses to typical interview questions. These tips will help you succeed in a telephone interview:

1. Post your resume and 60-Second Commercial where you can refer to them easily and eliminate all distractions.

2. Focus on why you are interested in working for the prospective employer (on the basis of your research and understanding of the employer's products or services, current developments, philosophies, and so on).

3. Be courteous and friendly; let the caller lead the conversation, but add questions of your own.

4. Stand up, smile, and speak directly into the mouthpiece while you're talking; this gives your voice more energy and a pleasant tone.

5. Beware of yes/no answers. They give no real information about your abilities.

6. Be factual in your answers; be brief yet thorough.

7. If you need time to think about a question, avoid using repetitive phrases to buy time; simply say, "Let me think about that."

8. Use the "clincher" technique described in Chapter 11: Ask what skills, knowledge, and qualities the employer

The Corporate Ladder Interview

Large organizations sometimes schedule *corporate ladder (or multilevel) interviews*. The first rung of the ladder is the human resources department interview, which screens for applicants qualified to progress to the next step. The next interview is usually with a divisional manager or department head and is more detailed and specific regarding your relevant qualifications, skills, and experience.

From this step, you might have one or two more interviews, perhaps with a department manager, followed by the immediate section supervisor for the position. Each step will be progressively more specific in evaluating your suitability for the job. If you are asked the same question by more than one person, try to elaborate creatively while maintaining consistency. The key is to keep your enthusiasm high. This is an endurance test, so keep fueling yourself with positive thinking and expectations. And lean on your support system!

is looking for in filling the position. As the interviewer answers, jot down the qualities you have that match; then describe them to emphasize how you meet the employer's needs.

9. As you wrap up the interview, ask what the next steps will be.

10. Follow up. Call back one or two days later, thank the interviewer for his or her time, and restate your interest in the position. If necessary, leave this message by voice mail, or send an e-mail or fax message.

The Computer-Assisted Interview

Some companies use *computer-assisted interviews* to screen applicants. The applicant is taken to a computer workstation and given instructions on how to take the interview. The interview typically consists of 50 to 100 computerized multiple-choice and true/false questions that are scored automatically. Some computer-assisted interviews include essay questions reviewed by recruitment specialists or managers. Answer questions just as you would in a face-to-face interview. Be sure to:

- Emphasize your related skills but don't exaggerate. Be concise, avoiding overly long responses or a negative focus on a topic.

- Be consistent in your answers; some programs search for contradictions.

- Avoid pausing too long to respond; some systems flag abnormally long pauses.

Benefits of computer-assisted interviews include ease and cost effectiveness of data collection, consistent gathering of information from all applicants to keep the playing field level, and avoidance of personal bias from the interviewer. The primary drawback is that computers are not able to assess personal qualities such as attitude and enthusiasm. However, these qualities can be observed in follow-up interviews.

The Internet Computer-Assisted Interview

The *Internet computer-assisted interview* is a version of the computer-assisted interview. The Internet interview is useful for long-distance applicant screenings because it saves travel time and other expenses.

In an Internet interview, the employer contacts you and gives you a password. Through the Internet, you log on to the company's in-house computer, using the password, and complete an interview that is essentially the same as a computer-assisted interview.

SUCCESS TIP

In computer-assisted interviews, be consistent in your answers and avoid long pauses for responses.

The Task-Oriented Interview

In the *task-oriented interview*, applicants are asked to demonstrate their skills by performing specific tasks. This style gives employers a chance to assess skills and knowledge in a realistic, rather than theoretical, way. It also gives applicants a chance to showcase their abilities and to assess their interest in the type of work they would be doing. If your target employer uses this style of interviewing, try to find out what types of skills you are expected to demonstrate and practice beforehand.

The Internet Video Interview

The *Internet video interview* involves using two-way video to conduct a "face-to-face" interview over the Web. The cameras are attached to computers at two separate locations. This method is being used more frequently to save money and time for organizations. Many major corporations and colleges and universities are set up to offer real-time video interviewing.

To save time and money, an employer may ask you to participate in an Internet video interview.

To succeed in this style of interview, follow the techniques outlined in Chapter 11 for standard face-to-face interviews. Be sure to dress appropriately, project energy, maintain eye contact with the camera, use positive body language, use good posture, and avoid fidgeting.

You may want to practice this type of interview with a member of your support group to increase your comfort level.

Complete Career Action 13-1

CAREER ACTION 13-1

Research Interview Styles

Part A: Personal Contact Research

Directions: Contact at least two organizations in your field similar to your actual job target, and arrange a brief meeting to research interview styles. Make certain they understand this is not a request for an interview. Follow the guidelines for conducting a successful outside assignment given in Chapter 7 in addition to the steps below.

1. During your meetings, ask your contacts to explain the style of interviewing they use to evaluate applicants for positions similar to the one you will be targeting.

2. Ask what criteria (skills, experience, education, attitudes, personal qualities, and so on) they use to evaluate applicants.

3. Ask for specific examples of positive and negative actions and comments of applicants.

4. Take notes of information you find useful.

5. As always, act professionally and thank the people who help you. Follow up with a thank-you note.

Part B: Internet Research

Directions: Use the following Internet resources or others of your choice to search for information on interview styles you expect to be most prevalent in your field. Summarize key points you find useful or print relevant articles.

Career Journal www.careerjournal.com

The Riley Guide www.rileyguide.com

Quintessential Careers www.quintcareers.com

HotJobs www.hotjobs.com

THE UNSTRUCTURED INTERVIEW

The unstructured approach to interviews is generally taken by people who are not professionally trained in interviewing. It tends to be more informal and conversational in tone. The unstructured approach is often used in small businesses and given by the owners or managers of the firms. In this case, interviewing job applicants is one of many responsibilities of the interviewer; it is not the primary job assignment, as in the case of a human resources specialist in a large organization.

SUCCESS TIP

In unstructured interviews, the most important point is to be sure you present your qualifications thoroughly. If an untrained or unstructured interviewer doesn't focus on extracting this essential information, make sure you bring it out!

Unstructured interviewing is often more successful at bringing out the personal qualities of an applicant (attitudes, feelings, goals, and human relations skills) than the structured interviewing. The questions are usually open-ended to encourage the interviewees to express their personalities, background, and goals. Interviewing success or failure in this type of interview situation is more often based on the ability of the job seeker to communicate than on the content of the answer.

Untrained interviewers, however, may be less skilled in discussing job qualifications; the conversation may get bogged down in unimportant details. In this case, you need to be the "professional interviewee." You can aid the interviewer by asking questions to learn about the full scope of the job and by communicating all your skills, experience, and attributes that apply to it.

PERSONAL BEST

Managing Stress

The ability to manage stress well is key to your success in today's ever-changing workplace. It's also key to success in stressful interviewing situations. If you can anticipate stressful situations ahead of time, you can manage the stress more effectively. These tips will help:

- **Rehearse.** Practice for a stressful event in advance so you can polish your performance and build confidence.

- **Plan.** How will you respond to the anticipated stress? Learn specific techniques for dealing with stress. Apply positive visualization.

- **Keep It in Perspective.** If an event seems big, put it in its place. How important is this event, really, in light of your ultimate goals? To put it in perspective, compare it in your mind with bigger events.

- **Get the Information You Need.** A lack of information can negatively affect your ability to perform. If you are uncertain about what's expected in your job or in an interview setting, ask for the information you need.

- **Think Positively.** Practice the Nine Success Strategies you learned in Chapter 1. Positive thinking, visualization, positive self-talk, goal setting, and self-esteem builders can all work together to combat stress.

- **Take Action.** Exercise, yoga, breathing exercises, good health, and nutrition can help you relax and release stress.

Physical activity is a good way to help you relax and keep up your energy for a successful interview.

THE BAD INTERVIEW

Some interviews are not good; in fact, some are grim. After learning the details of the job, you might be convinced you don't want it. The interviewer may be inept at interviewing, making it difficult for you to perform well. Do not stop trying.

Do your best to be the professional interviewee. You can always learn something beneficial, and it provides you the chance to polish your interviewing skills. Don't let down; it could cost you a future reference or a good job lead from the interviewer. If you have a bad interview, chalk it up to experience.

THE UNSUCCESSFUL INTERVIEW

As a general rule, a job applicant must have several interviews before a good job is offered. Getting a top-notch job is a full-time job that often requires several interviews and some rejections. Harness the energy of negative feelings from rejections, turning them into a positive force. Fueling your determination will help you land the job you want most.

Again, remember that you can learn from interviews. If you aren't offered the job, ask the interviewer to suggest ways you could improve your interviewing skills or whether you appear to be lacking in any area of skill, training, or experience. This information is the starting point for succeeding in your next interview.

Complete Career Action 13-2

CAREER ACTION 13-2

Summarize Interview Styles Pertinent to Your Field

Directions: Review all the information in this chapter and your findings from the personal contact and Internet research (Career Action 13-1 on page 233). Then prepare a written report that includes the following information:

1. Describe the styles of interviews you expect to be most prevalent in your field.

2. Describe techniques you have learned that would help you succeed in these interview styles.

✓ CHECKLIST:

Prepare for Any Interview Style

Check each of the actions you are currently taking to in-crease your career success:

☐ **Overly structured interviews:** Being friendly and positive to establish rapport and a relaxed tone

☐ **Behavioral interview:** Providing proof-by-example descriptions of capabilities

☐ **Screening interview:** Finding out what the next step will be and who makes the hiring decision

☐ **Board, panel, team interview:** Learning and using the names of all interviewers

☐ **Stress interview:** Remaining calm and not reacting

☐ **"Tell me about yourself" interview:** Focusing com-pletely on your job qualifications

☐ **Multilevel or corporate ladder interview:** Keeping answers consistent and maintaining energy

☐ **Telephone interview:** Posting your resume and your 60-second commercial close by; standing up, smiling, and eliminating distractions

☐ **Computer-assisted interview:** Giving consistent answers; avoiding long pauses

☐ **Unstructured interview:** Presenting qualifications thoroughly

critical thinking *Questions*

1. How can job seekers benefit by learning what style of interview is typically given by their target employers?

2. What benefits can you gain by trying to relax the atmosphere of a highly structured interview?

3. What style(s) of interviewing do you expect to be most prevalent in your job search? What techniques can you use to maximize your performance in the style(s)?

chapter 14

Navigate Interview Questions and Answers

"A long-term focus and commitment to succeeding are items I use to evaluate a prospective candidate. Specific questions regarding advancement opportunity and business development are key indicators that the individual is looking for a career, not merely a job."

Michael R. Slyby
Managing Director
MetLife Financial Services

The core of your interview is the question-and-answer period. It should include questions and answers from the interviewer and from you. To ace an interview, generally let the interviewer take the lead. Interviewers usually consider applicants' efforts to control the interview to be rude. You should, however, ask questions—for two reasons: (1) to verify that this is the employer you want to work for and (2) to demonstrate initiative and preparation. Chapter 14 presents a comprehensive overview of common interview questions, tips for answering these questions effectively, and samples of meaningful questions to ask.

FOCUS ON YOUR JOB QUALIFICATIONS

Persuasively discussing your strengths and how they can benefit the employer requires some preparation. Consider the positive capabilities and personal qualities your coworkers, supervisors, instructors, and others have recognized in you. Review your 60-Second Commercial (Chapter 11) and your resume. Write out examples of your positive performance related to the job target requirements.

What examples demonstrate your organizational skills and orderly mind? Have you developed better methods of performing tasks or working with people? How have you motivated people successfully? Can you cite examples of effective problem solving? Are you creative? Can you give examples of handling detail work well? Are you dependable and cooperative? What activities have you been involved in that demonstrate each of these? Are you flexible, able to work independently without regular supervision, and able to work effectively in a team? Choose these types of examples to showcase what you can do for the employer. Focus on proving your qualifications by example in the question-and-answer period of your interview.

PREPARE FOR INTERVIEWER QUESTIONS

Questions asked by interviewers generally fall into four categories:

- General information questions
- Behavioral questions
- Character questions
- Stress questions

The following lists include the most commonly posed interview questions. Study the questions and suggested answers; in Career Action 14-2, you will write your responses to these questions. Writing and rehearsing this script will help you answer questions successfully during an interview.

General Information Questions

General information questions are designed to obtain factual information about you. These questions usually cover your skills, education, work experience, and so on.

1. **Why do you want this job?** (Be prepared; every employer wants to know the answer.)

   Suggested Answer: "My skills and experience are directly related to this position, and my interest lies especially in this field." Then relate examples of your experience, education, or training that are pertinent to the job you are seeking; base this on your employer and job research. Emphasize your interest in developing your career in this area. Don't say you want the job because of the pay and benefits. If you are impressed with and knowledgeable about the reputation of the firm, say so; and add that you would be pleased to be a part of the organization. Don't overdo it, however. Keep your answer to the point, remembering that the point is what you can do for the company.

2. **What type of work do you most enjoy?**

   Suggested Answer: Play your research card; name the types of tasks that would be involved in the job. Demonstrate your research and how you are qualified for the position.

3. **What are your strongest skills?**

   Suggested Answer: Review your abilities and accomplishments and your 60-Second Commercial. Use these to develop your answer. Again, try to relate your skills to those required in the position for which you are applying.

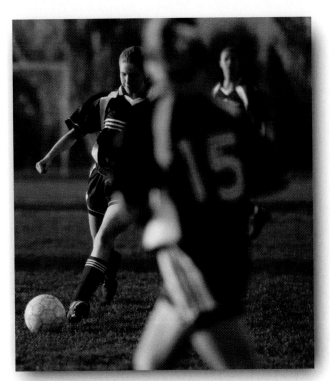

Use school or sports activities and accomplishments in other jobs to respond to questions about teamwork, character, and personal strengths.

4. **What are your long-range career goals, and how do you plan to achieve them?**

Suggested Answer: Although this is usually an information-oriented question, it can be a stress question if you trap yourself by appearing overly aggressive, too ambitious, or lacking in ambition. Employers look for a commitment in return for their training investment. They may not consider you if they think you won't be happy in the job for a reasonable amount of time and see the job only as a fast springboard to something better. Emphasize your strengths, state that your goal is to make a strong contribution in your job, and state that you look forward to developing the experience necessary for career growth.

Employers are impressed with people who show initiative because they often perform better than those who have no plans for self-improvement. Mention plans to continue your education and expand your knowledge to become a more valuable employee.

5. **Are you a team player?**

Suggested Answer: Teamwork is highly valued in today's workplaces, so a positive answer is typically a plus. Give examples of your successful team roles (as a leader, as a member, and as a partner) at school, on the job, and in clubs or other activities.

6. **Do you have a geographical preference? Are you willing to relocate?**

Suggested Answer: If the job requires relocation, this question is important. If you have no objection to relocating, make this perfectly clear. If you do have objections, this could be a stress question. Be honest in your answer. If you don't like being mobile, say so; otherwise, you will undoubtedly be unhappy in the job.

7. **Under what management style do you work most efficiently?**

Suggested Answer: "I am flexible and can be productive under any style. The management style I enjoy working with most is _____." (This shows you to be flexible and casts no negative connotations. It also answers the primary question.)

SUCCESS TIP

Prepare and rehearse responses to typical interview questions. The result can determine your interview and career success.

Behavioral Interview Questions

The behavioral job interview is used widely today and is based on the premise that past performance is the best way to predict future behavior. Behavioral questions probe specific past performance and behaviors through questions such as "Describe one of the most challenging assignments you've had. How did you handle it?" This may be followed by several more in-depth probes aimed at getting further details, such as "Explain what problems you encountered. How did you overcome them?" Some behavioral questions probe for negative experiences. In responding to these, focus on what you learned from the experience or what actions you took to improve the situation.

Experience Scenarios. To prepare for these interviews, recall scenarios of your experiences that illustrate how you have performed or behaved on the job. Write out examples that demonstrate good performance. Also be ready to describe how you have handled difficult situations. Students with little work experience should focus on class projects and group situations that illustrate their task performance and interpersonal behavior.

Behavioral Question Response Model. A good model for your answers is based on four elements:

- Describe the situation.

- Explain the actions you took.

- Describe the outcomes.

- Summarize what you learned from the experience.

   Example: Describe an accomplishment that demonstrates your initiative.

   Answer: "While I was working part-time as a computer lab technician for Seattle Technology College, our department received several complaints about service response time. I set a personal goal of answering all trouble-shooting calls within 90 minutes. I recorded the exact response time for each call and maintained the 90-minute response goal for one full semester. I was awarded the Customer Service Certificate for this performance."

Whenever possible, give positive examples that demonstrate measurable achievements. Or when describing a less positive experience, emphasize what actions you took to correct weaknesses or poor performance. By giving specific examples, you establish credibility and believability that can

> *"Each experience through which we pass operates ultimately for our good."*
>
> Raymond Holliwell

translate into a job offer. Some additional examples of behavioral interview questions are listed below.

- Tell me specifically about a time you worked under great stress.

- Describe an experience when you dealt with an angry customer or coworker.

- Give me an example that would demonstrate your ability to adapt to change.

- Tell me about a time you were forced to make an unpopular decision.

Character Questions

Character questions are used to learn about personal attributes, such as integrity, personality, attitudes, and motivation.

1. **How would you describe yourself?**

   Suggested Answer: Emphasize your strongest personal attributes, and focus on those relevant to your target job. Review your capabilities and accomplishments. Appropriate responses include these:

   "I'm punctual and dependable. At my current job, I haven't been late or missed one day in the last two years." "I get along well with others; in fact, I've been chosen by my coworkers to represent them in our company's monthly staff meetings." Give specific examples of your strengths. Don't just say "I'm a hard worker" or "I'm dependable"; give concrete examples. Other leads include "I learn quickly," "I like solving problems; for example. . . ," "I like contributing to a team," and "I like managing people."

2. **What rewards do you look for in your career?**

   Suggested Answer: Don't stress monetary rewards. Emphasize your desire to improve your skills, to make a valuable contribution to the field, and to become better educated. These show initiative, interest, and professionalism. You can also mention you expect an income that matches your performance.

3. **What accomplishment are you most proud of, particularly as it relates to your field?**

   Suggested Answer: Relate an accomplishment that demonstrates special effort and initiative—perhaps one that surpassed normal requirements. For example, at your last job, you recognized the need to improve communications within the organization. To identify the causes of miscommunications, you designed a questionnaire that was completed by representatives of every department. Management initiated the changes suggested, and communications improved in the areas identified.

   Another example: You purchased a computer with earnings from your part-time job and then used the equipment to start your own business preparing term papers, resumes, and other items for students and instructors from your school and community. The earnings paid for 80 percent of your school costs.

4. **Do you work well under pressure?**

   Suggested Answer: You might be tempted to answer with a simple yes or no, but don't. Those answers reveal nothing specific about you. Don't miss this opportunity to sell yourself.

   Be honest in your answer. If you prefer to work at a well-defined job in an organized, calm atmosphere (rather than one that involves constant decision making and pressure), say so. Otherwise, you may wind up in a job that is a constant source of tension. If you like the challenge of pressure, either in decision making or in dealing with people, make this clear.

   Keep in mind that a large company may have more than one working environment. For instance, an administrative support job in the customer relations department would likely involve more interactive pressure with the public than a support job in the data processing department.

Answer difficult questions honestly and directly. Address the employer's needs and concerns.

Stress or Problem Questions

Stress questions are asked to determine how you perform under pressure (controlled and composed or nervous and unsettled). They are also used to find out whether you are good at making decisions, solving problems, and thinking under stress.

Some questions may be aimed at clarifying issues the interviewer perceives as a possible problem, such as being overqualified or underqualified, having physical limitations, and lacking dependability (if your resume shows many different jobs).

Preparing Answers to Stress Questions. Prepare to answer any problem questions that are based on your resume or personal circumstances. Look at stress questions as an opportunity to demonstrate that the issue is not a problem as it relates to your ability to do the job. Career Action 14-2 will help you prepare by asking you to write out responses to possible stress questions. Then rehearse your responses. Either tape-record yourself giving the question(s) and prepared response(s) or ask a member of your support network to help you role-play the practice. Revise your responses based on feedback.

Prepare and practice for stress questions. Keep your cool, breathe deeply, use positive self-talk, and take time to think. Demonstrate stress skills by thinking the question through and remaining composed.

Remaining Cool Under Stress. Keep your cool; remain focused, take three to five calming deep breaths, and tell yourself "I can do this." If you get a question you are totally unprepared for, don't just blunder on. Use the "that's a good question, let me think about that for a minute" technique. This can buy you the time to prepare a well-thought-out response. Your goal is to demonstrate that you can handle stress—that you don't just react but you think through the situation and remain composed.

1. **Why do you think you are the best candidate for this job?**

   Suggested Answer: Prepare for this one. It might also be phrased "Why should I hire you?" Ask the interviewer to highlight the important objectives and challenges of the job. Then explain how you can handle them. Focus on how you can benefit the employer, giving examples of increasing productivity, saving money, increasing sales, and so on. Summarize accomplishments, skills, and experience pertinent to the job, followed by "How does that fit your requirements?" This now shifts the focus from you to the interviewer, helping reduce stress for you. The key is to get the interviewer involved in developing your answer. This buys you time to develop an appropriate answer.

2. **Why do you want to leave your current job?**

   Suggested Answer: This question is often posed to determine whether you have a problem with your current job. Accentuate the positive—you are seeking a new challenge, you have mastered your present job and are seeking advancement, you want to work for a company with stability, and so on. If you do have a problem with your current job, avoid discussing it. If you think you must discuss it, describe the situation briefly and unemotionally. Then return the interview to a positive tone, explaining that you think this organization would provide a good opportunity for career growth.

3. **Why have you held so many jobs?**

   Suggested Answer: Naturally, employers are impressed by a work history that implies stability and dependability. Often people have valid reasons for holding numerous jobs. Some jobs are seasonal (agriculture, landscaping, and recreation), some jobs involve frequent relocation (engineering, construction), and some jobs are profoundly affected by the general economy. You may have held a variety of summer jobs while completing your education. Capitalize on this; it shows initiative and provides you with broad working experience.

   You might also have accompanied your spouse, who was required to relocate frequently. If you did, in fact, change jobs frequently, mention that previously you wanted to obtain a broad base of experience but that now your goal is to apply this experience to long-term employment and development of a career.

4. **What is your greatest weakness?**

   Suggested Answer: "My weakest area is accounting (unless you are applying for an accounting position!), so I'm completing a beginning course at the college. It's going well and I plan to take the advanced course next semester." The point is to acknowledge any weak point and to explain your plan for improving in this area. Choose a weakness that is low on the employer's list of required skills and one that you are currently taking steps to improve (through practice, education, planning, and so on).

"Adopting the right attitude can convert a negative stress into a positive one."

Hans Selye

5. **Have you ever been fired from a job?**

   Suggested Answer: If you have been fired, use terms such as *laid off* or *terminated*; they sound less negative. Be honest about the reason for your termination. Briefly explain the situation and mention that you have learned from the experience. End your response on a positive note.

   If you have been laid off for a legitimate reason (such as a downsizing, a loss of company business, or a lagging economy), remember that this is not the same as being fired from a job. Therefore, you do not need to mention this in answer to question 5. If quitting a job was your own decision, remember to use more positive language, such as "I left" or "I decided to leave."

6. **Does your current employer know you are planning to leave?**

   Suggested Answer: If your current employer is aware of this fact, say so. If not, and especially if you depend on your current income, make this clear. Say you prefer that your current employer not be informed of your job search until a firm job offer is made and you will give at least two weeks' notice before leaving. (This demonstrates good ethics and a sense of responsibility—both pluses for you!)

Remember that some questions are not purposely posed to be stressful, but they may be stressful to you. For instance, if the interviewer asks, "Does your employer know you are planning to leave?" and the answer is yes because your spouse is being transferred, the question will not be stressful to you. If, however, the reason for leaving is that you can no longer tolerate working for your current employer, the question will probably be stressful.

The following Personal Best feature provides guidelines for handling illegal questions effectively. Review this information carefully and consider how you can apply it effectively if it becomes necessary in your own interview.

PERSONAL BEST

Handling Illegal Questions

The interview is going along well and then it happens: "Are you considering having children?" or "How long has your family been in this country?"

On the surface, questions such as these seem innocent enough. Yet the structure and format of the question may be illegal or, at the very least, inappropriate. Questions that focus on gender, age, race, national origin, or religion are inappropriate in a job interview because they can be used as a basis for discrimination.

So you've just been hit with an illegal question. What do you do? How do you respond?

If you complain about a question being illegal or unfair and refuse to answer, you probably won't be offered the job. You certainly have the right to refuse, but first weigh the situation. Is it worth jeopardizing the job over this question? Or does the interviewer appear so offensive that you don't want to work for the organization anyway?

The most effective approach is to answer the question in a polite, honest manner. Provide proof by example of your ability to meet the employer's expectations, as in the following example:

Interviewer: Do you have children?

Applicant: Yes, and appropriate child care is a top priority for me. I'm thorough in arranging dependable daily and alternative care. It pays off; I've never had to miss a day of work or school for child care purposes (emphasizing planning and management).

Anticipate the stress of illegal questions. Prepare and practice appropriate responses. This gives you the edge in demonstrating your ability to handle stressful situations calmly and skillfully—just the behavior employers want.

PLAN NOW: YOUR QUESTIONS COUNT!

Making the interview an effective two-way communication is important. Prepare to ask three to five well-chosen and appropriate questions. Prospective employers will respect what you inspect, not what you expect. Outline questions that will help you learn more about the employer and the position as well as questions that show initiative and preparation.

Don't ask all your questions at the end of the interview. Interject them naturally at appropriate intervals throughout the meeting. Keep your questions positive. Avoid asking any that could elicit negative reactions from the interviewer. Also, avoid discussing salary until a job offer is made (see Chapter 15).

Asking an employer if training is available for the position will demonstrate your interest in performing the job well.

Good Questions to Ask

Asking appropriate questions demonstrates interest, confidence, and intelligence. Study the following sample questions carefully; then write out your own questions as part of Career Action 14-2.

1. **Do you have a training program for this position. If so, would you describe it?** This demonstrates interest in the job and a desire to perform it well.

2. **Will you describe the duties and tasks in a typical workday for this position?** The answer will help you better understand the scope and emphasis of the job. It may be just what you want, or you may learn that it's not the type of work you are seeking. The information will be important to you in considering a job offer.

3. **May I have a copy of the written job description?** Getting a job description can help you tie your qualifications to those required for the job.

4. **Could good job performance in this job lead to career growth opportunities with the company?** This will help you determine whether this is a dead-end job or if employee career growth is encouraged.

5. **Will the responsibilities of this position expand with time and experience on the job?** The answer could also give you insight into whether this is a dead-end, no-growth job.

6. **Could you tell me about the people with whom I would be working?** To whom would I report, and who would be my peers and subordinates? The answer can help you evaluate how you might fit in this position.

7. **Do you require any more information about my qualifications or experience?** This gives you an opportunity to clear up any misunderstanding or lack of information. It also gives you another chance to run your 60-Second Commercial, reemphasizing just how well qualified you are.

SUCCESS TIP

Prepare and ask appropriate questions; this demonstrates interest, confidence, and intelligence.

Turnoff Questions to Avoid

Following are some questions most disliked by employers. Do not ask these; they make you sound uninformed and they diminish likability.

1. **What does this company do?** You should have done your research well enough to know exactly what the company does. This question will make you appear uninformed and unqualified. Employers are not looking for employees who know nothing about their business!

2. **How much sick leave and vacation time will I get?** Do not ask this during a first interview. Although employee benefits are important, asking specifically about vacations or sick leave projects a negative attitude. However, you should ask these questions before making a final decision about a job offer. Employers appreciate the importance of major benefits to prospective employees.

3. **Will I have an office?** This suggests too much emphasis on where you will work, rather than interest in the work.

4. **What time do I have to be at work in the morning? How long do you give for lunch?** These questions sound immature and do not project an enthusiastic interest in the work!

5. **How long do I have to work before I am eligible for a raise?** This question projects an attitude that tells the employer you are more interested in the salary than the job.

Complete Career Action 14-1

CAREER ACTION 14-1

Use the Internet to Search for Interview Question-and-Answer Tips

www **Directions:** Use the Internet to search for additional tips on interview questions and answers that could be useful. Summarize the key points or print relevant articles.

Check these web sites as well as your favorite search engines for tips on interview questions and answers. If you want to know more about handling illegal questions, include this topic in your Internet search.

- Net-Temps
  (Click on "Your Career"; then click on "Interviewing.")
  www.net-temps.com

- The Riley Guide
  (Click on "Networking, Interviewing, & Negotiating"; then click on "Interviewing" and select appropriate articles.)
  www.rileyguide.com

- Indiana University
  www.indiana.edu/~libpers/interview.html

- Virginia Tech
  (Select *Job Search*; then click on "Interviewing.")
  www.career.vt.edu

- JobWeb
  www.jobweb.com

APPLY Q-AND-A SAVVY STRATEGIES

Employers rate the following as top-notch strategies for interview question-and-answer performance.

- **Be enthusiastic.** Enthusiasm is a quality employers look for when hiring.

- **Pause to think before you reply.** If you're uncomfortable with a question, go back to the familiar. Stress your assets. Use the "thinking pause" to buy time to answer well. One of the following phrases can be used:

    "Could we return to this question? I'd like to think about it for a moment."

"That's a good question." or "Let me see. . ." (This works if you need only a little extra time.)

- **Be candid and honest.** Be realistic in expressing your preferences and dislikes. You won't be happy in a job that isn't a good fit.

- **Do not use canned responses.** Tailor your answers to fit your goals, objectives, and personality, as well as the goals and needs of the employer.

- **Be concise.** Keep your responses to the point, but avoid being curt or too brief.

- **Answer in complete sentences and speak correctly.** Speak in complete sentences. Avoid using slang, incorrect grammar, or repetitive terms. Speak clearly.

- **Be positive.** Positive thinking promotes positive behavior and speech, a positive image, positive responses, and a positive atmosphere. It also projects enthusiasm, self-confidence, and initiative.

- **Fill in gaps.** If you sense that the interviewer thinks you have an area of weakness, communicate how you plan to eliminate the weakness or round out your qualifications—perhaps by completing research or course work in the area.

Complete Career Action 14-2

CAREER ACTION 14-2

Create a Question-and-Answer Planning Sheet

Directions: Use the Question-and-Answer Planning Sheet on page 248 or on your Learner's CD to write answers to typical questions you anticipate during interviews. Also write sample questions you can ask during interviews. Use the suggestions presented in this chapter, the Career Actions for Chapter 3, and your 60-Second Commercial as references in writing your answers. Tailor your answers to your targeted job. Emphasize your qualifications for the job at every opportunity. Use positive, action-oriented words.

✓ CHECKLIST:

Interview Questions and Answers

Check each of the actions you are currently taking to increase your career success:

☐ Focusing on proof by example; responding persuasively to questions about abilities; giving examples of applying them in work, school, and other activities

☐ Preparing and rehearsing responses to typical interview questions

☐ Preparing and practicing for stress questions; staying cool, breathing deeply, using positive self-talk, and taking time to think; demonstrating stress skills—thinking the question through and remaining composed

☐ Preparing and asking appropriate questions

☐ Avoiding questions that diminish likability; these include questions that are too direct, that your research should have answered, or that make you appear immature or uncommitted to the job

critical thinking *Questions*

1. What should be your main objectives during the question-and-answer portion of the interview?

2. Why is it important for the applicant to pose some questions during the interview?

3. What specific types of questions do you need to prepare for most to be ready for your interviews? List two examples and include the answers you plan to give.

Question-and-Answer Planning Sheet

General Information Questions

1. Why do you want this job?

_____

_____

_____

2. What type of work do you enjoy doing most?

_____

_____

_____

3. What are your strongest skills?

_____

_____

_____

4. What are your long-range career goals, and how do you plan to achieve them?

_____

_____

_____

5. Are you a team player? Give examples.

_____

_____

_____

6. Do you have a geographical preference? Are you willing to relocate?

_____

_____

_____

Continued on next page.

CAREER ACTION 14-2 (continued)

7. Under what management style do you work most productively?

_____

_____

_____

8. What is important to you in a company? What things do you look for in an organization?

_____

_____

_____

Behavioral and Character Questions

1. What have you accomplished that demonstrates your initiative?

_____

_____

_____

2. How do you deal with an angry customer or coworker? Describe an experience you've had.

_____

_____

_____

3. How are you able to adapt to change? Give an example.

_____

_____

_____

4. How would you describe yourself?

_____

_____

_____

Continued on next page.

5. What rewards do you look for in your career?

_____

_____

_____

6. Of what accomplishment are you most proud, particularly as it relates to your field?

_____

_____

_____

7. Do you work well under pressure? Give an example.

_____

_____

_____

8. What do you think are the most important characteristics and abilities a person must possess to be successful? How do you rate yourself in those areas?

_____

_____

_____

Stress Questions

1. Why do you think you are the best candidate for this job? (or) Why should I hire you?

_____

_____

_____

2. Why do you want to leave your current job?

_____

_____

_____

Continued on next page.

CAREER ACTION 14-2 (continued)

3. Why have you held so many jobs?

_____

_____

_____

4. What is your greatest weakness?

_____

_____

_____

5. Have you ever been fired from a job?

_____

_____

_____

6. Does your current employer know you are planning to leave?

_____

_____

_____

7. What kinds of decisions are most difficult for you?

_____

_____

_____

Questions and Topics to Avoid

1. Why should you avoid asking "What does this company do?"

_____

_____

_____

Continued on next page.

2. Should you ask specifically about sick leave and vacation time? Why or why not?

_____

_____

_____

3. Why shouldn't you ask "How long do I have to be in the job before I qualify for a raise?"

_____

_____

_____

4. Why should you avoid asking "Will I have an office?"

_____

_____

_____

5. List below other questions interviewers dislike from applicants (based on your outside research or reading).

_____

_____

_____

Q-and-A Savvy Strategies

Review the "Apply Q-and-A Savvy Strategies" in this chapter. List those strategies that are most applicable to your job search. Add others you may have identified through your Internet research.

Your Questions

Review the questions in the section "Plan Now: Your Questions Count!" Then create the questions you want to ask during your interviews and save them in your Career Management File. Put the questions in your own words, and ask for help from a member of your support system, if necessary. Add questions that are pertinent to your job search, goals, and objectives.

chapter **15**

ACE EMPLOYMENT TESTS AND NEGOTIATIONS

In this chapter, you will:

www Use the Internet to research current salary information for your field.

- Identify and summarize employment testing procedures used and compensation packages offered in your field for the type of job you are seeking.

- Summarize guidelines for negotiating the compensation package.

- Summarize how to deal effectively with job offers.

"Our computerized preemployment tests help determine the marketability of each applicant. If the applicant does well on the assessment tests, we are more likely to place him or her in a position that requires more skills and pays better."

Jennifer Evans
Branch Manager
Kelly Services

Chapter 15 presents strategies to help you perform successfully in preemployment tests and drug screening, negotiating a fair compensation package, and evaluating and accepting job offers.

ACE EMPLOYMENT TESTS

Doing your homework is a sure way to improve educational test scores, and it also helps you succeed in employment tests. As part of your research, find out if the employer requires preemployment testing. Many employers don't use preemployment testing, but you may apply to one that does. If a test is involved, find out whether it's a written, oral, combination, or computerized test. Does it test technical knowledge, skills, manual dexterity, personality, special abilities, or other job-related capabilities? Try to find out what will be tested and how it will be tested.

Well in advance of asking for an interview, contact the employer, speak with a human resources staff person or the office manager, and ask the person to describe any testing procedures used.

Employer testing requirements vary. You could be asked to take a simple skills test or a more detailed technical test.

The Personality Test

The personality test is the one exception to the "do your homework" rule. Because this type of test is usually designed to determine whether your personal and behavioral preferences are well matched to the work involved, advance study doesn't apply. Technically there are no wrong answers to these tests. Most tests measure solitary or social tendencies, relative need for stability, preference for efficiency or creativity, style of goal achievement (flexible or fixed), and the tendency to accept others' ideas or stick to your own. Answer all questions honestly. If your personality doesn't match the job, you won't be happy in it.

The Skills Test

If you will be taking a skills test, start today to review, practice, and improve. No matter how good your skills are, you can improve with practice, which increases your employability. However, stop preparing one or two days before your test. Cramming until the last minute increases anxiety and often results in lower performance. Another benefit of polishing your skills is that you'll begin your new job with greater confidence.

The Technical Test

If you will be required to take an oral or written test for a professional position, try to get some samples of the technical questions that are asked. Resources for learning about the types of questions are the employer's human resources department, other employees in the company, people who have taken the test, and people who have taken similar tests in your field. Libraries and bookstores also have sample tests.

If you can find sample questions or even general topics that will be covered in the technical test, write out answers to the questions. The important thing is to be as complete as possible in your answers. The purpose of technical tests is to find out how much you know about the subject.

The Computerized Preemployment Test

The computerized preemployment test is useful for large applicant screenings because it saves time and other expenses. The test may be general in content, or it may be a skills or personality test.

Typically, applicants take these tests at the employer's site or at an employment agency if the applicant is working with one. You receive instructions on how to use the computerized test program and then are given a specified amount of time to complete it. The results are usually scored electronically and generated in a report. These results are then analyzed by human resources personnel. The best advice for performing well on these tests is to do your best; don't try to outwit the test. Also, avoid using absolutes such as *never* and *always.* These words can signal an extreme personality or lying. If it is a skills test, prepractice can help improve your score.

> *"In the book of life's questions, the answers are not in the back."*
>
> Charles Schulz

SUCCESS TIP

Research to learn what types of tests are given by your target employer. To sharpen your performance for skills tests, practice beforehand; for technical tests, study concepts. Don't try to prepare for personality tests; answer honestly to ensure a good match between you and the job.

Taking Employment Tests

Employment testing may be an important factor in an employer's hiring decision. Follow these guidelines to perform at your best:

- Eat properly before the test and be well rested. A sluggish body and brain diminish test performance.

- Do some physical exercise or yoga (or a similar activity) before your test to improve your circulation and your ability to relax and concentrate.

- Arrive 10 to 15 minutes early to avoid being rushed or tense.

- Most firms provide more than enough time to complete a test; so don't rush into poor performance. Ask, however, exactly how much time is allowed for the test.

- Before beginning, read the test carefully to clarify the instructions and to determine how many points are assigned to each question. If you run short of time, answer the questions assigned the largest number of points. If the points aren't indicated, ask the person monitoring the test how the questions are weighted.

- Ask whether points will be deducted for questions you don't answer. If so, answer every question. If not, don't spend a lot of time on questions you can't answer easily. (Save those until last!)

- Always clarify any directions or questions you don't understand before you start the test.

- Many tests are objective, often including multiple choice questions. In true-false questions, extreme statements are often false (for example, choices that contain the words *all, never,* or *always*). Moderate statements are often true.

- Double-check to make certain you haven't missed any questions. Remember, your first response is usually the correct one. Don't change answers unless you're sure you made a careless mistake.

- On general math tests, expect some simple addition, subtraction, multiplication, division, fraction, percentage, and decimal problems. Many math tests also include word problems.

- Advanced math tests will be geared to your field (engineering and statistical analysis, for instance). Consult others who have taken similar tests to determine what you should review. Educational and working experience are your primary preparation for this type of test.

- Oral tests or boards are generally given for advanced college degrees and senior management/supervisory positions. These test an applicant's technical knowledge.

Ask a colleague and/or an instructor in your field to meet with you to review important technical aspects of your field. Review and study major principles beforehand, and use the meeting to summarize these elements.

Prepare for Drug Screening

Drug screening as a preemployment requirement is commonplace. Be prepared for the possibility that you will be asked to take a drug test before being hired. Employers can refuse to hire you if you refuse to take the test.

Take drug screening seriously. Applicants who test positively for drug use or who admit to use of illegal drugs may be screened out of the job immediately. Never give flippant answers to questions about drug use. They could be interpreted negatively.

Policies for drug screening vary considerably from one employer to another. As part of your employer research, find out what the drug screening procedures and requirements are. Check with employers directly and with people who work with them. School career services counselors often have current information about drug testing procedures and may be familiar with those of many local employers.

To protect yourself, before you are tested, report to the employer any prescription or over-the-counter drugs you are taking. Some can result in a false-positive test.

Success Tip

Take drug screening seriously. Find out what the employer's drug screening procedures are. To avoid a false-positive result, report all over-the-counter drugs you are taking.

Research Salary and Benefits Ahead of Time

To optimize your ability to negotiate for the best possible salary and benefits, you must be as knowledgeable as possible about the going salary ranges and the types of benefits being offered in your field. You significantly reduce your salary and benefits bargaining power if you omit this step.

Success Tip

Postpone discussion of salary until you receive a job offer. This is your strongest bargaining strategy because the employer will already be convinced you are the person for the job.

The Compensation Package

Salary is not the only important factor in assessing the value of a job. The *complete compensation package* includes salary, potential for earnings growth, and all other benefits. All are important. Base your compensation considerations on the following:

- The trends in your field (based on research)

- Your worth (the value you can offer the employer)

- What benefits are most important to you: health/life insurance, retirement programs, flextime, dependent care, reimbursement for education or training, and so on

Research Compensation Trends in Your Field

Research the going rate. Increase your chances of being offered the best compensation by including these topics in your employer and industry research. Talk with leaders in your field, with people holding positions similar to your target job, and with area placement specialists. Also search online for salary and benefits information.

Some employers provide printed job descriptions that include a fixed salary listing, or they offer salary information on their Internet web sites. Other job notices include a salary range, or the salary may be open. Often you can find the range or approximate salary for the position from the employer's human resources department. In some cases, however, employers don't give out this information. They may give you only the bottom of the range—rarely the top figure. Having a general idea of the range is better than having no idea. Your career services office can help you research salary and benefits packages through local contacts and pub-

lications such as the *Job Choices* journal—an excellent publication by the National Association of Colleges and Employers.

If the salary is fixed, as may occur in some union or government jobs, you must decide whether it's acceptable to you. Also research salary and benefits information online. Check web sites of associations in your career field and use search engines.

If the salary is negotiable, try for a salary at the top of the range. (You can agree to accept a salary lower than the top level, but if you offer to take the lowest end of the range first, that's probably what you'll get.) Study the following section, "Negotiate for Top Salary and Benefits," and prepare to bargain your way up the pay scale.

> Complete Career Action 15-1

CAREER ACTION 15-1

Use the Internet to Research Current Salary Information

 Part 1 Directions: Access one of the two web sites listed below. Using the site's salary calculator, compute the cost-of-living differences between two cities in which you would consider working. Print the results.

1. Salary.com   www.salary.com

2. Homestore.com   www.homefair.com

Part 2 Directions: Access the following web site, and then complete the steps outlined in the paragraph below.

Occupational Outlook Handbook   www.bls.gov/oco

On the home page, click on the name of your general occupation; then click on your specific occupation. Finally, click on "Earnings." Print or summarize in writing the wage ranges listed for the occupation.

Note: For additional salary information, check out the valuable "Salary Info" at JobStar: www.jobstar.org.

NEGOTIATE FOR TOP SALARY AND BENEFITS

To gain the strongest bargaining position, try to postpone discussion of compensation until you receive a job offer. Bringing up the topic of compensation too soon could shift the focus too far from your qualifications and cost you the job. First concentrate on what the employer will gain (your skills, experience, personal strengths, and so on) before focusing on the price (your compensation). Review and apply the following strategies:

- **Whenever possible, let the interviewer bring up the topic of salary and benefits.**

- **Do not accept the job offer without discussing the salary and benefits.** You can bring it up by asking, "What salary range do you have in mind for the job?"

- **Aim for a salary that equals the peak of your qualifications.** The higher you start, the higher the offer is likely to be. State your requirement in a range (upper twenties, mid thirties), making it broad enough to negotiate. Don't specify a low end; if you do, the employer will likely select it.

- **If the interviewer asks what salary you want, a good response is "What figure or range is the company planning to pay?"** This gives you a starting point for negotiation. If it's higher than you expected, you help yourself by not stating a lower figure first. If it's lower, you now have a place to begin negotiations.

- **When the interviewer presses you for your salary requirement, refer to your research.** "The national average for a person with my experience, education, and training is $_____. Considering the cost-of-living factors here, I would expect a salary in the upper _____."

- **If the interviewer brings up the subject of salary too early in the interview** (before you adequately cover your qualifications), delay the topic, saying

"We make a living by what we get, but we make a life by what we give."

Winston Churchill

"Actually, the position itself is more important to me than the salary. Could we discuss the position a little more?"

- **While discussing salary, return to your assets.** Review all the benefits and qualifications you have to offer the company.

- **Once you state your salary range, do not back down,** particularly if you think it is equal to your qualifications. Base your range on careful research. The employer will respect confidence about the quality and worth of your work.

- **Do not discuss any other sources of income, and do not moan about your expenses.** Stay focused on this negotiation.

- **Discuss the fringe benefits** (insurance coverage, pension plans, paid vacations, and so on) along with the topic of salary.

- **Ask what criteria are used to determine compensation increases and the frequency of salary reviews.** If benefits and salary increases are good, they can offset a somewhat lower starting salary.

- **If the salary offer is made in a letter and the salary is too low,** arrange an appointment right away to discuss it. Bargaining power is far better in person than by letter or telephone.

- **If the salary isn't acceptable, state the salary you would accept,** and close by reaffirming your interest in the company and the job. If the interviewer says, "I'll have to think about your requirements," wait one week; then call back. You may receive a higher or compromise offer. If the interviewer gives a flat "no," express regret that you were unable to work out a compromise. Restate your interest in the job and organization; then send a follow-up thank-you letter within two days. It could swing the decision in your favor.

Complete Career Action 15-2

CAREER ACTION 15-2

Employment Test/Salary and Benefits Planning Sheet

Directions: This outside assignment will help you succeed in employment tests and negotiate effectively for fair salary and benefits. To prepare for your outside research in this assignment, complete Parts 1, 2, and 3 of the Employment Test/Salary and Benefits Planning Sheet, provided on the Learner's CD and also on page 263 of this text.

EVALUATE AND NEGOTIATE JOB OFFERS

Before deciding on a job offer, you must be sure it meets your career planning needs and goals. The following guidelines will help you assess job offers wisely.

Evaluate a Job Offer

Because the decision to accept or reject a job offer affects your lifetime career plans, consider this important decision carefully. Include the following factors in your evaluation of a job offer:

✓ **The job itself:** Is the scope acceptable? Is the work interesting to you? Will you work in teams or alone?

✓ **The organization and personnel:** Do you feel comfortable with the organizational structure and the people you have met?

✓ **The salary and benefits:** Does the salary match your education and abilities, and is it comparable with the competition? Does potential exist for increases?

✓ **Career development opportunities:** Will you have adequate opportunities for professional growth (through training, continuing education, and experience)?

✓ **The values and philosophies of management:** Are they compatible with your own?

✓ **Expense considerations:** What expenses are required for relocation, housing, living costs, and so on.

✓ **How the job meets your goals:** Consider carefully how this job fits into your long-range career goals.

✓ **The job market:** Are jobs in your field plentiful or in short supply?

Job offers are made by telephone, by letter, or in person. If the offer is made by letter, you have time to think it over carefully and less emotionally than if it's made by telephone or in person. You might want to discuss the job offer conditions with a member of your support system, a family member, a career specialist, or all of these people. Respond to the offer quickly so you don't jeopardize it in any way.

If the offer is made by telephone or in the interviewer's office, request time to think it over. Occasionally interviewers will offer to increase the salary or benefits if that appears to be your main concern regarding the job offer. This is particularly true if they are convinced you are the right person for the job and they don't want to interview any other applicants. If this should happen, more power to you! Even if this doesn't happen, it's still in your best interest to take at least one day to consider the advantages and disadvantages of the job offer.

Important: Make certain that waiting one day won't be an imposition. This helps avoid returning the next day to accept the offer and finding someone else has the job! Be sure you understand all conditions and aspects of the job before you decide.

When accepting a job offer, express your enthusiasm and interest in the job.

If you have absolutely no doubts or objections concerning the job offer, accept the offer on the spot with enthusiasm. This will reinforce the employer's confidence in your interest in the job.

SUCCESS TIP

Consider all aspects of the job offer (the job and company, compensation, growth opportunities, and expense considerations). Before accepting, negotiate to improve areas of concern and to provide the best career opportunity for yourself.

PERSONAL BEST
Negotiation Skills

You negotiate for things every day with employers, family members, businesses—with many people you encounter. You may negotiate for higher salary, better service, or a solution to a disagreement with a coworker. Regardless of the situation, these strategies by author and consultant Barbara Braham will help you handle negotiations more effectively:

- **Know yourself.** How do you feel about negotiation? Do you dread it? If so, you may give in too quickly or give away too much. Or do you want to win, no matter what the cost? If so, you may become adversarial and damage the relationship.

- **Think, think, think. Know what you want.** Anticipate what the other party wants. Also try to anticipate what the other party thinks you want.

- **Build trust.** Without trust, you'll have manipulation and suspicion masquerading as communication. Be trustworthy. Tell the truth.

- **Listen.** Pay attention to what's being said as well as to nonverbal messages, facial expressions, and voice inflections.

- **Know your BATNA.** BATNA stands for Best Alternative to a Negotiated Agreement. Before you begin a negotiation, know what your options are. Can you walk away from the deal? What other choices do you have? What are the pros and cons of each choice? Don't stop here. Also consider the BATNA of the other party.

- **Know what a win is.** What is your best-case scenario? What is your worst-case scenario? If you can reach an agreement within this range, that's a win! Don't drop below your bottom line. You'll feel bad about yourself and the deal later.

Source: Negotiation Skills,
www.bbraham.com/html/negotiation.html

Accept the Offer Professionally

If you accept the job offer verbally, follow up immediately in writing, summarizing your understanding of the conditions of the offer, stating the position title, starting date, salary, and other pertinent items. (Your employer might do the same, but this helps ensure mutual agreement regarding all conditions of the offer.)

Contact other organizations with which you have interviewed, and tell them you have accepted a job. You might deal with these people in your new job, or you might want to contact them in the future regarding employment.

Contact those who served as references or helped with your job search to tell them about your new job and to thank them for their help. People you thank are more likely to help in the future when you seek a new position or advancement in your career.

Reject the Offer Professionally

If you decide this is not the job for you, notify the employer by telephone first, if possible. Then politely decline the offer in a letter, thank the employer for the job offer, and wish the employer future success.

Consider How Economics May Influence Your Decision

Your final decision may be influenced by economics—the need to earn a living. If the offer meets most of your requirements but is not a perfectly logical career step, your decision still could be to accept the job. If so, take the job with a determination to excel. This is an opportunity for you to establish your reputation—all while taking home a regular salary. Accept the challenge and view it as preparation for the next step in your career development.

> **Complete Career Action 15-3**

CAREER ACTION 15-3

Planning for Dealing with Job Offers

Directions: Provide answers to the following items.

1. List every factor you should consider in evaluating a job offer. Be thorough in your answer. You might want to discuss it with a member of your support network, a placement counselor, or both. Include the factors that are specific to your personal job search, as well as the general factors discussed in this chapter that are relevant to your job search.

2. Explain how you can best respond to a job offer made in person:

   a. if you think you want the job.

   b. if you are certain you want the job.

   c. if you do not want the job.

3. How can you best respond to a job offer made by telephone?

4. List the follow-up steps you should take in accepting a job offer.

5. How should you professionally reject a job offer?

6. If economic conditions require you to accept a job that is not exactly what you are aiming for, how can you best approach this new job? What are the benefits of doing this?

✔ CHECKLIST:

Ace Employment Tests and Negotiations

Check each of the actions you are taking to increase your interview and follow-up success:

☐ Researching to learn what types of tests are given by a target employer; practicing beforehand to sharpen performance in skills tests; studying concepts for technical tests

☐ Taking drug screening seriously; finding out what drug screening procedures are used; reporting use of any over-the-counter drugs to avoid a false-positive result

☐ Postponing discussion of salary until after receiving a job offer

☐ Considering all aspects of a job offer: the job and company, the compensation package (salary and benefits), growth opportunities, and so on; negotiating to improve areas of concern before accepting a job offer

critical thinking *Questions*

1. Review "Ace Employment Tests" in this chapter. What are some pointers that apply to your job search campaign?

2. Is it more advantageous for the applicant to bring up the subject of salary first? Why or why not?

3. What is an appropriate response for you to make when an interviewer asks what salary you are looking for?

4. Base your answers to these questions on your salary information research: (a) What is the entry-level salary for the job you are seeking? (b) What salary range do you plan to seek in your job search? On what do you base this?

CAREER ACTION 15-2

Employment Test/Salary and Benefits Planning Sheet

Directions: Contact two employers in your field to learn about employment testing, salary ranges, and benefits offered for the type of job you are seeking. Answer the following questions.

Part 1: Employment Test Questions

1. Do you require prospective employees to take employment tests?

_____

_____

2. What kinds of tests are given (personality, skills, technical, computerized, other)?

_____

_____

3. Would you please describe the test (written, oral, skills, computerized, other)?

_____

_____

4. What types of questions are in the test (multiple choice, true/false, fill in the blank, essay, other)?

_____

_____

5. Would you please explain how the test applies to the job itself?

_____

_____

6. Could a person study for the test(s)? If so, could you recommend specific methods of study and resources?

_____

_____

7. Do you require prospective employees to take drug tests? If so, what is the procedure?

_____

_____

Continued on next page.

Part 2: Negotiating Salary and Benefits

Directions: Obtain and write out answers to the following questions.

1. Does this position have a fixed salary or a salary range?

   _____

2. If the salary is fixed, could you tell me the amount?

   _____

3. If the salary is in a range, could you tell me the range?

   _____

4. Is the salary negotiable?

   _____

   _____

5. What criteria are used for determining the salary for this position?

   _____

   _____

6. Are salary raises offered for excellent job performance? If so, what criteria are used?

   _____

   _____

7. What is in the typical complete compensation package (benefits)?

   _____

   _____

Part 3: Summary of Strategies for Negotiating Compensation

Directions: Review the strategies under the heading "Negotiate for Top Salary and Benefits" on page 258. Use a separate sheet of paper to summarize in your own words the tactics you plan to use in negotiating a compensation package (salary and benefits). Add additional tips you have found in Internet or other research.

chapter 16

PRACTICE FOR YOUR SUCCESSFUL INTERVIEW

In this chapter, you will:

- Review the techniques for successful interviewing and arrange a practice interview with a member of your support network.

- Arrange a dress-rehearsal interview with an employer in your field.

- Evaluate your practice and dress-rehearsal interviews.

"The interview questions I ask are designed to reveal traits and life priorities. Asking questions like, 'When and why did you decide to become a teacher?' gives insight into an applicant's motivation and commitment to the profession. I also like to ask potential employees what they hope to contribute to our organization. I always pose one last question: 'What would you like me to know about you that we have not discussed?'"

Susan Carter, Principal
Fairfax Elementary
Mariemont City Schools

Chapter 16 provides vital interview rehearsal activities, including interview practice with a member of your support network followed by a dress-rehearsal interview with an employer in your field. These activities sharpen your interviewing skills, boost your confidence, and increase your competitive advantage through carefully planned interview practices. The payoff could be just the job you are looking for!

GAIN COMPETITIVE ADVANTAGE THROUGH INTERVIEW PRACTICE

Users of *Your Career: How to Make It Happen* emphasize that the practice interviews improve their actual interview performance by as much as 100 percent! They say this valuable practice enhances their preparation, increases their self-confidence, improves the image of competence they project, and reduces their anxiety about the process—all of which improves their performance in actual interviews! Gain these valuable advantages yourself through your practice interviews.

REVIEW INTERVIEW TECHNIQUES

To prepare for your practice interviews, review Chapter 11, "Interview Like a Pro." Prepare and perform in your practice interview as if it were the real thing. A summary of key points for effective interviewing follows.

Prepare for the Interview

To ensure the best results from your practice interviews, prepare first.

- **Take the time to look your best.** Eat well and be rested, immaculately groomed, and appropriately dressed. Appearance has a major impact on interviewers. Make it positive.

- **Strengthen your performance with positive behaviors.** See Chapter 1 (positive self-talk and expectations, visualization, and so on).

- **Review the Career Actions in Chapters 2, 3, 9, and 11.** Focus on your capabilities, accomplishments, 60-Second Commercial, resume, and specific qualifications for your job target.

- **Assemble your Interview Marketing Kit** (see Chapter 11), and take it with you.

- **Allow travel time.** Arrive a few minutes early. If you're not certain how to get to your interview location, consider driving to the interview site the day before your meeting.

SUCCESS TIP

To improve actual interview performance and confidence, schedule and participate seriously in practice interviews.

For all interviews—practice or the real thing—make time to look your best. A positive appearance is essential!

Apply Interview Success Strategies

To polish your performance, follow these successful interview techniques covered in Chapter 11:

- **Remember, there is no time-out from the moment you enter the building until you leave.** Maintain good posture; project energy and enthusiasm; think good thoughts. Smile!

- **Use the interviewer's name** in your greeting. Identify yourself and the position for which you are applying.

- **Be likable and relax.** Be courteous and friendly and show interest in the position.

- **Remember, your body language and voice tone have a major impact in interviews.**

- **Stress your qualifications** and your interest in benefiting the company and advancing yourself.

- **Ask a few appropriate questions.**

- **Remain calm if asked a stress question.** Allow yourself time to plan an effective answer.

- **Close the interview skillfully.** Use the "clincher" (ask the interviewer to summarize the most important qualifications for the job; then stress your related abilities).

> *"The thing always happens that you really believe in; and the belief in the thing makes it happen."*
>
> Frank Lloyd Wright

SCHEDULE A PRACTICE INTERVIEW

Schedule a practice interview with a member of your support network (a friend, a family member, or an acquaintance), preferably someone experienced in interviewing who knows you personally. Ask one or two others to observe this practice interview, and get their recommendations for improving your performance.

If possible, arrange to have your practice interview videotaped. This will be the most valuable performance feedback you can get—firsthand review.

Complete Career Action 16-1

FOLLOW GUIDELINES FOR PRACTICE INTERVIEWS

The following interview guidelines will help you perform successfully in your practice interview.

- **Prepare and take your Interview Marketing Kit** (directions in Chapter 11). Practice showcasing relevant items from your portfolio at appropriate points in your practice interviews.

- **Dress as you would for an actual interview;** you will be rated on your appearance.

To get the most benefit from your practice interview, prepare for it as if it were real.

CAREER ACTION 16-1

Arrange Your Own Practice Interview

Directions: Schedule a practice interview with your support network members (one interviewer and one or two observers). Use the sample questions in Chapter 14 as a guide for your practice session. You can make a copy of them for the "interviewer" and include any stress questions (or others) you want to rehearse. Encourage the interviewer to expand on the questions, if possible, tailoring them to your job target to give you relevant interview practice. If possible, arrange to have your practice interview videotaped.

- **Provide your interviewer with your cover letter, resume, and employment application.**

- **Review the Interview Critique Form** (on page 274 of this chapter) to become familiar with the areas to be evaluated. This form is designed to give you an overview of your interview skills.

- **Give the interviewer and observers copies of the Interview Critique Form to evaluate your performance.**

- Send a thank-you letter to everyone who helps you.

Meeting with an employer for a practice interview also provides an opportunity to learn more about the company.

SUCCESS TIP

Ask your "interviewers" to evaluate your practice and dress rehearsals by using the Interview Critique Form.

PERSONAL BEST

Practice Interviewing with an Employer in Your Field

Some people have received job offers as a result of practice interviews with employers. Others have obtained leads that resulted in jobs. Everyone gains necessary interview experience, which is why this practice is so important.

Prepare now to participate in a dress-rehearsal practice interview with an employer in your field. This is your chance to rehearse and get feedback that will strengthen your actual interviews. Follow the guidelines below to schedule and participate in this important rehearsal:

- **Make an appointment for your interview dress rehearsal.** Explain that this is a course assignment and that you would appreciate the employer's help in completing it. Say you would like the interview to be as realistic as possible.

- **Ask whether it would be possible to get an employment application form.** If so, pick it up ahead of time, complete it carefully, and take it with you (along with your resume and cover letter) to the dress rehearsal.

- **Verify the address and other details about the meeting, and thank your contact** for agreeing to help you with the assignment.

- Take your Interview Marketing Kit and use it appropriately.

- Also take along a copy of the Interview Critique Form for the interviewer.

- Remember that any job offer should come spontaneously from the employer. Asking directly for a job contradicts your request for help in practicing your interviewing skills. If your contact makes an offer or provides leads or suggestions, however, follow up immediately if you are interested.

HAVE INTERVIEWERS FILL OUT CRITIQUE FORM

Make copies of the Interview Critique Form found at the end of this chapter. Give copies to the interviewer and observers of your practice interviews. After the interview, ask them to use the form to evaluate your performance, identify your strengths and weaknesses, and to give suggestions for improvement. Correct areas of weakness now—before your actual interview.

Complete Career Action 16-2

SUCCESS TIP

Summarize thoroughly what you learn from practice and rehearsal interviews. Send thank-you letters to everyone who helps.

Take your dress-rehearsal interview seriously. It can help you polish you interview skills and may result in job leads!

CAREER ACTION 16-2

Participate in a Dress Rehearsal Interview and Evaluate Your Performance

Directions: Contact an employer in your career field, and ask for help with a course assignment. Ask the employer to conduct a practice interview with you and to complete a copy of the Interview Critique Form.

1. Dress appropriately.

2. Take a copy of the Interview Critique Form (provided on page 274) with you, and ask the interviewer to evaluate your performance by completing the form during or after the interview.

3. After your rehearsal interview, evaluate your own performance; complete a copy of the Interview Follow-up and Evaluation Form (provided on page 271).

4. Within two days of your dress rehearsal, send a follow-up thank-you letter to the person who gave you the practice interview.

5. File your Interview Critique Form and Interview Follow-up and Evaluation Form in your Career Management Files Binder.

Practice interviews will build your confidence and help you prepare for real job interviews.

critical thinking *Questions*

1. Specifically how do you use the success strategies described in Chapter 1 (visualization, positive self-talk, affirmation statements, goal setting, and proactive and assertive behavior) in preparing for and participating in a practice interview? Which of these strategies do you find most useful?

2. Summarize any job search/career management advice or job lead information you received from the interviewer during your dress-rehearsal practice interview. What specific follow-up action do you plan to take with regard to this information?

CAREER ACTION 16-2

Interview Follow-up and Evaluation Form

Note: Duplicate this form for follow-up after every interview.

Directions: Record a summary of the interview as soon as possible to avoid forgetting important details. Supply the general information about the employer and the interviewer(s). Answer the questions as completely as possible.

Name of Organization: _____

Date of Interview: _____

Name(s) and Titles(s) of Interviewer(s): _____

_____

_____

Address:_____

Telephone: _____ Fax: _____

E-Mail Address: _____

Summary Activities and Questions

1. On a separate sheet of paper, write every question you can remember being asked during the interview. Take your time and be thorough. Do this before answering any of the following questions.

2. On the basis of the knowledge you gained in your interview and research, which of your qualifications would be the greatest asset in this job? Which of these qualifications do you think should be reinforced with the prospective employer in your follow-up?

_____

_____

_____

3. List any questions you think you answered inadequately. Then write out the best possible answer to these questions. Use additional paper if necessary.

_____

_____

_____

Continued on next page.

4. Did you forget to provide important information that demonstrates your qualifications for the job? Explain in detail.

   _____

   _____

   _____

5. What questions did you intend to ask but either forgot or didn't have a chance to ask? Write these out now.

   _____

   _____

   _____

6. How do you think you could have presented yourself more effectively (appearance, body language, verbal communication, enthusiasm, describing qualifications, and so on)?

   _____

   _____

   _____

7. In what area(s) do you think you performed best in your interview? Why?

   _____

   _____

   _____

8. In what area(s) do you think you performed poorly? What steps could you take to improve in these areas?

   _____

   _____

   _____

9. Describe information you learned about the interviewer that might be helpful in establishing greater rapport in the future (philosophy, current working projects or objectives, personal interests or hobbies, mutual interests, goals, and so on).

   _____

   _____

   _____

Continued on next page.

CAREER ACTION 16-2 (continued)

10. Should any point of confusion be clarified for the employer? Explain.

   _____

   _____

   _____

11. Are you scheduled for another interview with the organization? If so, record the date, time, place, and name(s) of the interviewer(s).

   _____

   _____

   _____

12. Record any other activities you offered to follow up on or were specifically asked to follow up on by the interviewer (for example, provide references, transcripts, certificates, or examples of work).

   _____

   _____

   _____

13. How does the interviewer prefer you follow up (by telephone, by letter, in person)?

   _____

   _____

   _____

14. By what date did the interviewer indicate the hiring decision would be made?

   _____

   _____

   _____

Continued on next page.

Interview Critique Form

Name of Interviewee: _____ Date: _____

Position Applied For: _____

Directions: Circle the appropriate rating of the interviewee (Excellent, Very Good, Good, or Needs Improvement) after each item listed below.

1. **Documentation** (Application for employment; resume; cover letter)

   Excellent　　　　　　　Very Good　　　　　　　Good　　　　　　　Needs Improvement

2. **Attitude** (Interested in position; self-confident; likable; pleasant tone of voice; smiling)

   Excellent　　　　　　　Very Good　　　　　　　Good　　　　　　　Needs Improvement

3. **Appearance** (Generally neat and tidy; appropriately dressed; alert; good hygiene)

   Excellent　　　　　　　Very Good　　　　　　　Good　　　　　　　Needs Improvement

4. **Job Qualifications** (Education, skills, and experience suitable for position; good personal attributes; human relations capability; dependable; punctual; industrious)

   Excellent　　　　　　　Very Good　　　　　　　Good　　　　　　　Needs Improvement

5. **Verbal Communication** (Speaks clearly with positive tone; uses proper English; avoids slang or repetitive words; emphasizes assets; is courteous; uses name of the interviewer)

   Excellent　　　　　　　Very Good　　　　　　　Good　　　　　　　Needs Improvement

6. **Nonverbal Communication** (Good body language; good eye contant; does not fidget)

   Excellent　　　　　　　Very Good　　　　　　　Good　　　　　　　Needs Improvement

7. **Listening** (Does not interrupt or respond too quickly; asks to have a question repeated, if necessary; takes time to think through important questions; calmly endures silence)

   Excellent　　　　　　　Very Good　　　　　　　Good　　　　　　　Needs Improvement

8. **Enthusiasm** (Demonstrates interest/energy through verbal and nonverbal communication)

   Excellent　　　　　　　Very Good　　　　　　　Good　　　　　　　Needs Improvement

Comments: On separate paper, please summarize any other observations you made during the interview. (Note favorable behavior and provide suggestions for improvement where necessary.)

chapter 17

INTERVIEW AND FOLLOW UP

In this chapter, you will:

- Review the summary of successful interview techniques.

- www Use the Internet to search for additional information on interview follow-up that could be useful to you.

- Prepare an outline for a follow-up telephone call that could be used after interviews.

- Compose a simple follow-up thank-you message to be used in addition to the follow-up telephone call.

- Prepare an outline of a formal follow-up letter that could be used after interviews instead of a telephone call.

"If you have not received feedback from a company that you interviewed with, don't hesitate to call. Persistence is often the key to furthering your career. Although I do not expect a follow-up call or letter after an interview, I am always pleased and favorably impressed when I do get one; it makes the candidate stand out from the rest."

Linda Stryker
Human Resources Manager
Square D/Groupe Schneider
www.squared.com

Previous Career Actions (completing employer research, practicing to interview, and applying the nine success strategies outlined in Chapter 1) have prepared you to succeed in your interviews. Chapter 17 highlights important points for succeeding in your interview and outlines interview follow-up actions that can tip the hiring decision in your favor.

INTERVIEW GAME STRATEGIES

To prepare for your successful interview, review the strategies covered earlier. Begin by reviewing all of Chapter 11, "Interview Like a Pro." Pay particular attention to Career Action 11-3, 60-Second Commercial; Career Action 11-4, Summary of Core Areas of Successful Interviewing; Career Action 11-5, Summary of Fine Points for Interview Success; and summaries of interview techniques. Also review Career Action 14-2, Create a Question-and-Answer Planning Sheet, and your research on salary negotiations and the suggestions presented in Chapter 15.

If you are asked to interview, the employer is interested in *you!* To connect most positively throughout your interview, focus on four areas:

- Be likable.
- Emphasize your qualifications.
- Show enthusiasm and interest.
- Use positive body language and voice qualities.

GOOD FOLLOW-UP MOVES

Interview follow-up can increase your chances of getting the job by 30 percent or more because many applicants don't bother to do it! Interviewers see follow-up by a job seeker as a proactive step that shows initiative and interest. When you *follow up,* you take action to evaluate your performance in interviews, you remind prospective employers of your qualifications for and interest in the job, and you encourage a speedy hiring decision (to hire you, of course).

Good follow-up reinforces your qualifications and helps you stand out favorably from the competition. Be patient during this stage of the job search. The hiring process often takes longer than the employer expects.

> *"Opportunity does not knock, it presents itself when you beat down the door."*
>
> Kyle Chandler

The key in follow-up is action. The steps include:

- Writing an evaluation of your interview performance.
- Sending a follow-up message to the interviewer by telephone, letter, or e-mail or through a personal visit.

Evaluate Your Interview Immediately

Within one hour of every interview (or at the earliest possible time), summarize and evaluate your interview performance in writing. Do this for interviews that went well and for those that went poorly. This is the best way to learn from the experience, to improve your performance, and to plan your successful follow-up strategies. Ask yourself the following questions:

- What positive impressions did I make? What negative impressions might I have left with the interviewer? Why did I make these impressions?
- Was there anything I should have said that I didn't?
- What other questions would I have liked to ask? What other questions should I have asked?
- What questions would I have answered differently? How would I have answered those questions differently?
- How did I feel about the interview immediately after it concluded? How do I feel about the interview now?

Plan Your Follow-up Strategies

After each interview, complete an Interview Follow-up and Evaluation Form (Chapter 16, page 271). Circle in red any notes that require follow-up (information you need to clarify or reinforce with the employer, questions you want answered, areas of weak performance and suggestions for improving, and specific actions you need to take).

A follow-up call, letter, or e-mail tells the prospective employer you are interested in the job.

Determine what method of follow-up is most appropriate. If, during your interview, you remembered to ask the interviewer how he or she wanted you to follow up, the decision has been made for you. If you forgot to ask this question, send a follow-up letter, rather than make a telephone call. If your cover letter and resume were sent to the prospective employer through e-mail, you may choose to follow up your interview with an e-mail message. If the interviewer approves of follow-up telephone calls, use that method. A telephone call is more personal and lively and gives you quicker feedback. But also follow up with a letter or an e-mail because it provides a permanent reminder of you!

Outline Your Follow-up Message. Regardless of the method you choose for follow-up, first outline the message and include these topics:

1. List any questions you need to ask.

2. Summarize pertinent information you omitted or covered inadequately in your interview.

3. State specifically how the organization could benefit by hiring you (a brief rerun of or an excerpt from your 60-Second Commercial).

SUCCESS TIP

Prepare a written script you can use for an interview follow-up telephone call.

Make your follow-up message brief and well polished. Include only the most important questions or information.

Time Your Call. Make your follow-up call within two days of your interview, while your name and the interview are still fresh in the interviewer's mind. Contact employers on days other than at the beginning or end of the week; Mondays and Fridays are the busiest business days. Just before lunch or closing are usually inconvenient times as well. Guidelines for a successful follow-up telephone call are outlined in the Personal Best feature on page 279.

Send a Brief Thank-You Message Too. Even if you make your initial follow-up by telephone, also send a brief thank-you letter or e-mail message within 48 hours of your interview to be sure your message is received during the decision-making stage. (The body of a thank-you e-mail would be similar to that of a thank-you letter.)

Thank-you messages should be written to each person who interviewed you. The letters can be basically the same, but try to vary each one in case the recipients compare notes. If you've already made a telephone call, do not restate your qualifications in this message; just thank the interviewer, with no strings attached! Send a thank-you note even if you're sure the job is not for you.

The thank-you letter brings your name before the interviewer one more time in a favorable light, reinforcing your name in his or her mind. It also provides a positive written record of you in the employer's files. Review the brief thank-you letter (Figure 17-1 on page 280) to be sent after a follow-up telephone call.

SUCCESS TIP

Draft a brief follow-up letter or e-mail message you can send after making a follow-up telephone call.

Send a More Complete Follow-up Letter When No Call Is Made or to Add Information. If the interviewer prefers follow-up in writing or if you think your interview performance was weak in any area and follow-up is important to getting hired, send a more complete follow-up letter. This letter should include the following:

1. Reference to your interview and the position you are seeking

2. Clarification of any pertinent information omitted during your interview

3. A brief version of your 60-Second Commercial

4. A thank-you for the interviewer's time

5. A statement of enthusiasm for the job

6. Encouragement of a speedy hiring decision

Review Figure 17-2 on page 281 to see how these items are presented in the sample letter.

NOTE: The follow-up letter provides a permanent written record of your qualifications and professional courtesy. The employer can review it anytime—an effective way to keep your "commercial" running!

Complete Career Action 17-1

CAREER ACTION 17-1

Search the Internet for Interview Follow-up Tips

WWW **Directions:** Search the Internet for additional tips on interview follow-up that could be useful to you.

When using search engines, try the following search strings: *interview follow-up letters, thank-you letters,* or *interview follow-up.* Summarize key points you find useful or print relevant articles.

Web Sites:

- Monster Trak   http://campus.monster.com
  (Click on "Career Guide" and then click on "Successful Interviewing.")

- CareerLab   www.careerlab.com
  (Click on "Cover Letter Library." These are excellent models. Then click on "Say Thank You with Class," and browse through the many samples provided.)

- Virginia Tech University   www.career.vt.edu
  (Click on "Students" to go to the Career Services page.)

- The Riley Guide   www.rileyguide.com/interview.html

A prospective employer will consider a recommendation favorably from someone he or she knows and trusts.

SUCCESS TIP

Draft a longer follow-up letter to add information or to use when no call is made.

Connect With Your Support Network Again. If a member of your support network is influential with your prospective employer, contact him or her to ask for additional support. A friendly follow-up call from this person to the employer could tip the scales in your favor.

An alternative to the follow-up call by a network member is a letter of recommendation sent to the employer from one or more people who can confirm your qualifications. Some employers routinely request letters of recommendation from former employers, managers, or supervisors of applicants. Arranging to have such letters sent on your own demonstrates initiative—another benefit for you!

PERSONAL BEST

Making a Successful Follow-up Telephone Call

If your interviewer approves of follow-up calls, you can set yourself apart from the competition with a well-timed, well-prepared telephone call.

- **Demonstrate courtesy.** "Do you have a moment?"

- **Begin with a greeting and self-introduction.** "Hello, Ms. Delgado. This is Gregory Tambascio calling."

- **Identify the position for which you interviewed and the date of your interview.** "I want to thank you for meeting with me yesterday to discuss the Data Processing Systems Analyst I position."

- **Provide important information you omitted.** "After reviewing our meeting, I realized I hadn't mentioned some pertinent information regarding my (education, work experience, qualifications, other)." Then give the specifics in a concise form.

- **Reemphasize your qualifications.** If necessary, give a short, targeted version of your 60-Second Commercial, emphasizing exactly how your qualifications can benefit the employer.

- **If necessary, ask questions to clarify any points not covered adequately.** This information may include a clearer description of the job responsibilities or clarification of work relationships.

- **Thank the interviewer, express your interest, and encourage a speedy hiring decision.** "Thank you again for the interview. I look forward to learning of your hiring decision soon. I believe we could benefit each other, and I'd be pleased to be a part of Mississippi Central Power Company."

Apartment 34
2440 Observatory Boulevard
Los Angeles, CA 90063
July 2, 20—

Ms. Stephanie Nolan
Manager, Auditing Staff
Nolan Henry O'Leary Public Accountants
1410 Granada Avenue, 7th Floor
San Francisco, CA 94115

Dear Ms. Nolan:

Thank you for the opportunity to interview for the position of Staff Auditor I with you
and your team. Your invitation to join the first hour of the weekly staff meeting made
me feel especially welcome—and sent me to the library to brush up on the finer points
of the state's tax credit program for employers who train welfare recipients!

I would enjoy being part of your team and look forward to your hiring decision.
Please call me anytime this week at 213-555-0128.

Sincerely,

Russell Thistlethwaite

Russell Thistlethwaite

Figure 17-1: Sample of a Brief Thank-You Letter

3493 Huntington Heights
Denver, CO 80202
August 23, 20—

Mr. Frederick J. Gray Wolf
Normandy Copiers, Inc.
3500 Main Street
Boulder, CO 80302-8715

Dear Mr. Gray Wolf:

The enthusiasm you shared this afternoon for the customer-centered philosophy behind the new Normandy Print Center is contagious! I know from experience how satisfying it is to break new ground and to achieve results that exceed all expectations.
The Normandy management system sounds unique, innovative, and challenging.

During our meeting, we discussed how I could contribute to your marketing plan, but
we didn't have time to talk about store operations. While I managed the parts and service operations of Reinassance Business Systems, our team achieved and maintained a
production efficiency rate that consistently placed us in the top 5 percent of the 160
shops nationwide. Sales of maintenance contracts increased every year I was in charge,
and we had the lowest return rate for products of all the centers.

Thank you for talking with me about the new opportunities at Normandy. Normandy
Copiers, Inc., will be a great success in Boulder, and I would like to contribute to that
success. As we agreed, I will call you next Thursday, but you can reach me before that
at 303-555-0171.

Sincerely,

Francesca Elena Valdez

Francesca Elena Valdez

Figure 17-2: Sample of a More Complete Follow-up Letter

WAITING-GAME STRATEGIES

Waiting to hear about a hiring decision is frustrating. Your best strategy is action!

Evaluate Your Performance and Identify Follow-up Activities

After you complete your follow-up telephone call and letter, review your notes on the Interview Follow-up and Evaluation Form (Chapter 16, page 271). Concentrate on the positive aspects of your evaluation to keep your self-image positive. Check to be certain you have completed all follow-up activities you underlined in red.

> *"Many of life's failures are people who did not realize how close they were to success when they gave up."*
>
> Thomas A. Edison

Complete Career Action 17-2

Call Back If You Don't Hear About the Decision

Check the last question on the Interview Follow-up and Evaluation Form: By what date did the interviewer indicate the hiring decision would be made? Call if you don't receive notice of the hiring decision by the date the interviewer gave you.

The following technique doesn't pressure interviewers:

"Hello, Ms. Delgado. This is Gregory Tambascio calling. You indicated during our meeting that you expected to make a hiring decision by July 30. I might have missed your call if you tried to get in touch with me."

This technique helps you with the waiting game by giving you current information about the hiring status. This demonstration of interest and initiative could also persuade the employer to hire you. It happens!

Remember the saying about the squeaky wheel getting the grease? Continue following up, especially if the employer has asked you to. Just be careful not to go overboard and annoy or bother the employer. You'll seem desperate for the job.

SUCCESS TIP

After each interview, evaluate your performance and identify ways to improve; list all necessary follow-up activities and complete them.

CAREER ACTION 17-2

Follow-up Telephone Call and Letter or E-mail

Directions: Access your Learner's CD or complete the follow-up telephone call and letter or e-mail activities on page 284.

✔ **CHECKLIST:**

Successful Interviewing and Follow-up

Check each of the actions you are taking to increase your interview and follow-up success:

☐ Reviewing interview success strategies: Chapter 11, 60-Second Commercial, and Career Action 14-2, Create a Question-and-Answer Planning Sheet

☐ Preparing a written script for an interview follow-up telephone call; if necessary, including questions not asked in the interview or adding information omitted

☐ Drafting a brief follow-up message to send after making a follow-up telephone call

☐ Drafting a longer follow-up letter to add important information or to use when no call is made

☐ After each interview, completing an Interview Follow-up and Evaluation Form; taking steps to improve areas of weak performance; completing all necessary follow-up activities

critical thinking *Questions*

1. What is included in a good interview follow-up?

2. What are the important topics applicants should include in their follow-up communication (telephone call, letter, or e-mail)?

3. What follow-up is required after your dress rehearsal practice interview (Career Action 16-2)?

Follow-up Telephone Call and Letter or E-mail

Part 1: Follow-up Telephone Call

Directions: Prepare a draft of a telephone call you can use to follow up an interview. Refer to the Personal Best feature for the items to be included in your telephone call. Practice making the call in a role-play situation.

_____

_____

_____

_____

_____

Part 2: Brief Follow-up Thank-You Message

Directions: Write a brief follow-up thank-you message to use after you have made your follow-up telephone call. This message may be sent conventionally by mail service or electronically, depending on the type of position or company you interviewed with or the type of initial contact you had with the prospective employer (for example, high-tech company or resume and cover letter were submitted electronically).

_____

_____

_____

_____

_____

Part 3: Complete Follow-up Thank-You Letter

Directions: Draft a letter you could use as a follow-up to your interview instead of a telephone call.

1. Write an appropriate greeting and a reminder of the position you interviewed for.

2. Include any pertinent information you omitted from your interview.

3. Summarize your job qualifications briefly with the short version of your 60-Second Commercial.

4. Express your interest in the job and your appreciation for the interview.

18 PREPARE YOUR NEXT MOVE IF YOU DON'T GET THE JOB

chapter

In this chapter, you will:

- Determine how to deal effectively with rejection in your job search.

- Evaluate your job search performance and identify methods of improving it.

"When things do not go the way you want them to go, it's time to ask yourself: What didn't work in the interview? What questions were you struggling with? What do you need to change? Ask people for honest feedback. Sometimes we need to check that the impressions we gave to others were what we intended."

Roxanne Pellegrino
Educational Services Manager
Philadelphia Job Corps

Getting a good job often requires more than one interview; it may take several tries before you land the job you want. Getting a rejection notice is not a great ego booster, but it's not a reason to stop your job search campaign. Think of it as a learning experience, and continue with your job search activities. Chapter 18 highlights practical strategies for reenergizing your motivation, reversing a rejection notice, and trying new angles to land a top job.

COUNTER REJECTION WITH SUCCESS STRATEGIES

To counter natural feelings of rejection, the best defense is taking immediate positive action.

- Maintain a positive attitude.

- Evaluate your performance and your self-marketing package.

- Connect with your network for support and rework your contacts.

- Plan your next job search steps and follow through.

Taking a short breather helps you renew energy and enthusiasm. Allow yourself one day to do something you enjoy and to relax—but no longer. And don't use rejection as an excuse for giving up. Simply regroup and rework your action plans!

Apply the Nine Success Strategies

Reread Chapter 1, focusing on the success strategies that project competence and strengthen self-esteem. Visualize yourself performing successfully in your next interview and on your new job. Also make a conscious effort to think and act positively and to use positive self-talk and affirmation statements.

Review your self-analysis forms from Chapters 2 and 3 (your talents, skills, qualifications, special accomplishments, and personal attributes). Also review your 60-Second Commercial. Remind yourself of your skills and positive accomplishments.

 SUCCESS TIP

After a job rejection, use positive thinking, actions, visualization, goal setting, and self-talk to recharge your motivation, to fine-tune your job search campaign, and to improve your performance.

Don't let a job rejection get you down. Use the tactics athletes use: Analyze your performance, visualize succeeding, and move on.

Persevere for Success

Winners in all fields agree: Perseverance is a major factor in their success. When they meet an obstacle, they find a way around it. Setbacks are not failures; you only fail when you quit trying.

No one can be right for every job. The right person for a job doesn't always get it. However, the best prepared and most determined person often does. While you may be responsible in part for the initial rejection, you still have the power to correct the situation and win the job offer. With belief in yourself, you can still succeed.

IS "NO" ALWAYS THE FINAL ANSWER?

Many job applicants have turned a first rejection into a job offer through effective follow-up. Sometimes interviewers get an inaccurate first impression of an applicant. You can revise that impression through follow-up; consider the following techniques:

- **Call and clarify.** Place a timely call to provide missing information, to correct misinformation, to clarify qualifications, or to restate interest. Doing so can turn rejection into employment.

- **Call and request a short follow-up meeting.** Explain that you have additional information, portfolio examples, or some other item you think the interviewer should consider before making a hiring decision. Ask for just 10 or 15 minutes to make your case. Do your homework and prepare your telephone script before you call. Make the call organized and concise. Speak with energy and enthusiasm.

SUCCESS TIP

Ask the interviewer to evaluate your performance. You need to base your rejection response on facts, not on assumptions; the information can help you identify areas that need improvement.

Get an Evaluation of Your Interview Performance

After receiving a rejection notice, if you're not sure where you fell short, call your interviewer and ask for an honest evaluation. If you are aware of the perceived shortcoming, though, prepare a strong written clarification you can refer to while making your rejection follow-up call. Here is a way of asking your interviewer for an evaluation:

"Hello, Ms. Nguyen. This is Aaron Goldman. I received your letter stating I had not been selected for the job, and I appreciate the prompt notification. Could you tell me which areas of my preparation and qualifications need to be strengthened, and could you suggest methods of improving in these areas?"

The interviewer may try to evade your question. Some employers are reluctant to offer specific opinions and are justifiably cautious about disgruntled applicants suing for unfair hiring policies. Even if you don't get concrete help, express your thanks.

Prepare and Respond. If the interviewer is willing to evaluate your performance and make suggestions for improvement, listen carefully and take notes. Accept the concerns the interviewer or company representative conveys to you. Their validity is irrelevant. The important point is that these concerns represent problem areas in the interviewer's perception of you. Develop ways to overcome each negative perception.

If you are prepared, briefly clarify your qualifications or clear up any misunderstanding during the telephone call. Use a friendly tone and do not react defensively. Remember, you asked for the opinion.

If you need more time to respond, after your call, write out an effective response to concerns identified by the interviewer. Then write, call, or visit in person to present your new information. A letter can become a permanent part of your application file and can be reviewed more than once, perhaps by someone else in the company who decides you have the required qualities.

Set Up Another Meeting. If the interviewer seems receptive, explain that you didn't convey your qualifications as completely as you had planned and suggest you meet once more to review them. Handled well, this approach demonstrates confidence, competence, and assertiveness.

> *"If opportunity doesn't knock, build a door."*
>
> Milton Berle

Ask for Referrals. If you reach a point where no further action would get you this job, ask for other referrals.

"Thank you again for your time, Ms. Nguyen. I have one more question. Could you recommend another department or company I might contact to discuss employment possibilities?"

Offer Additional Positive Information

Make your call or send your letter to add additional positive information and/or to clarify your qualifications. The purposes should be:

- To provide added positive information.

- To confirm your enthusiasm and interest in the job.

- To convince the interviewer you are qualified for the job.

Prepare your telephone script or letter, and review it with a member of your support network before going further.

Ask for a referral to another department within the organization. This department may have a position that better matches your skills and qualifications.

SUCCESS TIP

Prepare and deliver a response to a rejection notice. Provide additional information or portfolio samples. This follow-up may reverse the rejection.

REVERSE JOB REJECTION: A TRUE CASE

The following case illustrates how well-planned follow-up can reverse a job rejection. Steve was graduating in engineering from a private university. He applied to several companies, but his first choice was Silar Corporation.

His resume, cover letter, and application for employment got him an interview. He thought the interview was successful because he felt comfortable with the interviewer and solidly demonstrated how his qualifications fit the needs at Silar. He was encouraged by the positive feedback from the interviewer.

Steve was shocked when he received a cordial letter of rejection a week later. The letter emphasized that his 3.2 grade point average didn't meet that of the competition. Many applicants would have accepted the rejection as final proof that this particular job wasn't within their reach. Not so with Steve.

He discussed the subject with his professors and other members of his support network and decided a follow-up telephone call would be appropriate. Steve had not made it clear during his interview that he had worked full-time while earning his university degree. In addition, Steve's performance was below average in the first year while he clarified his degree objective and learned to develop good study habits—typical of many students. Because his grades were excellent the last three years, he thought an appeal to Silar based on demonstrated improvement and achievement was in order.

Review Steve's Success

Steve called the department manager with whom he interviewed at Silar Corporation. Steve said that he had received the rejection letter but added that additional circumstances might be considered. He explained that he had worked full-time during his four years in college and that he hadn't clearly identified his degree and career objectives until the latter part of his first year. After the first year, with clear goals in mind, his academic performance was excellent, including a 3.8 average in his engineering major.

Three days later Steve received a call from the department manager offering him a job! The manager explained that Steve's initiative and belief in his qualifications convinced him and his colleagues that Steve had the qualities they were seeking.

Model Your Success

Steve's technique (or a variation of it) has been used by thousands of applicants, and the results have been remarkably successful. You may have a perfectly valid reason for clarifying your qualifications. It takes courage and determination, but the possible reward for your effort is the successful conclusion of your job search. If you receive a rejection notice, you have nothing to lose and everything to gain by trying this tactic.

Word your rejection response carefully. Ask for help from a member of your support network who has strong communication skills. Work with this person to develop your rejection response using the guidelines in the Personal Best feature.

CONSIDER ANOTHER POSITION IN ANOTHER DEPARTMENT

If your rejection response doesn't land you this job, ask whether another position would be more suitable for you. Emphasize your enthusiasm for working for this employer, and ask whether you are more qualified to fill another position. This strategy encourages the interviewer to give you more consideration and can land you a "hidden job." If another position isn't available, ask for a referral to another employer. Employers are impressed by applicants who demonstrate initiative and confidence. If you project confidence and competence, you greatly increase your chances of convincing others of your potential.

PERSONAL BEST

Responding to Rejection

No one enjoys getting no for an answer. But your response to rejection can turn a potential negative into a positive for your job search.

To respond to a rejection notice:

- Describe in writing the shortcomings the interviewer perceives that resulted in your rejection.

- Summarize any misunderstandings you think contributed to your rejection.

- Summarize important information you omitted during the application or interview process.

- Draft your rejection response, clarifying any misunderstandings, adding information you omitted, and expanding on your qualifications.

- Make your response positive, active, and pleasant. Don't dwell on negatives.

- Review and practice the content with a member of your network.

Making this extra effort provides further proof of your initiative and interest in the job. This can be the factor that causes the interviewer to choose you.

SUCCESS TIP

Ask for referrals to another department or another company. Such leads often open new employment possibilities!

Don't Be Afraid to Reapply

If you don't get a job with your preferred employer now, don't give up. Even if you take another job for a while, opportunities can develop later. If an opening comes up in the future, you have the advantage of being known by the employer because a known applicant saves valuable time in recruiting a new employee. Besides, you never know how close to being accepted you were. You might be at the top of the list the next time an opening occurs. Keeping your name in front of the employer can put you first in line for the next opening. One way you can do this is by calling the interviewer every couple of months just to check in. Keep the phone call brief and polite. Your purpose is to keep your name at the top of the list. Consider the following true story.

"To keep a lamp burning, we have to keep putting oil in it."

Mother Teresa

Mercedes applied to a large, well-known corporation for a job as an administrative assistant in the human resources department. The department manager interviewed her. She knew she did well in the interview, but she didn't get the job because someone was promoted from within (another common practice).

A month later the manufacturing department manager found Mercedes' file and interview rating sheet in the human resources department. He noted the manager had decided not to hire her, despite excellent qualifications, because her personality was "too strong for the human resources department." The manufacturing department manager decided immediately that someone who was "too strong for the human resources department" was exactly what he needed in the manufacturing area. Result: The manufacturing department manager interviewed Mercedes and hired her at a higher salary than she would have been offered for the first position. Five years later she was promoted to a supervisory position with a salary 125 percent above her starting salary.

Be Persistent

Be persistent in pursuing your preferred job. Stay focused on your goal, and consider all the factors that may affect the status of the position for which you have applied.

Business conditions change daily and may include expansion, new product development, new government regulations, mergers and takeovers, and so on. Any one of these conditions could affect the status of your job target. These business conditions could result in the creation of new jobs; the modification of existing jobs; or in some cases, the elimination of jobs. Carefully consider how changes in business conditions may present new opportunities to you as a job seeker.

Many organizations and businesses keep applications in their active file for a specific period of time (usually six months). After that time, an application will not be considered for new position openings. Therefore, if you are interested in a position with a particular company, find out the organization's policy for keeping applications active. You may need to call a prospective employer periodically to keep your application active and to remind him or her that you're interested in new job openings.

Success Tip

Don't be afraid to reapply. You could be first on the backup list; employers save time and money hiring candidates from this list. Continue to check back to keep your name recognition high.

Business conditions change daily. These changes may represent new job opportunities for you.

FOLLOW UP ON YOUR JOB SEARCH PERFORMANCE EVALUATION

The keys to your success are preparation and positive thinking. Remember, it is necessary to plan and organize to succeed. Ask yourself these practical questions. Then take action to strengthen your job search effectiveness.

- Have I overlooked any skills, training, or competencies that support my job target?

- Have I checked with my support network to find out whether they have new job leads?

- Could my resume be improved or tailored to a new job target? How could it be improved? Who could do a good job of helping me with it?

- Should I make additional telephone calls/personal visits or write additional letters to prospective employers?

- Could my cover letters be improved? How could they be strengthened?

- Have I followed up on every interview—with telephone calls, messages, and personal visits? Have I followed up on the cover letters and resumes I mailed and on all job leads?

- Have I done thorough research on my current job leads—enough to talk intelligently and persuasively about me and the organization in an interview?

- Have I tried every possible job source?

- Should I reapply with any employers? When?

- Did I do a thorough job of interview follow-up?

- Have I scheduled my job search on my daily and weekly calendars?

Career Action 18-1 will help you outline practical actions to strengthen your job search effectiveness.

Complete Career Action 18-1

CAREER ACTION 18-1

Action Plans for Improving Your Job Search Campaign

Directions: Complete the Action Plans for Improving Your Job Search Campaign form on page 293. Complete the follow-up actions required to improve your job search techniques.

✓ CHECKLIST:

Recharging Your Job Search Campaign

Check each of the actions you are taking to increase your career success:

☐ Using positive thinking, actions, visualization, goal setting, and self-talk to recharge motivation and to improve the job search campaign

☐ Asking the interviewer to evaluate performance so responses can be based on facts and areas that need improvement can be identified

☐ Preparing and delivering a response to a rejection notice; providing additional information or portfolio samples and clarifying qualifications or misunderstanding as needed

☐ Asking for referrals to another department or another company

☐ Reapplying at a later date; calling back periodically to check the hiring status

critical thinking *Questions*

1. After a rejection, how should you approach your continuation of the job search?

2. Should you abandon your efforts to obtain a job with a prospective employer if, following your interview, you are notified that you were not selected for the position? Why or why not?

3. What can you gain from seeking an evaluation of your interview performance from an interviewer who rejected you?

4. If all your efforts fail to result in a job offer, what last request should you make of the interviewer?

CAREER ACTION 18-1

Action Plans for Improving Your Job Search Campaign

Directions: Review your complete job search campaign thoroughly. Answer each of the following questions in detail. Where necessary, include specific action plans you will take to improve. Check off each item as you complete the actions.

1. After reviewing my self-analysis activities in the Career Actions from Chapters 2 and 3, have I overlooked anything important that supports my job target? (List any items here and summarize needed research or improvement.)

   _____

   _____

   _____

2. Have I checked with my support network to find out whether they have new job leads? (List them here and follow up immediately.)

   _____

   _____

   _____

3. Could my resume be improved or tailored to a new job target? How could it be improved? Who could do a good job of helping me with it?

   _____

   _____

   _____

4. Should I make additional telephone calls/personal visits or write additional letters to prospective employers? (List detailed actions on a separate sheet of paper, and begin following up today. Don't put them off.)

   _____

   _____

   _____

5. Could my cover letters be improved? How could they be strengthened?

   _____

   _____

   _____

Continued on next page.

6. Have I followed up on every interview—with telephone calls, messages, and personal visits? Have I followed up on the cover letters and resumes I mailed and on all job leads? (List any follow-up needed in these areas.)

_____

_____

_____

7. Have I done thorough research on my current job leads—enough to talk intelligently and persuasively about me and the organization in an interview? (List any research that must be completed.)

_____

_____

_____

8. Have I tried every possible job source? (Refer to the list of suggested job sources in Chapter 6. List below any you could use now.)

_____

_____

_____

9. Should I reapply with any employers? When?

_____

_____

_____

10. Review Chapter 17. Did I do a thorough job of interview follow-up? (Make note of any follow-up activity omitted that might have improved your chance of being selected.)

_____

_____

_____

11. Have I scheduled my job search on my daily and weekly calendars? If not, do it now!

_____

_____

_____

chapter 19

YOU'RE HIRED! SUCCEED IN YOUR NEW POSITION

In this chapter, you will:

■ Review guidelines for adjusting successfully and achieving peak performance in a new job.

■ Evaluate your previous or current performance in a job, in volunteer work, or in another responsible activity.

 Search the Internet for job and career success tips.

■ Research your industry for tips on job success and promotion and on making a job change.

"While learning the essentials of a new position, also pay particular attention to those people around you who have contributed much to the organization. Glean knowledge and perspective from them. Watch how they approach new assignments. Observe how they handle tough situations. The more you learn about 'your' company, the bigger asset you become!"

R. E. Keiter
Manager
Wilson Associates

Chapter 19 presents guidelines for adjusting to and succeeding in your new job. These include techniques for developing successful interpersonal skills, achieving top work efficiency, quickly mastering new responsibilities, and learning how to prepare for a successful job performance evaluation. The importance of taking responsibility for achieving a high quality and quantity of work and for being adaptable to change is also emphasized. Once you master your job and are performing at your peak, you will likely be interested in working toward career development and advancement opportunities. This chapter also provides clear guidelines for earning a promotion and achieving career growth.

ADJUST TO YOUR NEW JOB

All workers who start new jobs have one challenge in common: adjusting to the job. Adjustment includes learning to perform specific job functions, learning how the job relates to the business as a whole, learning to work with others (superiors, team members or coworkers, and customers), and understanding the formal and informal chain of organizational command. Mastering all these elements takes time and effort on your part and training assistance from your employer.

> *"As for the future, your task is not to foresee, but to enable it."*
>
> Antoine de Saint-Exupery

Don't expect to achieve top efficiency overnight. It doesn't happen. Experiencing some anxiety in trying to learn so much new information and many new procedures is normal. Maintaining enthusiasm, eagerness to learn, and a positive attitude will help you adjust successfully.

Starting a new job is an important personal and professional step that shapes your lifetime career. Successful careers are developed through planning and determination to succeed. You will achieve peak success by being persistent and by accumulating skills, knowledge, and experience.

Your employer will want you to succeed; coworkers will help you get off to a good start. The following techniques will help you adjust to the organization and your job and to achieve a successful lifetime career.

Project a Positive Attitude: The Most Important Success Factor

Employers hire and promote employees who have good attitudes and demonstrate enthusiasm and a positive attitude. Employees who demonstrate a defensive, negative, or disinterested attitude are not promoted and may eventually be terminated. Two employees with equal job skills but vastly different attitudes often develop widely different career paths. The one with a strong, positive attitude progresses steadily; the one with a negative attitude stagnates.

Approach new tasks, colleagues, and superiors with the attitude that you will do your best and that you expect the best from them, while being patient with their constraints. People most often live up to the expectations others have of them.

Project a Positive, Professional, and Competent Image

People assume that the image you project is an example of the quality of work you do. Your image projects from three sources: your inner confidence, your outward appearance, and your verbal and nonverbal communication. Review the information on self-esteem, appearance, and communication skills in Chapters 1 and 11. Polish and apply these skills daily.

Expect that adjusting to your new job will take some time. Be alert, listen, and stay positive. Look, speak, and act professionally.

If you project an unsure attitude through your speech, appearance, and actions, you will be perceived as a tentative, unsure worker, even if your work is excellent. Purposely think, speak, dress, and act positively. This projects career-building confidence and competence.

Projecting a positive, professional, and competent image gives you a competitive edge. For example, if you make an error, your professional image influences people to be more accepting of the error as a part of learning, rather than as a result of incompetence. Successful people act positively, practicing the nine success strategies (Chapter 1) until these become habits.

Emulate the habits of successful people. Think of yourself, see yourself, groom yourself, and talk about yourself as a winner.

Develop and Practice Good Interpersonal Skills: Be a Team Player

Job success depends largely on the ability to work well with others. Studies repeatedly verify that job failure is most frequently based on poor interpersonal (behavior and attitude) skills, *not* on lack of skill.

Be a Team Player. Get along well with and assist others, show interest in their work, and work efficiently alone or with others. Team players are promoted first.

Be Tactful. The world's most successful people have these abilities in common: They are tactful, diplomatic, courteous, and helpful in dealing with other people.

Treat People the Way You Want to Be Treated.
Help others accomplish their assignments, compliment them on work well done, criticize tactfully only when necessary, and listen to what they have to say. This behavior encourages others to treat you the same way.

When you need help with a project or are in line for a promotion, your reputation for working well with others will more likely be rewarded. Treat all people (your employer, peers, the custodian) with respect.

SUCCESS TIP

Focus on three goals to help you adjust successfully to a new job: Keep a positive attitude; project a professional, competent image; and be a good team player.

GET OFF TO A SUCCESSFUL START

When you're hired, your employer expects you to have the basic knowledge and skills to do the job. You acquired these through your education and prior work experience. The challenge now is to apply them to the best of your ability in performing your job.

"The only certain means of success is to render more and better service than is expected of you, no matter what your task may be."

Og Mandino

Be a good learner and expand your abilities. You will be expected to become a productive employee within a reasonable training period. You can improve the quality and speed of your learning and performance by applying the following techniques for mastering a new job.

Pay Attention to Your Job Orientation

Your employer is responsible for informing you of your job duties and for providing an orientation to the work procedures. You should also be told about work hours, parking requirements, and related information.

Your employer should explain when and how your performance will be evaluated. To help focus your efforts and achieve the best possible performance evaluation, find out immediately *exactly how and when your job performance will be evaluated*. If your employer overlooks any of this orientation or job evaluation information, request an explanation.

Be Aware and Alert

Observe carefully the way work flows through your department, and be a good listener. This will help you adjust more quickly. Others appreciate good listening skills and not needing to repeat information. Also pay attention to subtle attitudes and unstated policies that influence work operations.

Learn the Organizational Culture and the Development of Your Area

Every organization has a unique personality and culture. To enhance your success, develop organizational savvy. Learn and adhere to culture values, including the expected work ethic and social norms. For example, are social activities in and out of the workplace the norm? Will you be considered aloof if you don't participate? Pay attention. Not all cultural norms are spelled out. You discover these through observation.

Use a Question-and-Answer Notebook

As you learn each aspect of your job, use a notebook to record all your questions and the instructions you receive. Ask your supervisor what times are best for discussing your questions (to avoid annoying your supervisor with poorly timed interruptions). Maintaining your notebook is important for several reasons:

- You will improve your efficiency by clarifying information that hasn't been explained fully.

- You won't have to repeat your questions.

- Your supervisor will appreciate your efficiency.

Remembering every detail required to master a new set of job tasks is impossible. A notebook provides a quick review and a reminder of tasks and procedures.

PERSONAL BEST
Managing Your Time

Managing your time effectively is one of the keys to becoming an efficient worker. Follow these time management tips to increase your productivity:

Be on Time. Be at your desk ready to work on time (or a little early) every day. Being on time gives you an edge of preparedness and an unhurried mind-set that improves work performance.

Determine Priorities and Plan Your Work Around Them. Ask your coworkers and supervisor what tasks are most vital to the successful operation of your department. Prioritize your work based on this information. Do your most important daily tasks first to avoid overlooking vital tasks during rush work periods. Reassess your priorities as new tasks are assigned, and review these with your team or supervisor periodically.

Use Time Management Tools: Calendars and Job-Tracking Forms. Keep your work calendar current, coordinate it with your work team, and check it daily. Keep a reminder notebook of tasks to be completed. Prepare a daily to-do list, and record the tasks in order of importance. Do your best each day to complete as many tasks on your list as possible.

Develop Good Time Management Habits. To gain maximum efficiency, group all tasks that are alike and complete them in one block of time. This focuses your attention and task performance rather than fragmenting it. For example, schedule one time block to prepare documents and another to place phone calls.

Keep Your Work Area Well Organized. If your work area is well organized, you can locate and use resources efficiently; this increases productivity, decreases frustration, and enhances your professional image.

Use time management and personal organization tools to keep track of your activities.

Be Dependable, Punctual, and Industrious

Be professional, hardworking, and accurate in performing your job. This sets a positive example for your coworkers. Employers value and look for these qualities in retaining and promoting people.

Maintain an Excellent Attendance Record.
Absenteeism causes work inefficiency, disruption of workflow, and lower productivity. It also places stress on workers who must cover for the absent employee, causing resentment and frustration. If you must be absent because of a severe illness, a serious emergency, or an unavoidable problem, let your employer know as soon as possible.

Chronic absenteeism is not tolerated by employers and is an eventual ticket out the door. *Abuse* is the key word. Patterns of questionable excuses raise questions in the employer's mind.

Be Punctual and Dependable. Be on time for work at the start of your day and after breaks or mealtimes. Be punctual for meetings. Those who make

an effort to be punctual do not appreciate your being late. Be on time! Being on time also means finishing projects and assignments when they are due.

Demonstrate Initiative. Personal initiative is a major factor affecting promotability. After you've finished your assigned duties, *don't sit and wait for more work to be assigned.* Find an appropriate task to perform on your own, or ask how you can help. Think creatively about better ways to do your job. Then research and plan how to implement your ideas. If a coworker is overloaded, offer to help.

Focus on People As Well As Job Duties

The way you relate to the people in your work will influence your career success as much as the quality of your job performance—no matter how skilled or educated you are. Make time for your coworkers, supervisors, employer, clients, or customers.

Be Courteous, Understanding, and Helpful. Spend time with coworkers during breaks and mealtimes. Network with others and get to know them. Don't let yourself become a loner; it won't enhance career success.

Be Aware of Organizational Politics. Every organization has formal and informal politics, which are impacted by changes in personnel. Learn who is respected (or even feared) in your place of employment. These people often influence office politics greatly and are usually powerful within the organization. Learn to deal with them successfully.

Note, however, that first impressions are not always accurate. Take time to observe and learn the office politics. Avoid affiliating closely with any individual or group that is not reputable and in harmony with your philosophy and the employer's.

Manage Yourself

Learn to deal with difficult people, control your emotions, and manage stress and conflict. Maintain a good fitness program and a healthy life balance.

Also manage your family and transportation; anticipate and prevent problems. Good books and classes are available on all of these subjects.

Build a Network

Actively build a network of people willing to help you understand how to work most efficiently and effectively in the organization. Whenever possible, reciprocate by helping people in your network. Also become involved in one or more professional, trade, or technical associations to expand your resources.

Seek Feedback and Accept Criticism

Actively asking for feedback from your supervisor demonstrates initiative and professionalism. Periodically ask your supervisor directly if your performance is meeting his or her expectations or if you need to improve. Ask for specific recommendations for improvement where necessary.

Because you are human, you will make an occasional mistake. Gasp! The challenge is to accept

Seek feedback and learn to accept criticism professionally. Consider criticism as an opportunity to improve.

criticism maturely. When you work for someone else, you agree to perform according to that person's standards. Because your employer pays your salary, he or she has the right to criticize your performance or behavior if it doesn't meet established standards.

If the criticism is deserved, don't deny fault. Accept the criticism professionally and make improvements. To learn from mistakes, request suggestions for improving from the person who criticizes you. If you don't think the criticism was justified, tactfully present the evidence that supports your opinion.

If your employer or supervisor continually criticizes you unfairly, particularly in front of others, request a meeting to discuss the reason. If the criticism continues even though you make the recommended improvements, consider seeking a position in another department or looking for a new employer.

Make Your Supervisor Look Good and Be Supportive

Find out what your supervisor needs to excel, and do what you can to provide it. Regularly using your initiative to meet these needs is a career booster!

In return for offering you a job and salary, the employer expects your support. Speak well of the firm and its personnel, products, and services. Speaking negatively about an organization harms the employer's reputation and may result in your being fired. If you're unhappy and see no way to gain satisfaction, move on.

Demonstrate Maturity

Be responsible for your actions. Perform at your best level, and expect the same from others you supervise. Be aware of your strengths and weaknesses. Capitalize on your strengths and make efforts to improve areas of weakness. Be self-reliant and self-disciplined. Maintain stable emotions in your workplace, leaving personal problems at home.

Prepare for Your Job Performance Evaluation

Learn how and when you will be evaluated on your job performance so you know where to focus your efforts to achieve a good evaluation. At the same time, you will avoid overlooking an area considered important by your employer. You also need to know how heavily the employer weights each performance area so you can concentrate on the important ones. If you don't receive this information, ask your supervisor to explain the process.

Even if your employer uses an informal method of job evaluation, ask what is considered good job performance and what criteria are used in determining promotions or raises. This will provide guidelines for your successful performance. As you become more knowledgeable about your job, demonstrate initiative. Set your own goals and deadlines for performance improvement and professional growth.

Many employers schedule annual, biannual, or quarterly meetings to review their employees' job performances in writing, orally, or both. Usually, the purpose of these evaluations is to identify strengths and weaknesses of employees and to establish short- and long-term goals of the employer and employee. A sample job performance rating form representative of those used by many organizations is the worksheet for Career Action 19-1.

> Complete Career Action 19-1

SUCCEED IN TODAY'S CHANGING WORKPLACE

As emphasized in Chapter 4, today's technology and increasing workplace competition are escalating the pace of work and changing the way it is performed. Employers need employees who are flexible, adaptable to change, and able to work independently in making decisions and solving problems. Competition requires increased efficiency.

Meet Your Employer's Quality Needs

Employers expect each worker to take responsibility for achieving maximum productivity while continuously looking for ways to improve quality.

CAREER ACTION 19-1

Job Performance Evaluation

Directions: Access your Learner's CD and complete Career Action 19-1, or use the Job Performance Evaluation form on page 307. If you have not held a paid job, evaluate yourself on volunteer work, internship work, or another significant activity in which you were responsible for carrying out assigned tasks and for working with, organizing, or directing others.

To meet your employer's expectations and achieve peak career success:

- Produce top-quality work.

- Produce the highest possible quantity of work.

- Be alert for problems and take action to prevent or solve them.

- Contribute efficiently and effectively as a team member.

Manage Change and Be Flexible

In addition to quality performance, focus on developing and improving your ability to be flexible and to adapt to change.

Be Flexible. Expect differences (some major) between the way your employer conducts business and the methods you learned in school or on another job. Schools often teach theories. However, supervisors interpret and apply theories and techniques (often developing their own) to accomplish specific work goals and tasks. Changing technology makes some textbook theories obsolete. Personalities also influence work methods. For example, an outgoing person typically uses different methods from those used by a shy person.

Employers value and seek employees who are flexible and adaptable to change.

A process may seem inefficient to you or may be different from the method used in your previous job. However, the process may serve a valuable organizational purpose that is not immediately apparent to you. Presenting a know-it-all image to your supervisor or others is a sure way to alienate yourself, perhaps permanently. If you think a technique could be improved, request a meeting with your supervisor to clarify the reasons for the technique. Using thoughtful questions is a good strategy to open the discussion.

There is a right time, place, and method for presenting your ideas or suggestions. Learn by observing how others present theirs. If the clarification by your supervisor still doesn't convince you that this is the most effective technique, explain the theory or technique you have learned or devised, offering it as a suggestion for consideration. Do not try to bulldoze your idea through.

Adapt to Change. Rapid technological, global economic, and other changes require continual changes in work processes, tools, and equipment. You must be flexible in evaluating the need for or adapting to changes in procedures, equipment use, and so on. Office automation affects the way business is conducted and the way work is performed. Keep an open, flexible attitude toward change. Don't make yourself obsolete by stubborn resistance; you may miss an open door to a career development opportunity. Continually keep your skills and knowledge current through education and training.

Complete Career Action 19-2

MANAGE YOUR CAREER DEVELOPMENT/ADVANCEMENT

Once you believe you've mastered your job responsibilities, you've overcome areas of weakness in your performance, and your employer is satisfied with your performance and understanding of the job, focus on managing your career development

CAREER ACTION 19-2

Use the Internet to Search for Current Job and Career Success Tips

 Directions: Search for articles on career success tips related to topics presented in Chapter 19 (adjusting to and succeeding in a new job, succeeding in today's changing workplace, and pursing a new career goal). Use any of the sites below or others you identify. Write a summary of at least two articles for this assignment.

1. CareerJournal   www.careerjournal.com

2. JobWeb   www.jobweb.com

3. Quintessential Careers   www.quintcareers.com

Some search terms to use on search engines and on web sites that have a search window: *career advancement, promotion, time management, performance evaluation, adapt to change,* and *mentor/mentoring.*

and seeking growth or advancement opportunities. You might want to work toward a new career goal—a lateral move or a promotion, for example.

Be Willing to Take on New Responsibilities

Find out what new responsibilities would be included in any new growth opportunities or position you seek. Outline required action steps; pursue them with expectation of success; and be willing to accept, learn, and carry out all new duties. Get any needed training to perform at the levels required.

SUCCESS TIP

To succeed in today's workplace, be a high-quality, top producer and a problem solver; adapt to and manage change; and be flexible.

Earn Your Advancement or Promotion

Keep in mind that you don't *get* a promotion or advancement opportunity; you *earn* it! When you know you're adequately prepared for advancement, start demonstrating your qualifications for it. The following guidelines will help you achieve this goal:

- **Maintain and update your career portfolio.** Continually add to the career portfolio you've created through the exercises in this text. This is your collection of documents and other items that provide evidence and examples of your work accomplishments, certifications, skills, qualifications, and more. Throughout your career, add records of all work-related achievements, including samples of exemplary work, letters of recognition for a job well done, and other documents supporting your good job performance, achievements, and related activities.

- **Seek a mentor.** A mentor is someone inside or outside your organization who can advise and coach you—someone respected and knowledgeable in your field. Seek advice from mentors experienced in the areas you need to improve. Don't limit yourself to seeking advice from just one mentor. Look for people who are sensitive to your concerns, who help you learn new skills, or who take time to explain organizational dynamics. Keep your relationship businesslike. A true mentor will develop an interest in you, make you aware of useful resources, and arrange opportunities for you to meet key people and grow professionally. Strive to meet your mentors' expectations for your performance.

> *"Perpetual optimism is a force multiplier."*
>
> Colin Powell

- **Develop expertise.** Identify your greatest working strengths and interests and build on them. Take advantage of all training in this area. Become known for your special expertise. This will help focus your career in a direction that best suits you and expands your career opportunities.

- **Be professional.** Think, act, speak, and dress professionally. If you want a promotion, act as if you already fit the part.

- **Expand your knowledge and skills.** Keep current in your job and industry knowledge (trends, technology, and improved methods of job performance). Correct any deficiencies immediately through reading, involvement in professional groups, training, and education. Submit reports of what you learn to your supervisor.

- **Do high-quality work.** Do the best possible job, and achieve the highest possible quantity and quality of work.

- **Increase organizational awareness.** Learn all phases of the organization, its goals, and how each job is designed to meet the overall goals.

- **Increase your visibility.** Get involved in organizational committees and cross-team projects in which you can excel. Show extra initiative and demonstrate leadership. Develop your speaking abilities.

- **Seek a promotion.** Once you've accomplished most of the items on this list, tell your supervisor you're interested in progressing and learning more. Demonstrate your ability to handle additional responsibility.

Complete Career Action 19-3

SUCCESS TIP

To achieve new career goals, take on new challenges, broaden your skills and knowledge, seek a mentor, keep your career portfolio current, network, and increase your visibility.

CAREER ACTION 19-3

Research Your Industry for Tips on Job Success and Promotion and on Making a Job Change

Directions: Access Career Action 19-3 on your Learner's CD, use the questionnaire provided on page 310, or design a custom questionnaire yourself. Survey knowledgeable people in your field, and record their answers on the form.

Increase your visibility. Get involved in organizational committees and cross-team projects, and develop your speaking abilities.

MAINTAIN YOUR NETWORK AND CAREER MANAGEMENT FILES

Once you're employed, send a thank-you note to all members of your network who helped you or expressed interest in your job search. Tell them about your new position. You want to keep your contacts for the next time you're ready to pursue a career goal. Realize that networking is not just a job search activity to be discontinued once you get your job. To achieve the greatest levels of career success, continual networking is a must.

Remember, staying networked all the time pays off! When you need important information or the time comes to seek a new job, you'll be leagues ahead of the competition that doesn't stay networked.

Keep your Career Management Files Binder current; don't abandon it. You've done a great deal of work in the exercises in *Your Career: How to Make It Happen.* Remember that this information will be useful throughout your entire career. Save your work (this book, the written assignments, and your computer files); you'll be glad you did!

✓ **CHECKLIST:**

Succeeding on the Job

Check each of the actions you are currently taking to increase your career success:

☐ Focusing on three goals to help adjust successfully to a new job: keeping a positive attitude; projecting a professional, competent image; and being a good team player

☐ Working efficiently, being dependable, focusing on people, and preparing for evaluation

☐ Being a high-quality, top producer; being a problem solver; learning to adapt to and manage change; and being flexible

☐ Taking on new challenges, broadening skills and knowledge, seeking a mentor, developing expertise, keeping a portfolio current, networking, and increasing visibility

☐ Keeping a career-building network active and maintaining your Career Management Files Binder to use in future career development activities

critical thinking *Questions*

1. On what is job failure most frequently based?

2. How can you most effectively learn a new job?

3. Why is it important to know how you will be evaluated on your job performance?

4. Why is it essential to adapt to change, and how can you demonstrate adaptability?

5. Once you have mastered a new job, what are specific actions you can take to increase your professional develop-ment and to make yourself promotable? List additional training or course work you could take to increase your knowledge and skills. Identify growth-oriented responsibilities you would be interested in pursuing. List other actions you could take to prepare for a promotion and increase your visibility.

CAREER ACTION 19-1

Job Performance Evaluation

Directions: Rate your job performance in your current or past work experience, in volunteer or internship work, or in another significant task-oriented activity. In the space to the left of each Performance or Behavioral Category, place the rating code you think most appropriately represents your performance (O = outstanding, V = very good, G = good, A = acceptable, U = unacceptable). On the line below each item, give one or two examples of the performance. Then go back and circle the items you rated acceptable or below; make these your targets for improvement.

Rating Code	Performance or Behavioral Category

Rating Code   **Performance or Behavioral Category**

_____ **ABILITY TO ACQUIRE AND USE INFORMATION AND FOLLOW INSTRUCTIONS**
(Uses initiative in acquiring, interpreting, and following instructions and using references)

List specific examples: _____

_____

_____ **INTERPERSONAL SKILLS** (Is tactful, understanding, and efficient when dealing with people)

List specific examples: _____

_____

_____ **BASIC SKILLS** (Is proficient in reading, writing, mathematics, listening, verbal and nonverbal communications)

List specific examples: _____

_____

_____ **JOB SKILLS** (Demonstrates command of required knowledge and skills)

List specific examples: _____

_____

_____ **THINKING/PROBLEM-SOLVING SKILLS** (Generates new ideas, makes decisions, solves problems, and reasons logically)

List specific examples: _____

_____

Continued on next page.

_____ **ABILITY TO COOPERATE WITH OTHERS** (Works well with team members and under supervision, exercises leadership, works well with people of diverse backgrounds)

List specific examples: _____

_____

_____ **QUANTITY OF WORK** (Does required amount of work)

List specific examples: _____

_____

_____ **QUALITY OF WORK** (Does neat, accurate, complete, and efficient work)

List specific examples: _____

_____

_____ **PRACTICES GOOD WORK HABITS** (Maintains good attendance and punctuality, is dependable, follows safety/work procedures)

List specific examples: _____

_____

_____ **ATTITUDE** (Demonstrates enthusiasm, interest, and motivation)

List specific examples: _____

_____

_____ **TECHNOLOGY** (Works well with technology—tools, computers, procedures)

List specific examples: _____

_____

_____ **PERSONAL QUALITIES** (Demonstrates responsibility, initiative, self-confidence, integrity, and honesty; practices good self-management; sets and maintains goals; exhibits self-motivation; is cooperative)

List specific examples: _____

_____

Continued on next page.

CAREER ACTION 19-1 (CONTINUED)

Overall Evaluation of Performance and Behavior

Directions: Review the rating codes (Outstanding, Very good, Acceptable, or Unacceptable) you placed in each category of your job performance evaluation on the previous pages. Place a check mark below next to the rating you recorded most frequently.

_____ Outstanding   _____ Very good   _____ Good

_____ Acceptable   _____ Unacceptable

Employee's Short-Term Goals: (List your short-term job or career goals here.)

_____

_____

Employee's Long-Term Goals: (List your long-term job or career goals here.)

_____

_____

_____

Suggestions for Improving Performance or Behavior: (List steps you can take to improve your work performance or behavior.)

_____

_____

_____

General Comments Regarding Employee's Job Performance: (Add any other appropriate comments to describe the quality of your work performance.)

_____

_____

Signature of Supervisor: (This is where your job supervisor would sign your performance evaluation.)

_____

Signature of Employee: (This is where you would sign the performance evaluation.)

_____

Date: _____

Research Your Industry for Tips on Job Success and Promotion and on Making a Job Change

Directions: Arrange meetings with knowledgeable people in your field to learn the following: (a) how the job performance of employees is evaluated, (b) what techniques help ensure success on the job, (c) how employees can earn a promotion, and (d) what methods are recommended for making a job change. Use the following questionnaire, adding pertinent questions relevant to your field. If you prefer, you can design and use your own questionnaire. Try to obtain sample job performance evaluations.

1. What advice would you give a new employee (in a position similar to the one you are seeking) to help him or her adjust quickly to the job, company, and people the employee would interact with?

   _____

   _____

2. What advice would you give this person to help ensure the highest degree of job success?

   _____

   _____

3. What criteria do you use to evaluate the performance of such an employee? Do you have a job performance evaluation form I could review?

   _____

   _____

4. How can such an employee earn a promotion here?

   _____

   _____

5. If an employee must leave your company, what steps do you prefer the employee take? How much notice do you expect? Do you prefer that the employee help train the replacement? Do you expect a letter of resignation?

   _____

   _____

chapter 20   MAKE SUCCESSFUL JOB AND CAREER CHANGES

In this chapter, you will:

- Focus on lifelong learning.

- Learn the difference between a job and a career; identify issues to consider when changing jobs or careers.

- Learn how to resign professionally.

- Identify factors to consider in relocating.

- **WWW** Use the Internet to research relocation and salary information.

- Recognize how to survive being laid off or fired.

"In today's business environment, career changes are inevitable. If you cannot find a suitable career opportunity in your field, give serious consideration to alternatives. Use your experience to expand a company's target market, placing yourself in a key position. In other words, if you can't find it, create it!"

Jerry Solomon
President
Engineered Environments, Inc.
www.eeihvac.com

This chapter defines the difference between a job and a career and presents strategies for determining whether you want to consider changing your job or your career. People rarely spend their entire lives working in the same positions for the same employers at the same locations. This chapter also explains the importance of lifelong learning in achieving career success. In addition, Chapter 20 provides guidelines for considering a job change or a career change. Methods are also presented for relocating successfully and for coping with being laid off or fired from a position.

KNOW THE DIFFERENCE BETWEEN A JOB AND A CAREER

A *job* involves performing a designated set of responsibilities and duties for a specific employer. A *career* encompasses a family of jobs. Your career is your life's work. Thus, *high school history teacher for Washington High School* is a job and *teaching* is the career. Similarly, *sportswear clerk for After Five Stores* is a job and *retail sales* is the career.

Many people don't consider the difference between a job and a career. As a result, they spend a great deal of time and money changing careers when they only need to change jobs. In other cases, people change jobs repeatedly and continue to be dissatisfied because they're not in the right careers.

Most people change jobs at least eight times during their working lives. With changes in technology and in their own values and interests, it's also common for people to change careers at least once during their lifetimes. If you realize your current employment situation is no longer satisfying, first consider whether the dissatisfaction is with your career or with your specific job.

If you're unhappy with your supervisor but enjoy your work, you may need to change jobs. It doesn't mean you need to change careers. However, if you don't like the basic kind of work you're doing, you may want to consider a career change.

SUCCESS TIP

Before you change your job or career, analyze whether your discontent is from your specific job or from your career choice. Don't change your career just because you don't like your supervisor, and don't keep changing jobs when you really aren't well suited for your career.

PERSONAL BEST

Be a Lifelong Learner

Rapidly changing technology and a global economy have created a fast-changing world. Jobs and careers are changing dramatically. To have a successful career and to distinguish yourself from the pack, you must update and add skills quickly and continuously. In short, you must make learning a lifelong pursuit. You need to develop and sustain the habit of continuing your education to avoid being left behind.

You can become a lifelong learner by:

- Participating in workshops and training programs.

- Taking college- or graduate-level courses.

- Subscribing to journals related to your field.

- Joining professional associations related to your career.

Distance learning programs offered on the Internet make lifelong learning opportunities more accessible than ever. Online instructional services such as Extreme Learning (www .extremelearning.com), NETg.com (www.netg.com), University of Phoenix (http://onl.uophx.edu), and Element K (www.elementk.com) can help you find online continuing education related to business and management, college studies, technology, training, graduate studies, and more.

To ensure your continuous and future employability, make sure you have the skills required to meet the demands of the changing workforce. To remain a viable employee in the twenty-first century, you must make lifelong learning a part of your career management plans.

Complete Career Action 20-1

CAREER ACTION 20-1

Lifelong Learning Considerations

Part A: Identify a career for which new training has become necessary for a person to remain employable. Describe the career process change, and identify the type of education or training required to meet the changing need.

Part B: Think about the career you're planning to pursue. List at least two likely changes or situations in this career field that will require further education or training.

SUCCESS TIP

Keep yourself on the cutting edge of the workforce by continuing your education. Lifelong learning is the ticket to continued employment in a rapidly changing world.

UNDERSTAND WHEN YOU SHOULD CHANGE JOBS

You might want to consider a job change if:

- Your current employer can't offer you advancement.
- A poor economy requires layoffs.
- You want to move to a new location.
- Your department is dissolved.
- Your philosophy conflicts with that of your current employer.
- You simply want a new challenge.

Never Quit a Job Before You Have a New One

If possible, begin and complete your job change while still employed. Because being employed is current proof that you do a job satisfactorily, you're considered more employable when you're currently employed. As the mountain-climbing instructor says to students, "Never let loose of your support before you have hold of another one."

Don't Rush Into a Job Change Without Adequate Planning

Give any change of job serious thought and planning. You'll regret a hasty decision to take a new job if it turns out to be worse than your current one. The job might look good, but without proper research, you could find yourself in a situation that is as bad as or worse than your current one. Evaluate your current job by asking yourself, "Is there room for advancement to a higher position, or are other important opportunities available?" If the answer is no and you will not be happy staying in the same position, you have strong grounds for considering a new employer. If the answer is yes, there may be advantages to staying with your current employer.

Know the Advantages of Staying With Your Current Employer

Seeking advancement or growth with your current employer can offer many advantages, including the following:

- Staying is less risky because you are already established and don't need to repeat the process of adjusting to new surroundings and people.

- Your reputation for job stability is improved by staying, rather than moving frequently from one employer to another.

- You won't lose accumulated benefits, such as vacation time, retirement, and profit sharing.

Success Tip

Change to a new job after carefully considering the advantages and disadvantages of staying in your current one. Avoid quitting your current position until you have obtained a new one.

Know What You Can Gain by Changing Employers

Changing employers can also offer many advantages, including the following:

- You increase job interest by becoming involved with new challenges, surroundings, and people.

- A job change can result in quicker advancement than you could achieve through seeking a promotion within the same organization.

- You gain knowledge, broaden your experience, and increase your support network, expanding your career growth opportunities.

- You start with a clean slate as you develop your reputation for good job performance.

Never let loose of your support before you have hold of another.

Know When You Should Change Careers

If, after thorough consideration, you decide you aren't happy in your work and a change to another job within the same field would not bring satisfaction, you might want to consider a career change. Ask yourself the following questions:

- **Have I changed positions several times only to find I'm still unhappy?** Repeated changes of employment that don't improve job satisfaction may indicate a career problem, not a job problem.

- **Are my problems the result of personality or philosophical conflicts with my supervisor or fellow employees?** If so, it's more likely you need a new employer instead of a new career. The exception occurs when the type of people usually found in your career field, regardless of the organization, don't fit your personality or philosophy.

- **Am I unhappy with the work environment?** If you don't like to work constantly at a desk, decide whether this is common to your career field or only to your job. Would you prefer outdoor work? You might want to look at other careers if your career doesn't provide the opportunity for this kind of work. Is the problem with the work environment common to the career or only to some jobs within the career field?

- **Am I constrained in expressing my values?** Again, is this a function of your job or your career?

- **Is this position interesting?** What are your interests? Are you unable to meet them in your career or just in your current job?

- **Am I frustrated that I'm not using my skills and abilities?** Is this a job-related or a career-related problem?

Even if you determine that your unhappiness is related to your career rather than to your current job, you still have to weigh the pros and cons of making a career change. Rarely can you just jump into another career without making sacrifices, such as taking a lower salary. You need to evaluate the advantages and disadvantages and whether you're gaining more than you're losing.

> *"An investment in knowledge pays the best interest."*
>
> Benjamin Franklin

SUCCESS TIP

Change to a new career if you determine that your unhappiness is related to your career (not just to your current job) and that an alternative career is realistically available and will meet your needs.

Reassess

First, determine what alternative careers fit your interests and abilities. Study the options to decide which you would prefer. Apply the strategies presented in Chapters 2 and 3. Then after you have selected an alternative career, find out what additional education or training you need, how long it takes to prepare for this field, and what it will cost. Also determine whether the education or training is available nearby and whether you can get the necessary skills while continuing your current job or if you need to return to school and/or relocate.

Be Realistic

What are the job opportunities in the new field? Are those jobs in a desirable location, and will the pay meet your requirements? Be aware that when you change careers, you often have to start over at the entry-level salary.

What kind of risk taker are you? Are you willing to give up the security of your current position and career and take a chance? Do you expect to be significantly more satisfied in this new career? In the final analysis, decide whether the probable advantages sufficiently outweigh the disadvantages and whether you are willing to assume any risk involved.

You must also be prepared to discuss your decision persuasively with prospective employers who may question whether you will be happy with such changes. It is important to convey to employers that you have considered and planned for this change carefully and that you believe the advantages outweigh the disadvantages.

Complete Career Action 20-2

Plan for Career Development Alternatives

Directions: Consider your career development.

1. List the name of your current targeted career; then list three jobs you might hold within that career field.

2. List two issues you would need to consider if you were evaluating a career change. List two issues you would need to consider if you were evaluating a job change.

RESIGN PROFESSIONALLY

Resigning professionally is good career insurance. Make every effort to leave your current employer with good feelings; do not leave in anger or with hostility, no matter how dissatisfied you might be. Throughout the rest of your career, references from your past employers will be requested each time you seek a new job. For this important reason, leave a job gracefully, pleasantly, and professionally.

Follow these guidelines to ensure that your resignation results in feelings of goodwill and a willingness by your employer to provide a good reference for you.

- Find out how your current employer typically reacts when learning that someone is looking for a new position. Does your employer become upset and fire that person or try to make it difficult for him or her to find new employment? Does your employer respond positively by offering to support the person in finding new employment? Or even better, does your employer provide positive inducements (such as pay raises or promotions) to keep the person within the organization? If this is the case, you need to consider whether you're willing to accept a pay increase and stay.

- If your current employer responds positively to people leaving, it's advantageous to discuss your plans immediately. The employer might provide you with references,

helpful suggestions, or even a better opportunity where you are.

- If your current employer resents losing employees and even fires those seeking other opportunities, do not give notice that you are planning to leave until you have another firm offer. You don't want to jeopardize your current position. Remember, you are more employable when you are currently employed,

- Do your current job to the best of your ability through your last day on the job. You're most likely to be remembered by how well you performed at the end of your employment. This can greatly influence the quality of future references from this employer.

- Update your career work portfolio before you leave. If appropriate, request letters of recommendation from supervisors. Assemble samples of your work and documentation of your achievements that are pertinent and exemplary.

 SUCCESS TIP

Resign professionally. Your future could depend on it!

- Plan for an orderly and efficient transition of your responsibilities to the person taking your place. If asked to help train your replacement, be as thorough as possible, taking care to explain your duties clearly and completely. Where appropriate, provide written instructions to help your replacement carry out the duties of your position.

- Give your employer at least two weeks' written notice before you leave your current job. This is common courtesy and important in maintaining good standing with your employer. Giving less notice is considered unprofessional. You should submit a formal letter of resignation. An appropriate sample is shown in Figure 20-1.

> Complete Career Action 20-3

UNDERSTAND WHEN YOU SHOULD CONSIDER RELOCATING

Sometimes deciding to relocate is easy. You might not have commitments keeping you in your current location, the job in the new location offers such great benefits that you can't afford to turn it down, or you just prefer to live elsewhere. On the other hand, the reasons you can't relocate may be compelling and require a difficult decision. You may need to weigh several important factors to decide whether relocation is best. The most important issues are personal or family considerations and the impact on your career goals.

Impacting Loved Ones

The impact of relocation on your loved ones generally is the most difficult decision regarding relocation. Your spouse or partner may have an excellent career position that would be lost if you relocated. You may have aging parents who require that you remain nearby. You must weigh the advantages of relocation against a possible negative impact on your spouse, children, or other important people in your life.

Good communication among all those most affected by this decision is important. If you're married and your spouse works, you need to discuss openly the advantages and disadvantages to each other's careers. If you have children, you should consider how they feel about moving, the quality of schools, and the availability of other resources important to your family in the new community.

Considering Your Values and Interests

Another important factor in considering relocation is determining whether your values and interests are being met in your current location. For example, if you're living in Florida but love to snow ski and have an opportunity to live in Denver, clearly you can list one advantage of moving to Colorado.

To help make the best decision, make a list of the pros and cons regarding all aspects of relocation.

CAREER ACTION 20-3

Write a Letter of Resignation

Directions: Review Figure 20-1 on page 318. Then practice by preparing a letter of resignation for a position you currently hold or have held.

March 9, 20—

Mr. George Diallo
Henson-Standlin Company
1414 Cromwell Avenue
Memphis, TN 38115

Dear Mr. Diallo:

This letter is to serve as notice that I will be leaving the Henson-Standlin
Company on March 31. I have taken a position as service manager with
Gantry and Sons in Salem, Oregon.

I have truly enjoyed working for Henson-Standlin and view my employment
here as a valuable experience and an opportunity for professional development. Thank you for your guidance and assistance during the past three
years; I sincerely appreciate it.

Best wishes to you for continued success.

Sincerely,

Kelli Sullivan

Kelli Sullivan

Figure 20-1: Sample Letter of Resignation

Affording Relocation

The other main personal consideration is economic. What will relocation cost? Don't look just at the cost of a moving van. Expenses include utility connections and other start-up costs required to move into new living quarters. If offered a job in another location, what portion, if any, of these costs will your employer provide? Also research the differences in living costs.

The cost of housing, transportation, utilities, food, taxes (state, local, sales), insurance, and other portions of your budget may vary greatly from place to place. The Internet is a valuable source of research on this topic.

Get copies of the local newspaper from all communities you are considering. Review grocery advertisements, classified listings for houses and apartments, and other indications of costs in the area. Classified listings of many newspapers are also available on the Internet. Also use your support network to identify individuals you can contact who may be familiar with this location.

 The following web sites can also help you in making important relocation decisions:

- **JobStar** (www.jobstar.org) links to some general and specialized surveys. Click on "Salary Info."

- **Realtor.com** (www.homefair.com/calc/salcalc.html) provides a cost-of-living calculator and links to comparisons of crime rates and other considerations and to links that help with calculating moving costs.

- **Monstermoving** (www.monstermoving.com) provides a wide variety of relocation information and online tools.

- **Homestore.com** (www.homestore.com) offers an "Apartments & Rentals" link for information on rental costs in various locations and tips for evaluating specific rental properties.

Use the Internet to find helpful relocation information.

SUCCESS TIP

When making relocation decisions, consider the impact and possible benefits on your career goals, the impact on your loved ones, your values and interests, and the costs involved.

Impacting Your Career Goals

Another important area of concern is the impact on your career goals. Will this move provide the opportunity to gain valuable experience and advancement not currently available? How will the move look on your resume if, later on, you look for another new position? Is education or training available at the new location (but not available where you are now) that would provide added benefits? Will you be exposed to new people who can help your career growth? Review your career plans. Will relocating better help you realize those goals?

Your decision will vary depending on your personal goals, needs, and circumstances. Base your relocation decisions on thoughtful and careful consideration.

USE RELOCATION TO GROW, NOT TO START OVER

Assume you have decided to relocate. What can you do to make this move as smooth and positive an experience as possible? How do you ensure you will continue to move forward in your career?

Moving companies often provide free pamphlets describing the steps you need to consider, including handy checklists. Check the Internet and your library for information on moving. Some important career-related issues are discussed below to help you get off to a good start in your new location.

See How Research Pays Off

Learn as much as you can about your new community before you move. If you belong to professional associations, find out whether they have chapters in the new community and arrange to transfer your memberships. If your association has a web site, check it for links to local chapters. This will help

you get professionally involved immediately and expand your support network to your new location. Subscribe to a newspaper to become familiar with your new area.

Most communities have web sites providing comprehensive information on the surrounding area. Just enter the name of the community in a search engine. Learn all you can about the new location before you actually move.

Complete Career Action 20-4

SUCCESS TIP

Make your relocation smooth and positive by researching the new community prior to your move, and build a new support network immediately upon your arrival.

CAREER ACTION 20-4

Use the Internet to Research Other Work Locations

  Directions: Check the web sites listed below to learn more about a community you might consider. Prepare a written report summarizing your answers to the following questions:

1. How does the climate/weather compare with the climate/weather where you live now?

2. What kinds of recreation and cultural opportunities are highlighted?

3. Is information on educational opportunities provided?

4. What cost-of-living information is provided?

5. What medical facilities are available?

DataMasters	www.datamasters.com
Salary.com	www.salary.com
USA CityLink	www.usacitylink.com
Monstermoving	www.monstermoving.com

Expand your support network.

Build a Support Network Branch

When you arrive in the community, work at establishing a broad support group. Get involved in the community. Volunteer to work in a charity or an organization that fits your interests. This is an excellent way to become involved in the community and to build your support network. You also have the opportunity to learn new skills or enhance old ones through volunteer work. Make this effort as soon as possible to speed the process of meeting new people, making new friends, and developing a healthy social network.

> *"When one door closes, another door opens; but we so often look so long and so regretfully upon the closed door, that we do not see the ones which open for us."*
>
> Alexander Graham Bell

KNOW WHAT TO DO IF YOU LOSE YOUR JOB

For many reasons, you might find yourself unemployed. Rapidly changing technology, economic downturns, and corporate mergers are a few of the reasons you might be laid off. Many people face this at some point during their working years.

Sometimes employees are fired. Firing may occur as the result of a personality conflict, office politics, lack of skills, poor attitude, absenteeism, or other unpleasant circumstances. You may never actually be fired, but it does happen. Regardless of the fairness of the situation, the results are the same—unemployment and the need to find a new job.

If you receive the proverbial pink slip as a result of being either laid off or fired, these are some immediate do's and don'ts to follow:

- **Do** try to have a calm and nonthreatening conversation with your supervisor to clarify the reason for your termination if you don't already know. Ask your supervisor for advice and support. Find out whether the organization offers outplacement assistance. By responding professionally, you can limit or eliminate a negative reference. You may even receive a positive reference and assistance in finding another position.

- **Do** give yourself a day or two (but no longer) to reflect on what happened and to put it into perspective. Begin to think about a positive future.

- **Do** review all of Chapter 1. Consider how you can apply the nine success strategies to strengthen your job search and career planning activities. Focus on positive self-talk, visualization, effective goal setting, proactive action planning, and assertiveness. This will energize your job search campaign.

- **Do** reestablish and rebuild your personal support system. You need it now more than ever.

- **Do** connect with and add to your network. Begin contacting people, asking them to refer you to several others to get a strong network established again. Repeat the process you used to get your last position.

- **Do** review this text and all the information you developed and stored in your Career Management Files Binder and your Learner's CD to complete the exercises. Update your resume and begin the job-hunting process anew. Carefully consider whether you need a new job or an actual career change.

- **Don't** make things worse by verbally (or physically) attacking your supervisor or anyone else before leaving. Prospective employers are likely to contact your previous employer for references. Do not add to your problems now.

- **Don't** begin applying for jobs the same day you get the bad news. You won't be in the right frame of mind to make good decisions or to present a confident and positive image to another employer.

Dealing With a Layoff or Downsizing

In the case of permanent layoffs or downsizing, some notice is usually given. *Before* the actual layoff is the time to reapply the job-seeking skills presented in earlier chapters of this book. Acting quickly is important because being employed is one factor that makes getting hired easier.

Use the term *laid off* rather than *fired* in your responses when you have a job interview; *laid off* has a less negative impact than *fired*. Discuss the situation briefly as positively as possible. Avoid negative statements about your former employer. Instead, emphasize positive things you have learned from the experience that will make you a valuable employee.

Surviving Being Fired

There is life after being fired! Should this misfortune be your fate, take heart in knowing that literally hundreds of thousands of people who lost their jobs

"A sense of purpose generates action and movement in the direction of dreams and goals. Set your sights on what you want in your career and then make it happen. Now, what are you waiting for?"

Joan C. Borgatti
RN, MEd, Editorial Director,
nursingspectrum.com

sometime in their past are now happily and successfully employed. You can also successfully survive a job loss if you focus on looking for new opportunities. Also keep the following pointers in mind:

- **Do** analyze objectively what you learned from this experience. What did you gain from the work experience? What can you improve or avoid in future situations to make you a good employee for someone else?

- **Don't** focus on how unfairly you were treated and begin to identify all the injustices your former employer committed against you and other employees.

- **Do** remember that many people have been fired and have gone on to enjoy successful careers. This is the beginning of new opportunities, not the end of the world.

Using Your Career Management Files Binder and Your Learner's CD to Speed Up Your Job Search

Keep this book and your Career Management Files Binder containing all of your completed assignments. They provide a solid foundation that will make your next job search easier and more efficient. Update and revise your job search documents as necessary. This will help you greatly through the process of finding a new job—after a layoff or by your choice. Immediately reactivate and rebuild your network groups. Start by contacting people with whom you are close. Ask each of them to provide you with the names of two more people you can contact to expand your network.

Complete Career Action 20-5

CAREER ACTION 20-5

Review Your Proactive Success Action Plan

In Chapter 1, Career Action 1-5, you accessed the *Your Career: How to Make It Happen* web site and completed a Proactive Success Action Plan. You completed the form by identifying a goal that was most important to you at the time. In addition, you were to identify success strategies described in Chapter 1 that you could use to accomplish the goal you identified. You then were directed to file your completed Proactive Success Action Plan in your Career Management Files Binder.

Directions: Retrieve and review your Proactive Success Action Plan. Review it carefully and then note exactly what progress you have made on this plan since you first wrote it. If you applied the strategies you outlined on the form, you should have made some clear progress.

Keep in mind the importance of using the nine success strategies throughout your career to reach your fullest potential!

CONCLUSION

The average American makes a minimum of eight job changes in a lifetime. (Some career changes are included in this number.) All the work you have done in this book to assess and document your experience, education, interest, goals, objectives, and capabilities and to develop resumes, cover letters, and other career management documents will be useful to you now and in the future. This information will give you a decided competitive edge throughout your career.

As you progress in your career throughout your life, continue to set your sights on what you want and then make it happen. You have all the tools—now go out and do it!

Set your sights on your goals, and then make them happen!

✓ **CHECKLIST:**

Making a Successful Job and Career Change

Check each of the actions you are currently taking to increase your career success:

☐ Staying on the cutting edge of the workforce by continuing with education

☐ Before changing jobs or careers, determining whether discontent is job-based or career-based

☐ Considering the pros and cons of staying in a current job before making a change; not quitting until after securing another job

☐ Changing to a new career if it's realistically available and meets one's needs

☐ Resigning professionally

☐ In relocating, considering the impact on loved ones, values and interests, costs involved, and the impact on career goals

☐ In relocating, researching the new community before moving; building a new support network immediately upon arriving

critical thinking *Questions*

1. Why has lifelong learning become crucial?

2. What are at least two benefits you can gain by changing employers when seeking a job change?

3. What actions should you take to resign professionally?

SAMPLE BUSINESS LETTER AND E-MAIL FORMATS

To project professionalism in your job search and career development written communications, use appropriate business formats. Listed below are guidelines for formatting a business letter and an e-mail message. Illustrations of these document formats follow the guidelines.

Business Letter Format (see model on page 326):
Use the following guidelines to format your business letters correctly:

1. Prepare standard business letters on 8 1/2- by 11-inch letterhead. If you don't have your own letterhead stationery (not expected for an individual) use a high-quality bond stationery.

2. Use the block style letter format illustrated on the following page. General guidelines for the placement of the letter parts are indicated on the illustration. A few specific tips are emphasized below.

3. Place the return address and date based on the length of the letter.

   For an average-length letter, begin the return address at the left margin at approximately the 2-inch top margin point. If the letter is long, place this section higher on the page to achieve a more balanced placement. Place the date directly under the return address and at the left margin.

4. Key a double space (two hard returns) between the salutation and the body of the letter, between each paragraph, and between the last line of the body of the letter and the complimentary close.

5. Key four hard returns between the complimentary close and the name of the sender.

E-mail Message Format (see model on page 327):
Follow the guidelines below to format an e-mail message correctly:

1. **Format:** Use a heading similar to that of a standard business memo. Include the To, From, Date, and Subject information to communicate clearly and quickly. Most e-mail programs contain a form at the top of the message screen for filling in this information.

2. **Case:** Use the standard mix of upper- and lowercase letters. (Using all caps is like **SHOUTING ON THE NETWORK!**) Entire messages in all capital letters are also extremely hard to read.

3. **Brief but complete:** Keep e-mail messages short and focused on one subject, but be sure to include all information necessary for the recipient to take appropriate action and to reach you.

4. **Professional:** As with hard-copy documents, your professional reputation is reflected in e-mail:

   a.   Plan and organize the message.

   b.   Prepare a draft, proofread, and revise.

   c.   Be courteous.

   d.   Use correct spelling and grammar.

1008 North Lindsey Avenue   (Begin writer's address at left margin at
Boise, ID 83706   approximately the 2-inch top margin point.
January 25, 20—   Starting line varies based on letter length.)
                                         (Date)

(4 line spaces, 3 blank lines)

Mr. Benito Suarez   (Letter address at left margin)
1235 Lake Hazel
Boise, ID 83709

(Always 2 line spaces, 1 blank line)

Dear Mr. Suarez: (Salutation)

(Always 2 line spaces, 1 blank line)

**** ***** **** * **** ** **** *** ** *** ** **** *** **** ***** *** ****** (Body of letter)
**** * ***. ********* ****** * ******* ***** *** ***** *** * ******* *** **** *
***** ** *** ** **** ********* **** ** ***********.

(All lines start at left margin.)   (Always 2 line spaces, 1 blank line)
**** ***** **** **** *** * *** **** ** **** ** *** ********* *** * **** ** **** *****
***** **** *** * *****.

(Always 2 line spaces, 1 blank line)

****** ***** **** ** * ***** *** **** **** *** **** *** ***** *** *** * ****** *** ** *
******. **** ** * ********* *** ******** ******** ** *** ******** ** **** *** ***
*************** **** **** ******* *** **** ********.

(Always 2 line spaces, 1 blank line)

Sincerely yours,   (Complimentary close at left margin)

(4 returns)

Ashley Curie   (Sender's written signature here)

Ashley Curie   (Keyed name of sender at left margin)

Business Letter Format

Date:	May 8, 20—	(E-Mail heading,
From:	Joe Ming	usually a form fill-in)
To:	Cheryl Yordy, MacroTech Corporation	
Subject:	Confirmation of Meeting, May 12, 20—	(Include a subject.)

This message is a confirmation of *** * ****** ******* **** ***** ** ******* *** *****
* ** ******* ****** ******** ** ******** **** ****** **** ****** ****. *** ****** ****

*** ********* *** ***** ***** ** ***** ****** **** ****.   (Body of message)

** ***** ******* **** ** ***** ****** *** ***** **** **** **** **** **** *** ** ** *** *** **** **
******* **** ** ***** ****** ***.

* **** *** **** **** *** * *** ***** *** ******** *** **** *** ** **** ***** **** * **** ***
**************.

Contact Information:
Joe Ming
E-mail address: ming@enterprise.com
Web site: www.jming.com
Fax number: 707-555-0180
Telephone: 707-555-0181
Mailing address: 8200 Whitney Avenue, Vacaville, CA 95688

E-mail Message Format

CAREER MANAGEMENT AND MARKETING TOOLS

Three important career management and marketing tools are recommended to help you reach your full career potential: (1) a Career Management Files Binder, (2) a career portfolio, and (3) an Interview Marketing Kit. These tools are discussed in various chapters throughout this text and are further summarized below as a convenient reference.

CAREER MANAGEMENT TOOL 1: CAREER MANAGEMENT FILES

In using this textbook, you will develop information and documents you can use throughout your life to help achieve each new job and career goal. This material will consist of information you record in your *Career Actions* as well as drafts of job search documents you create in these assignments, such as your resume, cover letter, networking lists, and more. Altogether this valuable career data will form your Career Management File. This data provides the essential base of career information you will need throughout your career. This information will also be in a format that is easy to retrieve and update any time you seek a new position in your career.

Compiling Your Career Management Files

1. **Organize Your Data—Create a Career Management Files Binder.** Set up a system for collecting, organizing, and updating your career information. You will need most of this data whenever you seek a new job, advancement, or a new career. Use a ring binder to serve as your Career Management Files Binder. Place 20 binder divider tabs, labeled Chapter 1 through Chapter 20, in this binder.

2. **File Completed Career Actions.** Place all completed Career Action forms or other written assignments (such as your resume, cover letter, and other career documents you develop) behind the corresponding chapter tab in your Career Management Files Binder. You can also use additional tabs with specific topic labels, such as "network list," "references," "resume," "cover letter," and so on.

   IMPORTANT: Look for this icon at the bottom of selected Career Actions:

   Career Management Files Binder. This icon indicates that the completed assignment should be printed and stored in your Career Management Files Binder.

3. **Use Your Learner's CD or the Career Action Forms in Your Text.** Many of the Career Action forms in the text are also available on your Learner's CD. Use the electronic version of these forms on the CD whenever possible (although you can use the paper forms included in your textbook). The new Learner's CD increases the convenience of preparing Career Action forms because the forms are interactive Word files you fill out using the keyboard.

   IMPORTANT: Look for this icon appearing with selected Career Actions:

   This icon indicates that the information you record for the Career Action can be accessed and prepared using your Learner's CD.

4. **Back Up Your Career Action Work:** Save your completed Career Action forms from your Learner's CD as well as the other career documents (resume, cover and other letters, reference sheet, and so on) you create in this course onto your hard drive or network drive. Much

of this information will be useful to you throughout your career for use in revising and updating your career documents and reference data. Also copy your files onto a personal diskette or back them up on a CD for use throughout your career.

File your Learner's CD and personal backup media along with the printouts of your assignments in your Career Management Files Binder. In this way, you will be creating an electronic "Career-to-Go" of data you can take with you and easily update or revise any time you seek a promotion or a job or career change.

CAREER MANAGEMENT TOOL 2: CAREER PORTFOLIO

The Career Portfolio is an organized master collection of items demonstrating job-specific skills and work qualifications. Some examples of appropriate portfolio items include your resume; an official copy of your transcript(s); exemplary samples of your work, such as business writing, graphic arts samples, and printed samples from software presentations; evidence of sophisticated computer usage, such as desktop publishing and web site creation; awards and commendations; work performance evaluations; and letters of reference.

Portfolio samples can be from paid or volunteer work, internships, cooperative education, clubs, community activities, and more. A comprehensive list of appropriate items and ideas for building your portfolio is included under the heading "Sample Portfolio Items," which appears in the next column.

Note: You will likely want to file original documents, such as school transcripts, in your Career Management Files Binder (described in preceding paragraphs) and include copies of these documents in your Career Portfolio. This way you will retain a clean master and still have a copy for demonstration during interviews.

Identifying Items for Your Portfolio

Begin by identifying your skills and experiences that relate directly to your job target. Then consider carefully what you have done or accomplished that best demonstrates those qualifications. For example, if you are seeking an accounting job, include your transcripts listing appropriate course work; a diskette or CD containing samples of budgets you developed or accounts receivable or accounts payable reports you prepared; a letter of recommendation from an employer for bookkeeping or accounting work you performed; and so on. See a comprehensive list of ideas for portfolio items under the heading, "Sample Portfolio Items," which appears below.

Assembling Your Portfolio

For a traditional portfolio, use a professional-looking three-ring binder that holds 8 1/2- by 11-inch pages. File and categorize all of your portfolio documents behind tabbed sections in the binder. Use sheet protectors, diskette protectors, and other accessories to display and protect your portfolio items. Larger portfolios (17 by 22 inches) are appropriate for art designers, journalists, advertising specialists, and technical writers to store and categorize oversized documents and credentials.

Sample Portfolio Items

Examples of portfolio components include:

- Paper documents.

- Diskettes and CDs containing text-based documents.

- Multimedia CDs containing sound or video clips and other presentation content.

- Video- or audiotapes.

- Pictures/photographs.

- Other items that can be used to demonstrate your qualifications.

To aid in assembling your portfolio, review the following list of ideas for appropriate components. However, don't limit yourself to these. Use your imagination and strive for a close match with your target job.

To Demonstrate Work Experience, Work Performance, and Credentials

- **Resume:** Include error-free copies of your resume printed on quality paper. This should be the first item in your portfolio.

    Note: Include in your portfolio a computer disk or CD copy of your scannable paper resume and your electronic resume for employers who prefer the disk format. Place the media in a protective jacket or case.

- **Employer or Internship Performance Reviews:** Include copies of these reviews, providing all comments are favorable.

- **Licenses:** Include for professions requiring a license to work in the field.

- **List of References:** Include a listing of references' names, addresses, and phone numbers and their association to you. Past employers, direct supervisors, and instructors are all good references.

- **Letters of Recommendation/Commendation:** Include these letters since they speak for themselves.

Education, Training, Degrees, and Certificates

- **Diploma/Degree:** Place a copy of your diploma(s) or degree(s) in your portfolio; place originals in your Career Management Files Binder.

- **Transcripts:** If your academic performance was good, keep copies of your transcripts in your portfolio to demonstrate this strength. Place your original transcripts in your Career Management Files Binder.

- **Certificates:** Include professional certification (CPA, CPS, CET, PE, teaching certificates, and so on) since this

is evidence of lifelong learning. Certificates of completion for continuing education, specialized training, workshops, seminars, and so on, are important because they, too, demonstrate career development.

- **Awards:** Include awards showing perfect attendance on the job and in school; academic accomplishments; or employee of the month, quarter, or year. Awards are proof of outstanding accomplishments and are of interest to employers.

Samples of Work, Use of Technology and Information

- **Design Work:** Include computer or manual drawings in the field of drafting to prove technical ability in mechanical, architectural, structural, or electrical designs. Include computer-aided drafting design (CAD) examples where appropriate. Interior design work as it pertains to decorators can also be demonstrated through drawings, photographs, and videotapes.

- **Artwork:** Include samples of sketches, drawings, and paintings; photographs or video footage; or computer-generated items in your career portfolio.

- **Writing Samples:** Showcase your best work if you are an author, an editor, or a reporter. Include samples of technical writing, reports, articles, business plans, instructional or training materials, institutional improvement plans, proposals, written content for web sites, and mission statements you have composed. The ability to communicate is important to employers.

- **Software-Generated Documents:** Include your best examples from school if you're preparing to graduate and lack related job experience. Provide such items as electronic spreadsheets, database documents, newsletters, or presentation documents. If you have on-the-job work experience, include relevant copies of your actual work.

- **Publicity/Press Coverage:** Include articles highlighting your work, volunteer, community, or professional activities or other special accomplishments. Sources for these are school, employers, or professional publications such as newsletters, newspapers, journals, magazines, and so on. Use printed and online resources.

Other

- **Examples of Community Service:** Include any materials that demonstrate active involvement in community service.

- **Forms of Identification:** Place front and back photocopies of a valid driver's license, social security card, or photo ID in your portfolio for easy retrieval. Many employers request at least two forms of identification to process your application.

- **Proof of Citizenship.**

Web E-Portfolio

For some career industries, a career portfolio developed as a web document is appropriate. This is called an e-portfolio or web portfolio, which contains documents formatted for display on the Internet. Virtually everything you could assemble in a standard portfolio (described above) can be formatted as pages of a web portfolio. If you develop a web resume or personal web site, you can include a link to your web portfolio. Use your favorite search engine to find samples of web portfolios and articles on web portfolios that may provide useful ideas for you. Enter the search string *web portfolio* to initiate your search. You can also include web addresses for your web site and web portfolio in your cover letter and on your resume and business card.

CAREER MANAGEMENT TOOL 3: INTERVIEW MARKETING KIT

The Interview Marketing Kit is a professional-looking folder containing items from the master Career Portfolio. You select the items from your master portfolio to meet the specific needs of each employer. In other words, your Interview Marketing Kit should be tailored and assembled using Career Portfolio items selected specifically for each interview. During interviews, you can extract appropriate portfolio items from your Kit that demonstrate your qualifications. This tangible evidence of abili-

ties often gives candidates a winning edge in competing for a job. Choose items that match the needs of the specific target employer. After your interview, you can refile the items in your master Career Portfolio.

The kit should also contain an "Interview Survival Pack." These are supplies that can bail you out of a situation that could diminish your confidence and performance. They include rescue items such as a comb, a toothbrush, breath freshener, and a spare tie for a man or an extra pair of nylons for a woman.

Selecting Portfolio Items to Place in Interview Marketing Kit

Before each interview, select items from your Career Portfolio that best pertain to this specific job target. Don't use every item in your primary portfolio for every interview. Place the items you select in your Interview Marketing Kit. Arrange the portfolio items in your Interview Marketing Kit in the order that best demonstrates how your abilities relate specifically to the employer's needs. Examples of appropriate items for your Interview Marketing Kit are as follows:

1. Items from your Career Portfolio that best support the needs of the organization with which you are interviewing:

   - Job-related samples of your work, if applicable (from your work, educational, or training experience)

   - Required certificates, licenses, transcripts, or other related documents

   - Spare copies of your resume

   - Letters of recommendation

   - List of references appropriate for the job

2. Your 60-Second Commercial summarizing your qualifications for the job (see Chapter 11)

3. A list of pertinent questions you can ask during the interview (see Chapter 14)

Note: Review items 2 and 3 just before your interview. Don't read from them during the interview.

Using Portfolio Items During Your Interview

Ask if the interviewer would like to see samples from your portfolio before displaying anything. Even if the interviewer prefers not to review them, having portfolio items conveys that you are professional and organized. During the interview, you may still have an opportunity to offer a portfolio sample if the topic suggests it. Employers typically ask questions about your resume. At this point, you can use your portfolio items to support your responses. Do not misrepresent yourself in the portfolio items; the work must be your own. Be prepared to reproduce the work if requested to do so during preemployment testing.

To make a good first impression and to capture the interviewer's attention, refer to one of your most impressive accomplishments first. Provide evidence of the accomplishment with an appropriate portfolio item. Save another exceptional item for the end of your interview to leave a memorable final impression.

Have a friend conduct a mock interview with you, and practice referring to your portfolio items at key points during the questioning process. This will prepare you to make a smooth delivery during your actual interviews.

REFERENCE READING

JOB SEARCH AND CAREER MANAGEMENT

Bolles, Richard N. *What Color Is Your Parachute 2003?* Berkeley, CA: Ten Speed Press, 2002.

Chapman, Jack. *Negotiating Your Salary: How to Make $1000 a Minute.* Berkeley, CA: Ten Speed Press, 2001.

Cook, Marshall J. *Time Management: Proven Techniques for Making the Most of Your Valuable Time.* Holbrook, MA: Adams Media Corporation, 1998.

Criscito, Pat. *Resumes in Cyberspace.* Hauppauge, NY: Barron's Educational Series, Inc., 2001.

Decker, Bert. *Speaking With Bold Assurance: How to Become a Persuasive Communicator.* Broadman and Holman Publishers, 2001.

Dikel, Margaret Riley and Frances E. Roehm. *Guide to Internet Job Searching, 2002-2003.* New York: VGM Career Books, 2002.

Dixon, Pam. *Job Searching Online for Dummies.* IDG Books, 2000.

Ferrara, Thomas. *Job Seeker Secrets: Making the Internet Work for You.* Cincinnati, OH: South-Western Educational and Professional Publishing, 2003.

Goleman, Daniel. *Emotional Intelligence.* DesPlanes, IL: Bantam Books, 1997.

Jennifer, James. *Thinking in the Future Tense: Leadership Skills for a New Age.* New York: Simon & Schuster, 1996.

Job Choices. Bethelem, PA: National Association of Colleges and Employers 2003. (Annual publication, usually available at college career centers.)

Johnson, Spencer and Kenneth H. Blanchard. *Who Moved My Cheese? An Amazing Way to Deal With Change in Your Work and in Your Life.* New York: Putnam Pub Group, 1998.

Judy, Richard and Carol D'Amico. *Workforce 2020: Work and Workers for the 21st Century.* Indianapolis, IN: Hudson Institute, 1998.

Karl, Shannon and Arthur Karl. *How to Get Your Dream Job Using the Web.* Albany, NY: Coriolis Group Books, 1997.

Kelly, Robert E. *How to Be a Star at Work: Nine Breakthrough Strategies You Need to Succeed.* New York: Random House, 1999.

Kennedy, Joyce Lain. *Job Interviews for Dummies.* New York: Hungry Minds, Inc., 2000.

Kennedy, Joyce Lain. *Resumes for Dummies.* New York: Hungry Minds, Inc., 2000.

Kennedy, Joyce Lain and Thomas J. Morrow. *Electronic Resume Revolution.* New York: John Wiley and Sons, Inc., 1995.

Parker, Yana. *Damn Good Resume Guide, Fourth Edition.* Berkeley, CA: Ten Speed Press, 2002.

Snodgrass, Jon. *Follow Your Career Star: A Career Quest Based on Inner Values.* New York: Kensington Publishing, 1996.

Wahlstrom, Carl and Brian Williams. *College to Careers: Your Road to Personal Success.* Cincinnati, OH: South-Western Educational and Professional Publishing, 2004.

White, Aggie. *Interview Styles and Strategies, The Professional Development Series.* Cincinnati, OH: South-Western Educational and Professional Publishing, 2003.

Yate, Martin. *Cover Letters That Knock 'Em Dead.* Holbrook, MA: Adams, Inc., 2000.

Yate, Martin. *Knock 'Em Dead: The Ultimate Job Seeker's Handbook.* Holbrook, MA: Adams, Inc., 1999.

PERSONAL MOTIVATION, COMMUNICATION, AND ASSERTIVENESS

Alberti, Robert E. and Michael L. Emmons. *Your Perfect Right.* San Luis Obispo, CA: Impact Publishers, 2001.

Baer, Jean. *How to Be an Assertive (Not Aggressive) Woman in Life, in Love, & on the Job: The Total Guide to Self-Assertiveness.* New York: NAL Ford-Dutton, 1991.

Bennett, Carole. *Business Etiquette and Protocol, The Professional Development Series.* Cincinnati, OH: South-Western Educational and Professional Publishing, 2001.

Briles, Judith and John Maling. *The Confidence Factor: Cosmic Gooses Lay Golden Eggs.* New York: Mile High Press, 2001.

Brown, Patricia. *Electronic Presentations, 10-Hour Series.* Cincinnati, OH: South-Western Educational and Professional Publishing, 2001.

Burnell, Ivan. *The Power of Positive Doing—12 Strategies for Taking Control of Your Life.* Center Ossipee, NH: IPO Publishing, 1999.

Carnegie, Dale. *How to Win Friends and Influence People.* New York: Simon & Schuster, 1998.

Cooper, Ann. *Professional Image, The Professional Development Series.* Cincinnati, OH: South-Western Educational and Professional Publishing, 2003.

Covey, Stephen R. *The 7 Habits of Highly Effective People: Powerful Lessons in Personal Change.* New York: Simon & Schuster, 1990.

Davidson, Jeff. *The Complete Idiot's Guide to Assertiveness.* Old Tapan, NJ: MacMillan Publishing Company, 1997.

Frankl, Viktor. *Man's Search for Meaning.* Boston, MA: Beacon Press, 2000.

Goldsmith, Joan and Kenneth Cloke. *Resolving Conflicts at Work.* San Francisco: Jossey-Bass, 2000.

Gordon, Douglas, Career Solutions Training Group. *Self-Management and Goal Setting, Quick Skills Series.* Cincinnati, OH: South-Western Educational Publishing, 2000.

Gray, John. *How to Get What You Want and Want What You Have.* New York: Harper Trade, 2000.

Heim, Pat, Susan Murphy, and Susan Golant. *In the Company of Women: Turning Workplace Conflict into Powerful Alliances.* J.P. Tarcher, 2001.

Hill, Napoleon. *Think and Grow Rich.* San Francisco, CA: Wilshire Publishing, 1999.

Kaye, Kenneth. *Workplace Wars and How to End Them.* New York: AMACOM, 1994.

Knight, Sue. *NLP at Work.* Naperville, IL: Brealey, Nicholas, 2002.

Peale, Norman Vincent. *Positive Principles Today.* New York: Fawcett Books, 1996.

Peale, Norman Vincent. *The Power of Positive Thinking.* New York: Random House, 1996.

Peoples, David. *Presentations Plus.* New York: John Wiley and Sons, 1992.

Peters, Thomas. *In Search of Excellence: Lessons From America's Best-Run Companies.* Thorndike, ME: GK Hall & Co., 1997.

Phelps, Stanlee and Nancy Austin. *The Assertive Woman.* San Luis Obispo, CA: Impact Publishers, 2002.

Robbins, Anthony. *Unlimited Power: The New Science of Personal Achievement.* New York: Simon & Schuster, 1997.

Rokes, Beverly, Career Solutions Training Group. *Advancing Your Career, Quick Skills Series.* Cincinnati, OH: South-Western Educational and Professional Publishing, 2002.

Rokes, Beverly, Career Solutions Training Group. *What Your Employer Expects, Quick Skills Series.* Cincinnati, OH: South-Western Educational and Professional Publishing, 2002.

Rozakis, Laurie. *The Complete Idiot's Guide to Public Speaking.* New York: Alpha Books, 1999.

Siegel, Bernie. *Prescriptions for Living.* New York: HarperTrade, 1999.

Tracy, Brian. *Focal Point: A Proven System to Simplify Your Life, Double Your Productivity, and Achieve All Your Goals.* New York: AMACOM, 2001.

Tracy, Brian. *Maximum Achievement: Strategies and Skills That Will Unlock Your Hidden Powers to Succeed.* New York: Simon & Schuster, 1995.

Tracy, Brian. *Thinking Big: The Keys to Personal Power and Maximum Performance.* Simon & Schuster, 1997. (Audiocassette)

Waitley, Denis. *The New Dynamics of Winning.* New York: Morrow, William, & Co., 1995.

Waitley, Denis. *The Psychology of Winning.* New York: Simon & Schuster, 1995. (Audiocassette)

Ziglar, Zig. *See You At the Top.* El Toro, CA: Pelican Publishing Co., 2000.

Functional resume, 118, 140
Functional skills, 227

G

Gatekeeper barriers, 221
General information questions, 238–239, 248
Globalization, 53–54
Goal setting, 6–7
GPA, 125
Graph, applicant-rating, 100
Growth areas, employment, 57

H

Hidden job market
    finding, after rejection, 289
    uncovering, 221–222
High school inventory, 22
Hoteling, 55
Human resources department
    addressing cover letter to, 177
    government, 38
    screening interview with, 222, 226–227

I

Image
    interview and, 191–193
    positive. *See* Positive image
Income
    tracking, 52
    See also Salary
Industry research, 109, 183
Information interview. *See* Career information survey
Information sources
    career/job fairs, 102
    libraries, 102
    local and small businesses, 104
    people resources, 101–102
    professional associations, 105
    trade associations, 105
Interests, on resume, 162

International Organization of Standards (ISO), 53
Internet
    career planning resources on, 39
    cover letter strategies on, 180
    hiring procedures research on, 93
    interview follow-up tips on, 278
    interview question-and-answer tips on, 245
    interview strategies on, 208
    job ads on, 76, 78
    job interview strategies on, 222
    job listings and information on, 78
    job research on, 104
    networking tips on, 71–72
    privacy limitations on, 56
    Proactive Success Action Plan on, 13
    relocation research on, 320
    researching workplace issues on, 64
    responding to jobs posted on, 219
    salary information on, 257
    security for, 55
Internet computer-assisted interview, 232
Internet video interview, 232–233
Interpersonal skills, as workplace competency, 38
Interview
    appearance for, 191–193
    attitude for, 190
    avoiding blunders in, 205
    bad, 235
    behavioral, 227
    board, 229
    body language for, 195–198
    campus, 229
    closing, 206–207
    corporate ladder, 231
    critique form, 269, 274
    direct requests for. *See* Interview requests
    dress rehearsal, 269
    emphasizing qualifications at, 199–200
    first 30 seconds of, 190
    focus on interviewee in, 190
    follow-up. *See* Interview follow-up
    game strategies, 276
    image and, 191–193
    Internet computer-assisted, 232
    Internet video, 232–233
    listening skills for, 199–200
    multilevel, 231

O

Online job openings, 183
Online job search, steps for, 182–183
Online self-assessment test, 20
Organization awareness, 304
Organizational activities, inventory of, 16, 24
Organizational culture, 298
Organizational politics, 299
Organizer, networking, 70
Orientation, job, 297–298

P

Panel interview, 229
Performance evaluation, for new job, 301
Personal career inventory, 16–18, 22–34
Personal data, on resume, 126
Personal finances, managing, 52
Personal qualities
    assessing, 33–34
    in SCANS report, 38, 48–49
    self-assessment of ideal, 19
Personality test, 254
Personality types, 8
Personal support system, 66
Portfolio
    defined, 40, 329
    for interview, 203–205
    items for, 41, 329
    for online job search, 183
    See also Career portfolio
Position objective, 166
Positive affirmations.
    See Affirmation statements
Positive self-talk, 5–7
Positive visualization, 4, 7
Posture, 196
Practice interview, 267–268
Privacy, respecting others', 59
Proactive behaviors, 12–13
Proactive Success Action Plan, 13, 323
Promotion, 303–304
Proof-by-example descriptions, 227
Prospective employers

compiling list of, 82
records of, 83, 87
research questions about, 110
researching, 99–112. *See also* Research
Public agencies, 79
Publications, career planning, 38
Punctuality, 299

Q

Quality
    employer's need for, 301–302
    teamwork and, 57
Quality assurance programs, 53–54
Question-and-answer planning sheet, 246, 248–252

R

Rating form, interview, 228
Reapplication, 290
Reference books, 82, 102
References
    on employment application, 168, 170
    establishing, 70–71
    on resume, 126, 162
    See also Job references
Referrals, asking for, 287
Rejection
    countering, with success strategies, 286
    evaluation of interview after, 287
    learning from, 235
    responding to, 289
    reversing, 288–289
    turning first, into job offer, 286
Relocation, 317, 319–321
    affording, 319
    research for, 320
    support network branch, 321
Research
    advantages of, 100
    applying your, 106–107
    areas of, 101
    industry, 109, 183
    information sources for, 101–102

This page constitutes an extension of the copyright page. We have made every effort to trace the ownership of all copyrighted material and to secure permission from copyright holders. In the event of any question arising as to the use of any material, we will be pleased to make the necessary corrections in future printings. Thanks are due to the following authors, publishers, and agents for permission to use the material indicated.

Chapter 1. 5: © Getty Images/PhotoDisc; 9: © Getty Images/PhotoDisc

Chapter 2. 18: © Getty Images/PhotoDisc; 19: © Getty Images/PhotoDisc

Chapter 3. 41: © CORBIS; 42: © Getty Images/PhotoDisc

Chapter 4. 52: © Getty Images/PhotoDisc; 53: © Getty Images/EyeWire; 56: © Getty Images/PhotoDisc

Chapter 5. 68: © Getty Images/PhotoDisc; 71: © Getty Images/PhotoDisc; 72: © Getty Images/PhotoDisc

Chapter 6. 75: © Getty Images/PhotoDisc; 79: © Getty Images/PhotoDisc; 81: © Getty Images/PhotoDisc; 85: © Getty Images/PhotoDisc

Chapter 7. 90: © Getty Images/EyeWire; 94: © Getty Images/PhotoDisc

Chapter 8. 101: © Getty Images/EyeWire; 104: © Getty Images/PhotoDisc; 107: © Getty Images/PhotoDisc; 108: © Getty Images/PhotoDisc

Chapter 9. 115: © Getty Images/EyeWire; 118: © Getty Images/PhotoDisc; 120: © Getty Images/PhotoDisc; 125: © CORBIS; 127: Deanna Ettinger; 131: © Getty Images/PhotoDisc; 134: © CORBIS; 137: © Getty Images/EyeWire

Chapter 10. 164: © Getty Images/EyeWire; 176: © Getty Images/EyeWire; 177: © Getty Images/PhotoDisc; 179: © Getty Images/EyeWire; 182: © Getty Images/PhotoDisc; 186: © Getty Images/EyeWire

Chapter 11. 190: © Getty Images/PhotoDisc; 193 (right): © Getty Images/PhotoDisc; 193 (left): © Getty Images/EyeWire; 197: © Getty Images/Digital Vision; 200: © Getty Images/PhotoDisc; 205: (007317B) Wallace Garrison

Chapter 12. 214: © Getty Images/PhotoDisc; 216: © Getty Images/PhotoDisc; 220: © Getty Images/PhotoDisc; 223: © Getty Images/PhotoDisc

Chapter 13. 227: © Getty Images/PhotoDisc; 231: © Getty Images/PhotoDisc; 233: © Getty Images/EyeWire; 235: © Getty Images/PhotoDisc

Chapter 14. 239: © Getty Images/PhotoDisc; 241: © Getty Images/EyeWire; 244: © Getty Images/PhotoDisc

Chapter 15. 254: © Getty Images/Digital Vision; 260: © Getty Images/PhotoDisc

Chapter 16. 266: © Getty Images/PhotoDisc; 267: © Getty Images/PhotoDisc; 268: © Getty Images/PhotoDisc; 269: © Getty Images/PhotoDisc; 270: © Getty Images/PhotoDisc

Chapter 17. 277: © Getty Images/Digital Vision; 279: © CORBIS

Chapter 18. 286: © Getty Images/PhotoDisc; 288(left): © Getty Images/EyeWire; 288 (right): © Getty Images/EyeWire; 291: © Digital Vision

Chapter 19. 296: © Getty Images/EyeWire; 299: © Getty Images/PhotoDisc; 300: © Getty Images/PhotoDisc; 302: © Getty Images/PhotoDisc; 305: © Getty Images/PhotoDisc

Chapter 20. 314: © Getty Images/PhotoDisc; 319: © Getty Images/EyeWire; 321: © Getty Images/PhotoDisc; 323: © Getty Images/PhotoDisc